Management in Service Industries

Management in Service Industries

EDITED BY PETER JONES

EDITED BY PETER JONES

Pitman

PITMAN PUBLISHING
128 Long Acre, London WC2E 9AN

A Division of Longman Group UK Limited

© Longman Group UK Limited 1989

First published in Great Britain 1989

British Library Cataloguing in Publication Data
Jones, Peter
  Management in service industries.
  81. Service industries. Management
  I. Title
  338.4

ISBN 0 273 03121 x (Cased edition)
ISBN 0 273 02953 3 (Paperback edition)

Printed & bound in Great Britain

Contents

Preface

This text is about service. More specifically it examines those sectors of the economy that deliver services and asks the question: 'What is the nature of management in service industries?'. Implicit in this question, and in the fact that this text has been published, is the fundamental assumption that managers of services face different problems and act differently from managers in the manufacturing sector. But this assumption is contentious. Since at least the early 1970s, there has been debate about the proposition that 'services' are in some way different from 'goods'. And even if they are, there has been even more debate about whether it makes any difference to the way in which managers behave. I do not intend to pursue this debate here. The book itself, with its many contributors, throughout its chapters continually examines aspects of the debate and the arguments for and against the basic assumption. Indeed, one of the reasons for asking so many diverse people to write for this text is to provide a range of opinion about what is important in relation to the management of services.

However, I must admit that my own view tends towards the belief that, somehow, services are different from manufacturing, and that managers of services should both act and be different from managers of factories and processing plants. This belief may be biased. I spent my childhood working in my parents' corner shop, the first half of my career in the hotel and restaurant business, and the second half in education. I can therefore claim to have first-hand experience of retailing, hospitality management, teaching and consultancy – a fairly good cross-section of service industries. It can therefore be argued, perhaps rightly, that, because my experience does not include non-service activity, it cannot provide me with a perspective or balance that enables judgement to be made.

Nonetheless, the principal factor that underpins my assertion that services and managing services are different is the role of people. In services, both managers and workers meet the consumer face to face. From the top to the bottom of a service organisation, from the chief executive to the lavatory attendant, the workforce must deliver directly to the paying customer. And not just a handful of major customers, but often hundreds and thousands of customers every week. Just add up how many people right now might be travelling on British Rail, be using a Trusthouse Forte hotel, visiting a Barclays bank, eating in a McDonald's, or visiting a DHSS office and the number could be in excess of 10 million people. At a recent conference, where representatives of local authorities and contract caterers were present, a quick calculation revealed that there 40 organisations were responsible for serving over 5 million meals every weekday.

Whilst it is true to say that the contributors to this text are diverse, in the main they, too, believe that services are in some way different. Some of them, in particular Brian Moores and Gary Akehurst, have held this view for a long time. Others have only considered this question because they were asked to contribute to this text. What emerges is that, whilst they agree that there is a difference, they do not agree on the cause or importance of this difference. Some focus on the people issue I have identified above. Others regard the intangibility of services as being the key issue. Almost all the contributors accept that any difference that exists between products and services is not clear cut, a black and white division. They refer to a variety of sources that regard products and services as a continuum or as a 'bundle'. It then follows that, depending on the extent of the differentiation or bundling, the way in which service managers behave will be radically different from, or quite similar to, the way in which manufacturing managers behave.

Therefore this is not a prescriptive text. It does not claim to provide the definitive view of what services are and how managers should behave in order to perform well. Rather the text has two aims. The first aim is to identify the scale and nature of service activities in the UK. The second aim is to provide a range of views about the issues managers face and what they are doing or could do about them. The book is arranged into four sections. Part I looks at the size and scale of the service sector in the UK and examines the key trends in services that will be affecting these industries into the 1990s. This is followed by Part II which is concerned with strategic and organisational issues facing service organisations. The third section, Part III focusses on the nature of functional management in service organisations, with chapters on each of the principal functions – operations, finance, personnel and marketing. Finally, Part IV identifies key issues that service organisations must address and examines their responses to these issues.

P. J.

List of contributors

BRIAN ADAMS, Director, Grant Thornton Management Consultants Limited

PROFESSOR GARY AKEHURST, Head of Department of Catering and Hotel Management, Dorset Institute, Poole

DR JON BAREHAM, Head of Department of Service Sector Management, Brighton Polytechnic

DR MICHAEL Z BROOKE, Managing Director, Brooke Associates (Manchester) Limited

FRANCIS BUTTLE, Lecturer in Marketing, Department of Hotel, Restaurant and Travel Administration, University of Massachusetts/Amherst

PAUL COLEBOURNE, Executive Consultant, Grant Thornton Management Consultants Limited

DR PAUL FIFIELD, Director, The Winchester Consulting Group

NORMAN FLYNN, Lecturer in Public Sector Management and Chairman of the Public Sector Management Area, London Business School

PROFESSOR PAUL R GAMBLE, Charles Forte Professor of Hotel Management, Department of Management Studies for Tourism and Hotel Industries, University of Surrey

ROBERT JOHNSTON, Lecturer in Service Operations Management, Warwick Business School

PETER JONES, Principal Lecturer, Brighton Business School

ANDREW LOCKWOOD, Lecturer in Hotel and Catering Management, Department of Management Studies for Tourism and Hotel Industries, University of Surrey

DR ROBERT CHRISTIE MILL, Professor of Hotel and Restaurant Management, University of Denver

PROFESSOR BRIAN MOORES, Professor of Management Science, University of Stirling

DR DAVID REA, Research Associate, The Centre for Research on Organisations, Management and Technical Change, Manchester School of Management, University of Manchester Institute of Science and Technology

SUE RICKS, Department of Service Sector Management, Brighton Polytechnic Business School

SUSAN SEGAL-HORN, Lecturer in Strategic Management, Cranfield School of Management

DR LEIGH SPARKS, Lecturer, Institute for Retail Studies, Department of Business and Management, University of Stirling

PROFESSOR JOHN STANWORTH, Director, Future of Work Research Group, London Management Centre, Polytechnic of Central London

DR DAVID TARGETT, Senior Lecturer in Decision Sciences, London Business School

DR PAUL WILLMAN, Lecturer in Industrial Relations, London Business School

Acknowledgements

I would like to thank all the contributors to this text who have conscientiously and patiently developed their chapters. Most are 'academics' (whatever that is), some are consultants, and some are both. Each has his or her own particular style and has approached the topic in his or her own distinctive way. Some contributions are pragmatic and down to earth, others adopt a more rigorous academic approach. But all of them are informative, well-informed, challenging and stimulating. It has been my pleasure to meet, discuss and sometimes argue with these colleagues. This is their book.

Part I
Service industries in the United Kingdom

This book begins by examining the size and scale of the UK's service economy and the various service industries that make up the service sector. The exact scale and relative importance of services is difficult to establish. As Gary Akehurst discusses in Chapter 1 there are definitional problems and some controversy as to how to measure services. But whatever approach is adopted, it is clear that 'services' are a more significant proportion of most western economies than ever before and that they are continuing to grow. Some commentators have observed that these economies are going through the same sort of structural shift that occurred during the industrial revolution when in the space of, relatively, a few years, nations changed from largely rural, agricultural economies into urban, industrial ones. Today, it is the industrial, manufacturing sector that is in decline and people-oriented services that are growing. There are even some predictions that services will represent 90 per cent of economic activity in the USA by the year 2000.

Central to understanding the impact of this growth and the underlying causes is an understanding of the consumer. In Chapter 2, Jon Bareham explores how consumer needs have changed in recent years and the likely impact these trends will have on service provision. These general trends can be seen to be having quite specific impacts on the various sectors examined in the remaining four chapters of Part I.

The four sectors evaluated are what can be termed consumer service industries, although the financial sector also has a considerable role as a producer service industry. Between them, these four sectors constituted about 47 per cent of the UK's gross domestic product in 1985 and 60 per cent of the total employees in employment in 1985. All of them have faced, and continue to face, very similar challenges from the environment, and there are some common themes running through these sectors. The challenges include significantly greater levels of competition, largely encouraged by government policies of deregulation, more liberal employment/retailing/licensing laws, and 'privatisation'; significant demographic changes in the market place, with a rapid decline in the numbers of younger people and a steadily ageing population; the impact of information technology; and consumers with more money to spend and more sophisticated tastes.

Common trends within these industries, partly as a response to these changes in the environment, are greater industry concentration, some conglomeration of organisations across a range of services, and more sophisticated marketing, especially in terms of market segmentation and branding. In Chapter 3, Paul Fifield explores the idea of 'convergence', whereby the traditional barriers between banks, building societies, insurance companies and finance houses are breaking down. The same sort of trend is seen in the retail sector in Chapter 4, as Leigh Sparks outlines the nature and growth of 'multiples'. Likewise, in Chapter 5, Andrew Lockwood discusses the extent to which firms in the travel and hospitality sectors are forging new links or even merging to create large-scale, one-stop travel organisations. Even the public sector is being subject to these same trends, although of most significance is probably the blurring of the distinction between public and private service providers. Norman Flynn in Chapter 6 identifies four main issues: decentralisation, the shift to the private sector, contracting out and performance measurement.

Part I therefore aims to set the scene with regards to what is actually happening in service organisations in the UK. It should not be forgotten, however, that what is happening on these shores is happening on a global scale. Indeed, one other major trend is the growth of multinational service firms.

1 Service industries

PROFESSOR GARY AKEHURST

Introduction

Britain is not alone in experiencing a rapid transformation of its economy. Other advanced economies are experiencing a similar phenomenon, particularly in Europe, North America and Japan. Various labels have been attached to this process of economic development including 'the third industrial revolution', 'the new information society', 'deindustrialisation', 'the post-industrial society' and 'the service economy'. We must not, however, imagine for one moment that services or service industries are a twentieth-century development. Shops, inns and financial services existed in medieval times. What makes the current structural shifts towards services particularly important are the profound economic and social implications of these changes. Of particular note are:

1   the rapid internationalisation of traded services encouraged in part by deregulation, increasing specialisation of services and the activities of multinational corporations, especially in tourism, banking and the capital markets;

2   the emergence of information technologies which are leading to an international division of labour and greater operating flexibilities;

3   the hopes that service industries which are labour-intensive will increase employment opportunities.

In addition, in the European Economic Community the goal of a single internal market by 1992 holds out the promise of increased competitiveness and a freedom from national regulations and restrictions.

It is rapidly becoming clear that services lie at the very heart of the commercial, economic and technological changes occurring not only in Europe but throughout the world. These changes affect all manner of processes, products, markets, jobs and activities. Ochel and Wegner (1987, pp 5–6) summarise some of the principal features of these changes:

Old features	*New features*
Standardised output/assembly lines	Customised goods and services/increased variety and bundling of goods and services
In-house production or internalisation of services	Increased externalisation of services, increased networking and interlinkages
Local and national markets	Growing internationalisation and competition
Vertical integration of production/large corporations	Vertical disintegration, small and medium sized firms and large transnational conglomerates
Rigid embodiment of technical progress	Flexible production modes for goods and services
Material inputs and outputs	'Immaterial' investments and human resource and knowledge-based inputs
Factory/blue-collar employment	White-collar/office/home employment
Sectoral regulated service functions	New forms of regulation

Controversies, definitions and classifications of services

Changes of these magnitudes and complexities are inevitably painful as older, more traditional industries undergo transformations and sometimes contraction. Major industrial and social change brings with it bitter controversy as politicians and industrialists alike debate the issues from a frankly inadequate knowledge base. There is a serious lack of statistical information and the difficulties of defining, classifying and measuring services is a major obstacle to innovation and prosperity. It is a common prejudice that services are in some way a 'residual' and a drag factor with negative influences on economic growth and productivity, often labelled 'deindustrialisation'. Such views have been around for a long time. Adam Smith (1776) considers that the labour of manufacturing adds, generally, to the value of the materials which is worked upon, while the labour of the menial servant adds to the value of nothing. Smith obviously had in mind those employed in service activities. But lest the reader feels he or she is exonerated, Smith goes on to write 'in the same class must be ranked some of the gravest and most important, and some of the most frivolous professions: churchmen, lawyers, physicians, men of letters of all kinds, players, buffoons, musicians, opera-singers, and opera-dancers, etc.' The Smith argument, therefore, assumes that most if not all service workers are a definite drain on a country's productive capacity. As such, any expansion of the service sector is definitely a 'bad thing, to be avoided at all costs'. McKenzie has written: 'The emergence of the "service economy" in the United States has given birth to public policy worries that the country is in the process of being reduced to a nation of orderlies, fast-food workers, and bus boys.' (McKenzie, 1987).

Such distinctions between the usefulness or otherwise of services and goods are based on beliefs rather than facts and owe much to the arbitrary categories and classifications of statisticians. To an increasing extent goods and services are no longer demanded separately or individually but are bundled as part of a 'product package'. Marketing researchers have suggested that the generic term should be 'products' with services constituting a subset (Middleton, 1983). Foxall, however, suggests that the most appropriate generic concept is surely that of a 'service'; '. . . the suggestion that a single conceptual basis should be found for both "products" and "services" is sound in view of the fact that customers are interested in obtaining the same thing – benefits, satisfactions or services – whether or not they are supplied via a physical entity . . . Marketing analysts should recognise that that which is exchanged for customers' money in a market transaction is a *service* (or a bundle of services) which may or may not involve the transfer of a physical entity.' (Foxall, 1984). McKenzie (1987) illustrates well that, no matter how carefully definitions of 'goods' and 'services' are constructed, the allocation of GNP and employment is largely arbitrary:

- a hamburger sold at a fast food restaurant is part of a service but a hamburger sold in a supermarket is a good;
- a computer is a manufactured good when sold to a household but part of a service when leased by a corporation;
- a truck driver is a manufacturing worker when he or she transfers intermediate products between plants in the same firm but is a service worker when he or she, operating an independent business, enters into a contract with the same firm to make the very same deliveries.

All this is compounded by the antics of researchers attempting to provide a comprehensive listing of the apparent characteristics of services such as intangibility and non-storeability; consumption and production are simultaneous and inseparable; the benefits of services are difficult to describe; the consumer is a central actor in the transfer and exchange process; a general lack of homogeneity and problems of controlling service quality (particularly in replicating a service). A 'service' can then, it is argued, be defined by reference to these necessary and sufficient characteristics or conditions. This functional approach sometimes argues that *all* these characteristics should be present when distinguishing goods from services; at other times it is argued that only *some* of these features should be present (Akehurst, 1987). As Blois (1983) points out, it is not absolutely clear or obvious as to which of these characteristics is absolutely fundamental nor 'how many of these characteristics must apply to a product before it is considered to be "a service"'. Of course, what these characteristics merely demonstrate are the preconceived, self-selected features which the researcher or policy maker, in his or her experience as a consumer, believes to be distinguishing features of services compared with goods. Surely we must observe differences both within and between 'services' and 'products' but should 'not force these observations to fit a spurious analytical dichotomy' (Foxall, 1984).

All this suggests that while it is necessary to categorise to make some sense of an increasingly complex universe, nevertheless official statistics must be treated with caution. McKenzie adds a further note of caution: 'The emergence of the service economy may be as much an artifact of the classification system as it is a real phenomenon'. The fact is that an economy exists and is designed to satisfy needs and wants regardless of whether those needs are met by tangible or intangible devices.

When it comes to identifying a group of service industries there is much more unanimity than may appear at first sight despite the difficult conceptual and measurement problems. Generally included under the label 'service industries' are: retail and wholesale distribution, banking, finance and insurance, other business services (legal, advertising, marketing, etc.), hotels and catering, tourism, health, education and welfare services, public administration and defence, recreational and cultural services, transport and communication services, other personal services (e.g., laundry, repairs). It is a matter of debate whether construction activities are included, although Riddle (1986) argues that the professional services of engineers, architects, etc., are important in international traded services. Table 1.1 lists some of the main classifications used.

The US Office of Technology Assessment has proposed an alternative classification system for service providers based on a division between producer services (provided for intermediate markets of businesses and industry) and consumer services (provided for final markets, largely to private citizens) (Table 1.2)

Kuznets (1938) divided goods into consumer and producer goods which are further divided into those with perishable, durable or semi-durable

Table 1.1 Classifications used

Output- or production-based

Fisher (1935); Clark (1940):
  Primary (agriculture and extractive industries)
  Secondary (manufacturing)
  Tertiary (the residual)

Fuchs (1968)
  Agriculture
  Industry (mining, manufacturing, transport, public utilities)

Sabolo (1975)
  Primary (agriculture and fisheries)
  Non-primary
  High use of capital and skills (mining, manufacturing and transport)
  Low use of capital and skills (trade)
  High use of skills, low use of capital (finance)

The International Standard Industrial Classification (ISIC) identifies four main service divisions at single digit level subdivided by outputs into more detailed two digit level classes. The British Standard Industrial Classification (SIC) revised in 1980 identifies four main service divisions:
  Distribution, hotels, catering and repairs
  Transport and communications
  Banking, finance, insurance, etc.
  Other services (includes public administration, education, recreation)

NACE-CLIO (Nomenclature des activités dans les Communautes Europeennes) classifies goods production, market service sectors and non-market service sectors

Consumption/expenditure-based

Singer (1981) with respect to services:
  Production services
  Collective consumption
  Individual consumption

Function-based

Katouzian (1970)
  Complementary services (transport, finance, commerce)
  New services (education, health, entertainment)
  Old services (domestic)

Browning and Singelmann (1975)
  Distributive services (transport, communication, commerce)
  Producer services (professional, financial)
  Personal services (domestic, hotels, restaurants, leisure)
  Social services (education, health, defence)

Source: based on Riddle (1986)

attributes depending on the length of time over which the service yields utility. Daniels (1985a, p 6) illustrates these attributes with examples of consumer services:

Table 1.2 Classification scheme for service providers

Producer services (intermediate markets)

Financial services
  banking, insurance, leasing

Shipping and distribution
  ocean, rail, trucking, air freight, wholesaling, warehousing, distribution

Professional and technical
  technical licensing and sales, engineering design services, architectural design,
  construction management and contracting, other management services, legal services,
  accounting

Other intermediate services
  computer, data processing, communication services (including software), franchising,
  advertising, other (commercial real estate, business travel, security, postal services,
  contract maintenance, etc.)

Consumer services (final markets to private citizens)

Retailing
Health care
Travel, recreation, entertainment
Education
Other social services, including Government
Other personal services (restaurants, home repair, laundry, etc.)

Source: Office of Technology Assessment, Washington, DC., USA.

perishable	visit to a hairdressers, use of a launderette
semi-durable	advice from lawyers, assistance from accountants in completing tax forms, a course of dental treatment
durable	educational training, architectural advice and assistance with the design of a new family house.

Producer services can be similarly classified.

Comparatively recently attention has been given to the international trade in services. McRae (1987) mentions that the traditional view of services in trade models is that they are non-tradeable and therefore, of secondary interest to trade in goods. The characteristics of services ensures that service industries' outputs, prices and inputs are determined within the domestic economy. The demand for these non-traded services (such as retail and personal services) is considered to be local, supported by income generated by the exporting physical goods industries. This model breaks down when faced with the global information technologies revolution, the continued development of transnational corporations, together with management and franchising contracts. 'In service sectors such as accounting, advertising, information storage and retrieval, legal services, financial services, and insurance, it is now possible for suppliers in one market area to serve clients in another, thus breaking the need for buyers and sellers to locate in the same geographical area' (McRae, 1987).

Services in the development of societies and economies

The generally held view at the present time is that there is no general and valid theory which alone explains the complex shifts towards services. Clearly these changes are not a painless process of long-term evolution to some 'mature' society or economy. The traditional model of development (developed by Fisher (1935) and Clark (1940) among others), where an economy moves from being predominantly agriculturally based to manu-facturing-based (the industrial revolution phase) and finally moving to a predominantly services-based economy (the post-industrial phase) is now known to be somewhat of an over-simplification. If the income elasticity of demand for services is higher than that for manufactured goods resources will shift to the service sector as income levels rise. Unfortu-nately this model focused particularly on consumer services rather than producer services; neither could Fisher nor Clark (and this is not a criti-cism) foresee the massive changes in technologies or the globalisation of corporate activities.

The second concept, of the post-industrial society concentrating in part on the quality of life and households as both production and consumption units (prosumers) with respect to services has been a major stimulator of research activity (Bell, 1974; Gershuny and Miles, 1983). Households demand time saving final consumer services but as income rises so there is a tendency to replace this demand for final services by physical goods and the household's own labour, that is, the internalisation of services or self-services. There are trade-offs between the relative prices of goods and services, the utility maximising mix of leisure and work (income), the scarcity of time (paid/unpaid work), the purchasing of time and the conflict between consumption and leisure. These trade-offs link the external decisions of households to internal decisions relating to domestic work and leisure. Some writers stress the transfer of more and more personal and social services, such as health and education, to the State or private companies. Such transfers need to be considered within the circum-stances of particular countries and their political and social institutions. Akehurst (1987) adds qualifications to these scenarios: 'First, there is clearly a limit to self-service (which can often be grossly inefficient) because of, for example, capital requirements and the possession of specialised skills. Second, employment in service industries continues to grow both relatively and absolutely due to household demand despite lower productivity. This alone suggests that self-service is not the major element in economic development but must be considered together with the growth of intermediate services provided by firms for other producers and the growth of firms which undeniably can be classified as service producers.'

Consumer services undoubtedly give rise to conceptual difficulties. Not only are they a heterogeneous series of activities but also a wide range of social, economic, demographic and institutional factors are at work. The demand and supply of final consumer services will depend on a variety of factors including:

leisure time trends;
changes in perceived lifestyle;
female participation in the work force;
disposable or discretionary income trends;
income distribution;
size of families;
age and other demographic factors;
the self-service economy mentioned above;
government taxation;
relative prices.

This is not an exhaustive list but indicative of some of the factors which need to be carefully considered.

Finally, the information economy theories (for example, Porat, 1976 and Touraine, 1971) emphasise the information technologies as a driving mechanism for change. Ochel and Wegner (1987) argue however, that 'the service and information economies are intertwined but not identical. The speed of diffusion of information technologies may be overestimated and be hindered by political decisions (infrastructures, macroeconomics and budgetary constraints), slow growth and social barriers'. These writers argue strongly that services are becoming much more of an integral part of developed economies with complex linkages across so-called sectors of economic activity.

The significance of service industries in the British economy

Given the statistical inadequacies and definitional problems any data may be indicative of possible trends but must be treated with caution. Broad trends suggest that the share of services in terms of gross national product (GNP) and employment is rising over time.

Table 1.3 indicates that the share of services in gross domestic product (GDP) at constant prices has risen from 48.5 per cent in 1973 to 53.2 per cent in 1984. Similarly, the share of services in civilian employment has risen from 56.3 per cent to 65.7 per cent in the same period. Interestingly, services have been less prone to cyclical fluctuations reflecting perhaps the general non-stockability of services.

Table 1.3 Percentage output shares of services in UK GDP and employment

	GDP at current prices	GDP at constant 1980 prices	Civilian employment
1973	51.3	48.5	56.3
1979	51.4	50.1	60.1
1984	54.5	53.2	65.7

Source: OECD

Table 1.4 shows GDP by industry. It is noteworthy that there is a relative decline of agriculture, manufacturing and transport and a relative increase in banking, insurance, finance, business services, energy and water supplies. Approximately half the growth in service industry shares in GDP is due to a relative increase in prices and the rest a volume increase, according to Kravis (1985)

Table 1.4 UK GDP by industry 1975–85*

	1975 £m	%	1985 £m	%
Agriculture, forestry and fishing	2,507	2.7	5,485	1.8
Manufacturing	27,638	29.9	76,800	25.2
Energy and water supply	5,041	5.4	34,335	11.3
Construction	6,299	6.8	18,651	6.1
Distribution, hotel and catering, repairs	11,927	12.9	40,384	13.2
Transport	5,263	5.7	12,913	4.2
Communication	2,509	2.7	8,044	2.6
Banking, finance, insurance, business services and leasing	10,010	10.8	42,473	13.9
Public administration, national defence, social security	7,321	7.9	21,599	7.1
Education and health services	9,012	9.7	26,187	8.6
Other services	5,000	5.4	17,978	5.9
Total	92,527		304,849	

* Contribution to GDP before providing for depreciation but after providing for stock appreciation, and before adjustment for financial services and residual error.
Source: CSO

Table 1.5 shows average annual percentage increases in real GDP, employment and labour productivity in services 1960–84. The fairly rapid growth of output and employment in the UK service sector can be explained in part by the decline in international competitiveness of manufacturing industries and the exploitation of traditional comparative advantage in financial services.

Table 1.5 Average annual percentage increases in real GDP, employment and labour productivity in services

	1960–68	1968–73	1973–79	1979–84	1960–73	1973–84
			Real value added			
USA	4.6	3.6	3.3	2.4	4.1	2.9
Japan	10.5	7.1	4.4	3.2	9.2	3.9
EEC	4.4	4.8	3.1	1.8	4.6	2.5
FRG	4.0	4.8	3.1	2.8	4.3	3.0
France	5.0	5.7	3.8	1.4	5.3	2.8
UK	2.8	3.2	1.7	1.5	3.0	1.6
			Civilian employment			
USA	2.5	3.4	3.2	2.2	2.8	2.7
Japan	2.8	2.4	2.2	1.9	2.6	2.2
EEC	1.7	1.9	1.7	1.3	1.8	1.5
FRG	1.0	1.7	1.1	0.7	1.3	0.9
France	2.5	2.6	2.2	1.1	2.5	1.7
UK	1.3	1.5	1.4	0.8	1.4	1.1
			Real value added per person employed			
USA	2.0	0.3	0.2	0.3	1.3	0.3
Japan	7.5	4.4	2.2	1.3	6.3	1.8
EEC	2.8	2.9	1.5	0.5	2.8	1.0
FRG	2.9	3.1	2.0	2.1	3.0	2.1
France	2.4	3.1	1.7	0.4	2.8	1.1
UK	1.6	1.8	0.4	0.7	1.7	0.5

Source: OECD

Table 1.6 gives a detailed picture of employment by standard industrial classification (SIC) divisions. The strong growth in employment in distribution, hotels, catering and financial services is clearly seen.

The fastest growing sectors have been producer services, except transport and distribution. Wood (1983) estimates that some 18 per cent of UK employment is in producer services but Daniels (1985b) estimates this proportion to be nearer 22 per cent. Commentators have, however, suggested that the UK together with West Germany have experienced relatively weak service jobs creation.

Table 1.7 shows the numbers of full-time and part-time employees in manufacturing and service industries.

Various statistics undoubtedly have their uses but what these trends cannot indicate are the causal factors in the growth process or answer the question whether the service sector can 'become the engine of growth in place of manufacturing' (Ochel and Wegner, 1987). However, productivity in the service sector has been observed to grow slowly compared with

Table 1.6 Employees in UK service industries

	SIC 1980 Division	1981 '000	1985 '000
Distribution, hotels, catering and repairs	6	4,167	4,471
of which:			
retail distribution		2,090	2,203
hotel and catering		949	1,058
repair of consumer goods and vehicles		204	211
wholesale distribution		888	960
other (scrap, waste merchants, commission agents)		36	39
Transport and communications	7	1,423	1,304
Banking, finance, insurance, etc.	8	1,740	1,971
of which:			
business services*		848	986
Other services**	9	6,121	6,266
of which:			
personal services		180	179
recreational and cultural services		432	438
Total employees in employment		21,870	21,466

* includes estate agents, professional services, advertising, computer services, etc.
** includes public administration, defence, national government service, local government, social security, police, education, etc.
Source: Annual Abstract of Statistics, CSO, 1987

Table 1.7 Numbers of full-time and part-time employees in manufacturing and services

		1971 '000	1984 '000
Manufacturing			
Males	full-time	5,475	3,916
	part-time	71	
Females	full-time	1,869	1,199
	part-time	471	361
Totals		7,886	5,477
Service industries			
Males	full-time	5,261	6,155
	part-time	473	
Females	full-time	3,418	3,584
	part-time	2,206	3,708
Totals		11,358	13,449
Total			
Males	full-time	12,840	11,741
	part-time	584	
Females	full-time	5,467	4,972
	part-time	2,757	4,172
Totals		21,648	20,885

Source: Social Trends, 1987, CSO

manufacturing, perhaps due to the labour-intensity of services and a certain unwillingness to change. There is an argument, however, that particular producer services 'play a strategic role in the improvement of productivity in other sectors and it seems very likely that the goods sector may be a net gainer from service activities' (Ochel and Wegner, 1987). Further research is needed to substantiate these views.

Conclusions

Service industries are often looked to as one way of reducing unemployment and creating more jobs. At the same time service industries hold out the promise of prosperity and innovation. Certainly there are hopeful signs in the internationalisation and liberalisation of traded services. But there are many problems. Despite a quickening of research on services after years of neglect nobody pretends that we fully understand these really rather complex macro-issues of definition, measurement, productivity growth, the diffusion of new information technologies, or the micro-issues of the management of service businesses, the externalisation of producer services, the quality of services or the quality of training of service personnel.

For years to come service industries will be surrounded by controversy:

- are services the way forward for a prosperous future?
- is the growing share of services in employment and GDP further evidence of a declining industrial base or the manifestation of a growing interdependence of national economies?
- will services offer hope to the millions of unemployed in the world?

I wonder what Adam Smith would make of all this?

References

Akehurst, G. P. (1987) 'The Economics of Services: an Introduction' in G. P. Akehurst and J. Gadrey (1987) *The Economics of Services*, Frank Cass, London.

Akehurst, G. P. and Gadrey, J. (1987) *The Economics of Services*, Frank Cass, London.

Bell, D. (1974) *The Coming of Post-industrial Society – a Venture in Social Forecasting*, Heinemann, London.

Blois, K. J. (1983) 'Service Marketing: Assertion or Asset?', *Service Industries Journal*, 3 (2) pp. 115–116.

Browning, H. C. and Singelmann, J. (1975) *The Emergence of a Service Society*, National Technical Information Service, Springfield.

Central Statistical Office (1987a) *Social Trends*, HMSO, London.

Central Statistical Office (1987b) *Annual Abstract of Statistics*, HMSO, London

Clark, C. (1940) *The Conditions of Economic Progress*, Macmillan, London.

Daniels, P. W. (1985a) *Service Industries, A Geographical Appraisal*, Methuen, London.

Daniels, P. W. (1985b) 'Producer Services in the Post-industrial Space Economy' in R. Martin and R. Rowthorn (eds), *Deindustrialisation and the British Space Economy*, Macmillan, London.

Fisher, A. G. B. (1935) *The Clash of Progress and Society*, Macmillan, London.

Foxall, G. (1984) *Marketing in the Service Industries*, Frank Cass, London, p. 2.

Fuchs, V. (1968) *The Service Economy*, Bureau of Economic Research, New York.

Gershuny, J. and Miles, I. (1983) *The New Service Economy: the Transformation of Employment in Industrial Societies*, Frances Pinter, London.

Katouzian, M. A. (1970) 'The Development of the Service Sector: a New Approach', *Oxford Economic Papers*, 22(3).

Kravis, I. B. (1985) 'Services in World Transactions' in R. P. Inman (ed) *Managing the Service Economy, Prospects and Problems*, Cambridge University Press, Cambridge.

Kuznets, S. (1938) *Commodity Flow and Capital Formation*, National Bureau of Economic Research, New York.

McKenzie, R. B. (1987) 'The Emergence of the "Service Economy": Fact or Artifact?' in H. G. Grubel, *Conceptual Issues in Service Sector Research: a Symposium*, The Fraser Institute, Vancouver, pp. 73–77.

McRae, J. J. (1987) 'An Organizational Overview of the IRPP's Research on the Tradeable Service Industries' in H. G. Grubel, *Conceptual Issues in Service Sector Research: a Symposium*, The Fraser Institute, Vancouver, p. 33.

Middleton, V. T. C. (1988) 'Product Marketing – Goods and Services Compared', *Quarterly Review of Marketing*, 8(4).

OECD (1986) *Economic Outlook*, 39, OECD, Paris.

Ochel, W. and Wegner, M. (1987) *Service Economies in Europe, Opportunities for Growth*, Pinter Publishers, London and Westview Press, Boulder, Colorado for the Commission of the European Communities, pp. 26–33.

Office of Technology Assessment (1985) 'International Competitiveness in the Service Industries', unpublished report, Washington DC.

Porat, M. (1976) *The Information Society*, Stanford University, Stanford.

Riddle, D. I. (1986) *Service-led Growth, the Role of the Service Sector in World Development*, Praeger, New York.

Sabolo, Y. (1975) *The Service Industries*, International Labour Office, Geneva.

Smith, A. (1776, 1937) *An Inquiry into the Nature and Causes of the Wealth of Nations*, Modern Library, New York.

Touraine, A. (1971) *The Post-industrial Society*, New York.

Wood, P. A. (1983) 'The Regional Significance of Manufacturing-Service Sector Links: Some Thoughts on the Revival of London's Docklands' paper presented at the Anglo-Canadian Symposium on Industrial Geography, Calgary, Canada.

2 Consumers of services

DR JON R BAREHAM

Introduction

Those who provide services need to understand what influences the decisions made by consumers, about what they might or do buy. For the provider the ideal would be to have so sophisticated an analysis of consumer needs, wants and behaviour as to be able to predict them. Then the provider would be able to supply adequately the relevant type and level of service required to meet demand.

Tuck (1976) has shown that in reality many providers rely on a mix of intuition and experience to guess consumer opinion and buying behaviour. It would seem that the guesses are not that accurate as witnessed by the high failure rate of services such as restaurants or holiday products. This suggests that prediction of consumer preference is not an easy matter. The major reason is that the causes of behaviour are often complex and hard to identify and understand.

This complexity has persuaded some academics to construct models of the buying process in an attempt to identify the range of variables involved. These models are summarised by Engel, Blackwell and Miniard (1986). Besides identifying the stages leading from initial recognition of need to the final acquisition of a service these models also contain an identification of the variety of cultural, social, psychological and economic factors which may have an influence on the actions of the consumer at each stage in the decision process.

Most models have therefore been developed by an eclectic selection from the disciplines of anthropology, sociology, psychology and economics. They appear on paper as elaborate systems diagrams with arrows linking a diversity of variables.

Despite this apparent sophistication and the value of such models to academic research both Foxall (1980) and Tuck (1976) have criticised their application to the real world and particularly their relevance to the marketing practitioner. Chisnall (1976) once described these models as 'like TV wiring' diagrams and about as useful to the uninitiated. Tuck (1976) has agreed that only the fairly precise mathematical relationship between attitude and behaviour elaborated by Fishbein (1980) is of useful practical value since it has some predictive power.

For all these criticisms and shortfalls models of consumer behaviour do nevertheless provide a constructive framework for the description and organisation of the range of factors which have an influence on consumer choice. In all the models there is a differentiation between the sets of factors which influence which consumers buy which services; where, when, how and why.

The major ingredients of all the models are similar but the organisation is different. It is possible to discern three sets of factors which have an influence on the buying process. These are referred to here as external environment, external stimuli and individual disposition. The external environment includes the cultural and social background of the consumer.

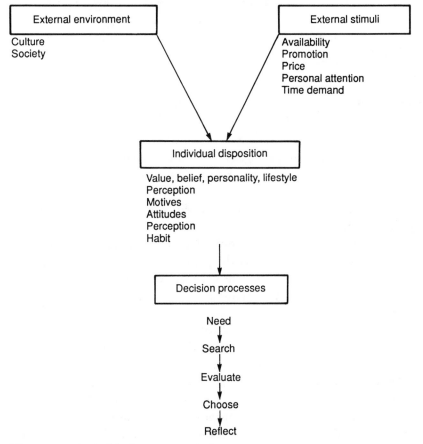

Figure 2.1   A model of consumer choice

The external stimuli from the provider of the service includes the availability of the service, which is in turn a consequence of geographical location and technological sophistication, promotional activity via the media and point of sale, price, the time use or time saving provided by the service, and the level of personal attention given by the provider. The individual disposition of the consumer takes account of psychological constructs such as values, beliefs, personality, lifestyle, motives, attitudes, perception and learning which can influence purchase behaviour.

These three sets of factors impact on the decision process of the consumer which in turn follows a series of stages from identification of need, to search, to evaluation of alternatives, to choice, to post acquisition evaluation. This model is illustrated in Figure 2.1.

Engel, Blackwell and Miniard (1986) take over 500 pages to describe the complexities of this process. This chapter cannot therefore do justice to what is even then a fairly non-sophisticated analysis. The attempt here is therefore to use this broad framework, but within it to identify a number of key trends which have an influence on the consumption process with examples drawn primarily from the tourism, hospitality and retailing industries.

Trends affecting service consumption

In the **external environment** the two major factors influencing consumer choice are cultural and demographic changes. Here as an example of cultural change the increased importance given to health is examined. This is followed by a brief analysis of some of the major demographic and economic influences which will also shape the overall pattern of purchase behaviour in future.

An individual learns the behaviour which is shared and transmitted by members of the society to which he belongs (Linton, 1947). Mainly the learning is from the family to which he belongs although social groups such as peers, and social institutions such as school and the media are also important.

The influence of the culture in which we live is not static but adaptive, changing and reflective of new values which society comes to recognise. In some cases these values become enforced through the legal system, or are faithfully followed with no legal force as customs or folkways.

The increased value put on health in our society is an example of an emerging cultural norm. The percentage of domestic income spent on food is now so low that, with a few exceptions, price elasticity does not exist. The factors of importance include value for money and quality attributes which are tied to perceived healthiness. Consumers in western countries now pay more for health-related foods, e.g., hormone-free meat or free-range eggs (Daly and Beharrell, 1988).

Over the last 100 years there have been vast changes in the food consumption habits of people in western countries, whether eating out or in. There has been a marked decrease in consumption of bread and po-tatoes but an increase in milk, dairy and meat products. More recently the decrease in bread and potato consumption has continued but there have also been falls in consumption of sugar, meat, dairy foods, eggs, liquid milk and total fat. However, these major trends hide some increases in consumption of foods which are perceived as healthy such as yoghurt, natural cheese, wholemeal bread, poultry, and fish (Daly and Beharrell, 1988). These trends are also true for Norway, USA, Belgium and Italy (Frank and Wheelock, 1988) so that throughout the western world, the increased cultural emphasis on healthy eating has resulted in changed consumption patterns for food eaten at home or away from home.

Similarly, interest in sport and leisure is a reflection of concern with health, but also a consequence of the decreasing working week. The percentage of adults taking part in active outdoor sport in the UK rose from 28 per cent to 31 per cent between 1977 and 1983 and in active indoor sport from 21 per cent to 25 per cent in the same period (General House-hold Survey, 1985). Forty-four per cent of adults had participated in active sport in the four weeks before the interview. Between 1931 and 1985 the average working week for manual employees fell from 48 to 44 hours per week and from 1971 to 1985 the percentage of manual employees with a basic holiday entitlement of over 3 weeks rose from 4 to 100 per cent (Social Trends, 1988).

This increasing emphasis on health and the increase in leisure time are examples of important but powerful influences on the consumption of many services such as facilities in hotels, types of holiday, preferred type and place for shopping, transportation and health services.

One of the most fundamental changes in western society is the changed population structure. After 200 years of population growth, Europe is reaching saturation point with a more or less static population size. The percentage of people under 15 is typically around 20 per cent in Western Europe compared with 35–40 per cent in Asia and South America. Simi-larly the population over 60 years old is 15–20 per cent in Europe, 21 per cent in the UK, but only 5–8 per cent in Asia and South America (Table 2.1, Social Trends, 1988).

In the UK the number of people over 60 was four times greater in 1985 than 1901. The number increased by 2.5 million between 1961 and 1985 and is expected to increase by a further 2 million to the year 2015. In

Table 2.1 Population and population structure: selected countries

	Estimates of mid-year population (millions)					
	1961	1971	1976	1981	1984	1985
United Kingdom	52.8	55.6	55.9	56.4	56.5	56.6
Belgium	9.2	9.7	9.8	9.8	9.8	9.9
Denmark	4.6	5.0	5.1	5.1	5.1	5.1
France	46.2	51.2	52.9	54.2	55.0	55.2
Germany (Fed. Rep)[2]	56.2	61.3	61.5	61.7	61.2	61.0
Greece	8.4	8.8	9.2	9.7	9.9	9.9
Irish Republic	2.8	3.0	3.2	3.4	3.5	3.6
Italy	49.9	54.0	56.2	56.5	57.0	57.1
Luxembourg	0.3	0.3	0.4	0.4	0.4	0.4
Netherlands	11.6	13.2	13.8	14.2	14.4	14.5
Portugal	8.9	9.0	9.7	9.9	10.1	10.2
Spain	30.6	34.1	36.0	37.8	38.3	38.6
European Community[3]	281.5	305.2	313.7	319.1	321.2	322.1
Sweden	7.5	8.1	8.2	8.3	8.3	8.4
Turkey	28.2	36.2	41.1	45.4	48.3	49.3
Australia	10.5	12.9	13.9	14.9	15.6	15.8
USSR	218.0	245.1	256.7	267.7	275.1	278.6
Egypt	26.6	34.1	37.9	43.5	47.2	48.5
Tanzania	10.6	13.6	16.4	19.2	21.1	21.7
Zimbabwe	4.0	5.5	6.3	7.4	8.0	8.3
China	671.0	840.0	908.3	1011.2	1049.7	1059.5
India	439.0	551.3	613.3	676.2	745.0	750.9
Japan [4]	94.0	105.7	112.8	117.6	120.0	120.8
Canada	18.3	21.6	23.0	24.3	25.1	25.4
USA	183.8	206.2	215.1	230.0	236.7	239.3
Brazil	71.8	95.2	109.2	124.0	132.6	135.6
Peru	10.3	13.8	15.6	17.8	19.2	19.7

1 Latest available year.
2 Includes West Berlin.
3 Includes United Kingdom, Irish Republic, Denmark, Greece, Portugal, and Spain throughout.
4 Includes Okinawa
5 Under 20.

Source: Government Actuary's Department; Demographic Year Books and Monthly Bulletin of Statistics, United Nations.

particular there will be increases in the numbers of very old people (Social Trends, 1988). Within the 1990s in the UK the 15–29 age group is projected to show relative decline, whilst there are increases up to the year 2000 in the 30–44 age group and beyond that for the 45–59 age group. These middle and older age groups are relatively affluent and take three or four holiday breaks a year. However, they do not wish to be identified as elderly, which has stopped Holiday Inns from targeting the 55+ age group as an identifiable market, but has not stopped Friendly Hotels and

Percentage[1] aged		Expectation of life at birth[1] (years)	
Under 15	60 or over	Males	Females
19	21	71.4	77.2
20	19	68.6	75.1
20	20	71.4	77.4
22	18	70.4	78.5
17	20	70.2	76.8
22	17	70.1	73.6
31	15	68.8	73.5
21	18	69.7	75.9
19	18	66.8	72.8
22	16	72.7	79.3
26	15	65.1	72.9
26	16	70.4	76.2
. .	. .	. .	. .
19	22	73.0	79.1
39	5	53.7	
25	14	71.4	78.4
36[5]	13	64	74
40	6	51.6	53.8
46	6	47.3	50.7
51	3	51.3	55.6
34	8	62.6	66.5
39	6	46.4	44.7
23	14	74.2	79.7
22	14	71.9	78.9
22	16	70.5	78.2
38	6	57.6	61.1
41	5	52.6	55.5

Stakis from expanding into the nursing and residential homes business (Table 2.2, Social Trends, 1988, Harmer, 1988).

At the same time as the age structure of the population is changing so, too, are the number and structure of households, with a declining number of people per household. One of the reasons is the increased divorce rate which rose from 2.1 per 1000 married people in 1961 to 13.4 in 1985 (Social Trends, 1987).

Between 1971 and 1981 the total number of households increased from

Table 2.2 Age and sex structure of the population

United Kingdom	0–4	5–14	15–29	30–44	45–59	60–64	65–74	75–84	85+	Millions All ages
Census enumerated										
1901	4.4	8.0	10.8	7.5	4.6	1.1	1.3	0.5		38.2
1911	4.5	8.4	11.2	8.9	5.6	1.2	1.6	0.6		42.1
1921	3.9	8.4	11.2	9.3	7.0	1.5	1.9	0.7		44.0
1931	3.5	7.6	11.8	9.7	8.0	1.9	2.5	1.0		46.1
Mid-year estimates										
1941	3.4	6.8	9.2	10.3	8.5	2.3	3.2		1.3	44.9
1951	4.3	7.0	10.2	11.2	9.6	2.4	3.7		1.3	50.3
1961	4.3	8.1	10.3	10.5	10.6	2.8	4.0	1.9	0.3	52.8
1971	4.5	8.9	11.8	9.8	10.2	3.2	4.8	2.2	0.5	55.9
1976	3.7	9.2	12.4	10.0	9.8	3.1	5.1	2.3	0.5	56.2
1981	3.5	8.1	12.8	11.0	9.5	2.9	5.2	2.7	0.6	56.4
1983	3.6	7.6	13.1	11.1	9.4	3.2	5.0	2.8	0.6	56.3
1984	3.6	7.4	13.3	11.2	9.3	3.3	4.8	2.9	0.7	56.5
1985										
Males	1.9	3.7	6.8	5.7	4.6	1.5	2.2	1.0	0.2	27.6
Females	1.8	3.5	6.6	5.6	4.7	1.7	2.8	1.9	0.5	29.0
Total	3.6	7.3	13.4	11.3	9.3	3.1	4.9	2.9	0.7	56.6
Projections[1]										
1987		10.7	13.5	11.6	9.2		8.0		3.8	56.9
1991		11.0	12.9	12.1	9.5		7.9		4.0	57.5
1996		11.7	11.6	12.6	10.5		7.7		4.2	58.3
2001		12.0	10.8	13.2	11.0		7.6		4.4	59.0
2006		11.7	11.0	12.6	11.6		7.9		4.5	59.3
2011		11.1	11.7	11.3	12.1		8.8		4.5	59.4
2015		10.8	12.0	10.6	12.6		9.1		4.5	59.6

1 1985-based projections.   Source: Office of Population Censuses and Surveys; Government Actuary's Department

18.3 million to 19.5 million with only a marginal rise in population. One-person households increased from 17 per cent in 1971 to 24 per cent in 1985, while the percentage of households with 5 or more people fell from 14 to 8 per cent (Table 2.3, Social Trends, 1988).

The nuclear family has all but disappeared. In 1984 only 5.2 per cent of households consisted of a male bread winner, an economically inactive wife and two dependent children (Table 2.3). Single-person households, reconstituted families and households with economically active females form the bulk of the social fabric (EOC, 1986). However, although in 1985 28 per cent of households contained married couples with dependent children, 45 per cent of people lived in such a way. Similarly the 24 per cent of one-person households represents just 10 per cent of the population.

The population is also becoming increasingly well educated with increased voluntary extension of school leaving age and more adult and higher education places. There is a consequent difference in the educational attainment of different age cohorts. Seventy-two per cent of the 25–29 age group in 1985 had an educational qualification but only 40 per cent of those aged 50–59 did so.

In addition to these general trends in the UK population there are particular variations amongst ethnic groups in which the age profile is younger. Over half the households headed by a person in the Pakistani or Bangladeshi ethnic groups contain five or more people compared with less than one-tenth classified as such in white ethnic groups. A much lower proportion of West Indian, Indian or Asian households are one-person (Social Trends, 1988).

Similarly in the USA the black population is growing faster than the white. Interestingly, the Hispanic population in the USA is now greater than the black population and makes up 10 per cent of the total population. Household size tends to be large and the median age well below the national average (Mahatoo, 1985).

There have also been dramatic changes in workforce, income and expenditure. The UK labour force grew by 1.7 million between 1971 and 1985 to number 26.6 million. The growth was almost entirely due to the increased number of females in the labour force. Another noticeable trend is the drop in male employment beyond 60 following vigorous early retirement schemes (Social Trends, 1988, Table 2.2). The UK labour force is expected to grow by nearly one million between 1987 and 1995 with most due to increased participation by women. The labour force will, however, become increasingly concentrated in the 25–54 age range with a 23 per cent decrease in the 16–19 age group. This is likely to be combined with increased participation in higher education (MSC Report, 1988). Many women will join the labour force not only because of increasing oppor-

Table 2.3 Households[1]: by type

Great Britain

	Percentages and thousands								
	Percentages						Thousands		
	1961	1971	1976	1981	1984	1985	1961	1971	1981
No family									
One person									
Under retirement age[2]	4	6	6	8	9	9	726	1,122	1,469
Over retirement age[2]	7	12	15	14	16	15	1,193	2,198	2,771
Two or more people									
One or more over retirement age[2]	3	2	2	2	2	1	536	444	387
All under retirement age[2]	2	2	1	3	2	2	268	304	535
One family									
Married couple only	26	27	27	26	26	27	4,147	4,890	4,989
Married couple with 1 or 2 dependent children	30	26	26	25	24	24	4,835	4,723	4,850
Married couple with 3 or more dependent children	8	9	8	6	5	5	1,282	1,582	1,100
Married couple with independent child(ren) only	10	8	7	8	8	8	1,673	1,565	1,586
Lone parent with at least 1 dependent child	2	3	4	5	4	4	367	515	916
Lone parent with independent child(ren) only	4	4	4	4	4	4	721	712	720
Two or more families	3	1	1	1	1	1	439	263	170
Total households	100	100	100	100	100	100	16,189	18,317	19,493

1 All data for 1961, 1971, and 1981 are taken from the 10 per cent sample analyses of the Population Censuses of those years, and do not necessarily agree with the 100 per cent figures in Table 2.2. Percentages for 1976, 1984, and 1985 are from the General Household Survey.
2 60 for females, 65 for males.

Source: Office of Population Censuses and Surveys

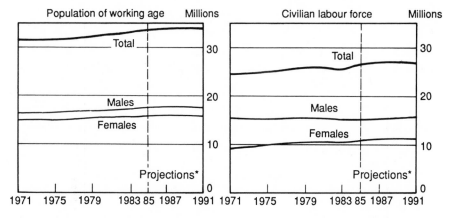

Figure 2.2 Population of working age and the civilian labour force (Great Britain). *The projected changes beyond 1985 are based on data up to 1984. The 1983-base population estimates have been adjusted to be consistent with more recent estimates. (*Source: Employment Gazette*, Department of Employment. Crown copyright. Reproduced with the permission of the Controller, HMSO)

tunity, but because most find housework boring and monotonous (Table 2.4). Although more are going to work they still only average 75 per cent of what is earned by men (Baron, 1988). Also, women are mainly moving into the expanding service sector which accounts for 76 per cent of womens' jobs. An interesting consequence of these changes is that people who are the consumers of services are in another respect the providers of those services. A further effect of these changes is the obvious need for expansion of services such as convenience food, labour saving devices in the home, and flexibility in retailing of goods and services.

Consumer expenditure is also some reflection of social trends. Since 1977, as Table 2.5 shows, expenditure on food has been relatively constant in absolute terms but has declined in relative terms. However, during a period of rising income and consumer credit, the main growth sectors in absolute terms are clothing and footwear, household durables, vehicle purchase, TV and video, expenditure abroad and other services (Social Trends, 1988). Future scenarios based on different economic projections show that demand will grow for leisure activities such as eating out, sport and recreation, viewing and listening, holidays (Martin and Mason, 1982).

Individual disposition

The second major area concerns individual disposition. A range of psychological states have an influence on consumer choice as indicated in

Table 2.4 Civilian labour force economic activity rates[1] and projections: by age and sex

Great Britain							Percentages All aged 16 or over
	16–19	20–24	25–44	45–54/59[2]	55–59 60–64[3]	60/65+[4]	
Males							
1971	69.4	87.7	95.4	94.8	82.9	19.2	80.5
1976	70.5	85.9	95.7	94.9	80.4	14.5	78.9
1981	72.4	85.1	95.7	93.0	69.3	10.3	76.5
1983	69.6	84.1	94.5	90.1	59.2	8.1	74.2
1984	72.9	84.6	94.4	89.1	56.7	8.2	74.2
1985	72.9	84.9	94.4	88.9	54.4	8.2	74.0
Projections[5]							
1986	72.8	85.3	94.6	89.5	59.2	7.0	74.3
1991	71.6	84.9	94.9	90.4	59.2	5.2	74.4
Females							
1971	65.0	60.2	52.4	62.0	50.9	12.4	43.9
1976	68.2	64.8	60.0	66.5	54.3	10.3	46.8
1981	70.4	68.8	61.7	68.0	53.4	8.3	47.6
1983	66.7	68.2	62.2	68.0	50.5	7.5	47.0
1984	68.7	69.0	65.1	69.1	51.1	7.6	48.4
1985	69.7	68.6	66.3	69.4	51.8	6.8	48.7
Projections[5]							
1986	69.9	70.3	66.3	70.0	51.9	7.3	49.1
1991	68.7	70.4	67.9	71.7	53.6	7.0	50.0

1 The percentage of the home population, or any sub-group of the population, who are in the civilian labour force.
2 45–54 for females, 45–59 for males.
3 55–59 for females, 60–64 for males.
4 60 or over for females, 65 or over for males.
5 1984-based

Source: Department of Employment

Figure 2.1. Of paramount importance is the underlying value system and personality of the consumer which will influence his or her lifestyle. Classifications of consumers according to lifestyle have, in market research, tended to replace or enhance more traditional methods of segmentation.

Early this century it was reasonably easy to categorise people according to criteria associated with social class, such as income and occupation, and to make some reasonable deductions about how they would behave. Some broad-brush demographic segmentation of consumers on these criteria is still attempted and gives some useful insights. In the 1950s, motivation research became fashionable as an attempt to get a deeper understanding of the subconscious psychological forces which might influence purchase decisions. Almost as an outgrowth of this work, the concept of lifestyle has come to the fore in the last 15–20 years as a way of trying to understand the rich diversity of factors influencing consumers.

Lifestyle is operationalised through the measurement of a number of psychological variables; activities; interests and opinions. In other words, the attempt is to differentiate consumers on the basis of the way they live and what they value rather than on how much money they earn or what job they have. Besides being able to do this for the individual, it is also possible to identify some general trends in lifestyle or cultural influences which seem to be of changed importance in society and hence will influence services which are purchased. Some of the general trends in lifestyle which appear to have an important influence on purchase behaviour can be identified.

The lifestyle of people is becoming increasingly varied reflecting divergence in levels of affluence and flexibility of working pattern.

Price is becoming less of a constraint. People will buy luxury holidays and seek high-class cuisine and hotels if they get value for money. Personal attention and care of the provider is an important signal of quality.

Time is valued, so products are bought which save time. As examples, consumption of Egg McMuffins is increasing while consumption of eggs is decreasing, people prefer using cash dispensers to queuing in a bank, and private health schemes mean less waiting than when public health care is provided. There is a trend away from fixed regular meals to eating convenience foods at convenient times, prepared often from the frozen state by microwave (Wood, 1988).

The shorter working week, smaller families and earlier retirement give more opportunity and energy for active leisure pursuits with increased eating out, DIY, travel and hobbies. More attention is given to personal ambition, life experience and meaning in work and less on success and achievement.

Table 2.5 Consumers' expenditure

United Kingdom	1977	1978	1979	1980	1981	1982	1983	1984	1985 Indices/ percentages	1985 £s million (current prices)
Indices at constant 1980 prices										
Food	96	98	100	100	99	99	101	100	101	29,950
Alcoholic drink	95	100	104	100	97	94	98	100	103	15,783
Tobacco	95	103	103	100	93	86	85	82	80	7,006
Clothing and footwear	86	94	101	100	99	103	110	117	125	14,894
Housing	94	95	98	100	101	102	105	107	109	31,711
Fuel and power	98	99	104	100	100	98	98	97	103	10,657
Household goods and services										
Household durables	87	94	105	100	99	103	110	113	118	7,622
Other	97	104	103	100	100	100	101	104	107	6,445
Transport and communication										
Purchase of vehicles	76	94	106	100	102	104	124	118	125	10,243
Running of vehicles	93	97	98	100	101	104	106	109	110	14,731
Other travel	91	93	99	100	100	98	101	106	111	6,892
Post and telecommunications	77	85	96	100	101	102	105	113	120	3,940
Recreation, entertainment, and education										
TV, video, etc	84	90	99	100	108	121	138	152	168	5,405
Books, newspapers, etc	98	99	100	100	97	94	91	90	89	2,964
Other	90	95	98	100	99	98	99	103	106	11,224
Other goods and services										
Catering (meals, etc)	99	98	101	100	93	91	99	100	104	12,339
Other goods	105	112	112	100	100	105	106	114	119	7,213
Other services	89	93	97	100	103	110	120	129	138	10,885
Less expenditure by foreign tourists, etc in the UK	122	114	110	100	91	89	103	111	121	6,228
Household expenditure abroad	51	63	80	100	107	106	107	108	110	4,444
Final expenditure by non-profit-making bodies	94	96	97	100	104	110	119	127	135	5,088
Consumers' expenditure	91	96	100	100	100	101	105	107	111	213,208

Percentage of total consumers' expenditure at current prices

Food	18.5	17.9	17.2	16.7	15.9	15.3	15.0	14.6	14.0	29,950
Alcoholic drink	7.6	7.3	7.3	7.3	7.3	7.2	7.3	7.4	7.4	15,783
Tobacco	4.2	3.9	3.6	3.5	3.6	3.5	3.4	3.4	3.3	7,006
Clothing and footwear	7.6	7.8	7.7	7.2	6.7	6.5	6.7	6.8	7.0	14,894
Housing	13.4	13.2	13.2	13.7	14.8	15.4	15.0	14.9	14.9	31,711
Fuel and power	4.9	4.6	4.5	4.6	5.1	5.2	5.1	4.9	5.0	10,657
Household goods and services	7.3	7.6	7.6	7.3	6.9	6.7	6.7	6.6	6.6	14,067
Transport and communication	14.7	15.4	16.3	16.4	16.5	16.5	16.8	16.6	16.8	35,806
Recreation, entertainment, and education	9.3	9.4	9.3	9.3	9.2	9.2	9.1	9.2	9.2	19,593
Other goods, services, and adjustments	12.6	12.9	13.3	14.1	14.0	14.4	14.9	15.6	15.8	33,741
Total	100.0	100.0	100.0	100.0	100.0	100.0	100.0	100.0	100.0	213,208

Source: United Kingdom National Accounts, Central Statistical Office

There is increasing pressure to do away with external restrictions on personal choice for example, on shopping hours and licensing laws.

A concern with the environment and harmful substances is reflected partly in changed attitudes to health, such as antagonism to irradiation of food and pressure for nutritional labelling (Wood, 1988). The growth of the 'Green Party' is evidence of mounting individual concern.

External stimuli

The final area relates to the effect of external stimuli. Obviously part of the decision about what people buy in the way of services depends on what is available and how it is presented to them. Increasingly, factors like design, presentation, environment, atmosphere, entertainment and facilities have become important. Companies are moving into the provision of new services to reflect this, e.g. department stores into estate agency and financial services, garages into food retailing, banks into personal financial services, financial houses into holidays, hotels into leisure and breweries into fast food and hotels.

There seem to be some underlying trends in services provided to customers; there is more emphasis on provision of a total package, quality is uppermost and customer care has been developed to provide a competitive edge. As an example, in the tourism and hospitality field total expansion of the service has been obvious. In the ten years up to 1987 short-break holidays increased by 7 per cent; conference and business tourism by 20 per cent. Incoming foreign tourism has increased by 5 per cent with an 8 per cent increase in real spend. Interests in having fun and making life fun, have led to an interest in products and services which allow this, such as the growth of packaged holidays to unusual destinations. In the next 15 years it is expected that growth of 50 per cent will occur in the number of heritage and cultural attractions in the UK with the best opportunities for those which meet consumer needs for high quality catering, retailing, entertainment, and design.

Mixed leisure developments are likely to increase with leisure provision seen as adding value. In Great Britain the need for indoor resort complexes has been established at the Blackpool Sand Castle and Rhyl Sun Centre. Wave machines, sun machines, leisure ice, children's theatre and other developments based on the Disneyland concepts applied to the European market are increasingly available.

In the past decade the accommodation sector has seen a shift from 54 to 59 per cent of nights self-catered at the same time as a decrease from 46 to 41 per cent in serviced, conventional accommodation. However, in the serviced accommodation sector there is likely to be growth in three areas; budget hotels as low cost extensions to pubs and restaurants, luxury hotels to provide for the rising expectations of the business market, and country house hotels with sport and leisure facilities to provide for over-seas and shortbreak markets. Bed and breakfast provision is likely to remain buoyed up by incoming tourists, numbers of which will increase with the Channel Tunnel opening in 1993 and decreased travel costs consequent on the Single Europe Act in 1992. In the UK the number of all year round holiday centres such as Centre Parc in Sherwood Forest, are expected to increase as a reaction to increased leisure time.

In the restaurant and pub sector themed restaurants and bars will increase and food courts, healthy food and regional recipes are likely to capitalise on some of the main consumer trends. Restaurants are likely to polarise into fast food at one end of the scale and luxury *haute cuisine* at the other end (Anon, 1988; Bramwell, 1988).

The holiday market is likely with the Single Europe Act to result in cheaper, less restricted travel and increased accessibility of places that have been till now difficult to get to. As a result the trend is likely to continue for people to take more than one holiday each of shorter duration.

In the home, increased computerisation is likely to mean increased opportunity for funds transfer between or within bank accounts, shopping, booking of holidays, searches of databases of information, buying and selling of goods and credit transfer.

All these changes, many intended to increase the quality of customer care, are also indicative of the fact that the customer will be part of a 'total experience' in buying. Increasing sophistication of technology will make it possible for the level of service to the customer to be improved, although the technology will not replace but release the provider of the service to give more personal attention to the consumer.

Summary

In summary the services provided to consumers in the future will have to meet the needs of an ageing population in which people will have shorter hours of work and longer holidays. The household structure will become increasingly dominated by divorced, remarried or one-parent families. More men than in the past will be economically inactive, whether unemployed, retired or part of the domestic economy. At the same time more women, especially married women, will become employed.

Overall, people will become better educated and their changed values will be reflected in lifestyles which are increasingly concerned with health, convenience, indulgence, conservation and quality. Perhaps more obvious will be a concern with individuality, so that individual and unusual services which provide for a particular market niche may best capitalise on emerging consumer needs.

Of course, changes consequent to the impact of information technology, better and cheaper transport and changed territorial barriers will mean that many new services will become available. Predicting how consumers will respond to these new facilities may be just as difficult in future as it is now, given the complex interaction of psychological state, physiological need and attributes of the service which have an influence on consumer choice.

References

Anon. (1988) 'Global Trends', *Caterer & Hotelkeeper*, 28th January.

Baron, P. (1988) 'The Changing Market for British Food', *British Food Journal*, 90, 1.

Bramwell, B. (1988) English Tourist Board Projections, CHME Conference, Stafford.

Central Statistical Office (1987) *Social Trends*, HMSO, London.

Central Statistical Office (1988) *Social Trends*, HMSO, London.

Chisnall, P. M. (1976) Personal communication, Sheffield City Polytechnic.

Daly, L. and Beharrell, B. (1988) 'Health, Diet and the Marketing of Food and Drink – Some Theoretical Problems', *British Food Journal*, 90, 1.

Engel, F., Blackwell, R. D. and Miniard, P. W. (1986) *Consumer Behaviour*, 5th edition, Dryden Press, Hinsdale, IL.

Equal Opportunities Commission (1986) *The Fact about Women is . . .*

Fishbein, M. (1980) *Understanding Attitudes to Predicting Social Behaviour*, Prentice-Hall, Englewood Cliffs

Foxall, G. (1980) *Consumer Behaviour*, Croom Helm, London.

Frank, J. and Wheelock, V. (1988) 'International Trends in Food Consumption', *British Food Journal*, vol. 90 No. 1, pp. 22–9

Harmer, J. (1988) 'Senior Citizens', *Caterer & Hotelkeeper*, 28th January.

Linton, R. (1947) *The Cultural Background of Personality*, Routledge, London.

Mahatoo, W. H. (1985) *The Dynamics of Consumer Behaviour*, Wiley, Chichester.

Manpower Services Commission (1988) Report.

Martin, W. H. and Mason, S. (1982) *Leisure and Work; The Choices for 1991 and 2001*, Leisure Consultants, Sudbury.

Office of Population, Censuses and Surveys (1985) *General Household Survey*, HMSO, London.

Segal-Horn, S. (1986) *The UK Retail Industry, Working Paper No. 10*, Department of Business Management, Brighton Polytechnic.

Tuck, M. (1976) *How do we choose? A study of consumer behaviour*, Methuen, London.

Unsworth, R. (1988) *The Times*, 16th April.

Wood, S. (1988) *The Financial Times*, 19th April

3 Consumer financial services

DR PAUL C FIFIELD

Introduction

In this chapter we will consider the UK consumer financial services sector. For an industry which has such a major impact on the UK economy and balance of payments and at the same time can count almost every one of us as a customer, this sector has a surprisingly confused image in the market place.

The term 'financial services' is comparatively new and was coined to help classify the variety of money-based services on offer to consumers at a time when the traditional barriers between the different suppliers looked like breaking down. Between 1945 and 1980 the industry could be divided into three separate sectors, each of which kept to its own area of business. Broadly, the three sectors were life and general insurance, controlled by the DTI and selling insurance related products; building societies, controlled by legislation and limited to taking deposits and lending on mortgage; and clearing banks, controlled by the Bank of England, who were effectively excluded from the housing market and the personal sector. During the 1980s, government proceeded to dismantle some of the restrictions enabling the banks and life companies to attack the mortgage market. The term 'financial services' is now used to cover everything from simple motor insurance through bank accounts to the most complicated investment plans.

As was highlighted in Chapter 1, the financial services sector is very important to the UK economy, responsible for 13.5 per cent of GDP and 9.2 per cent of employment in 1985. In addition, the financial services sector has always been an important exporter with the banks being major players in international markets.

Currently the financial services sector is undergoing a period of intense change; change to a degree never before experienced by the industry. During the 1980s a number of challenges have appeared to confront suppliers such as increased competition, legislation, industry convergence, technology, European harmonisation and a scramble for distribution outlets. How the providers of financial services respond to these challenges will largely dictate whether they survive in the industry of the 1990s. This chapter will explore most of these challenges in some detail, but we start with a brief analysis of the size and structure of the sector just as the first of the industry's challenges, the Financial Services Act (FSA), comes into force.

Size and structure

The collective term 'financial services' can generally be taken to include the following:

Clearing banks

The banking sector is dominated by a small number of what, by world standards, are massive banks. The 'Big Four' banks are Barclays, Lloyds, Midland and National Westminster and major among the next league are Bank of Scotland, Royal Bank, Standard Chartered and the Trustee Savings Bank (TSB). Since the ceiling control on bank deposits was lifted in 1981, the clearing banks have expanded out of traditional banking services into investment, insurance and mortgage lending. It is estimated that they now control 30 per cent of the personal mortgage market (from 8 per cent in 1980) and 60 per cent of unsecured loans. They have also spearheaded the credit card market with 'Visa' (Barclays) and 'Access' (Natwest/Lloyds/Midland/Royal Bank of Scotland). While the banks have made progress in the lending sector they have come under pressure in other areas and they have lost significant shares of the savings and deposit markets.

General insurance

This includes all aspects of protection against loss arising from accident or catastrophe. Cover can be arranged for motor, house buildings damage, home contents and personal valuables loss, etc.

Life assurance

Originally, life assurance companies aimed to offer security for dependents, but now the bulk of their business is investment-linked and products include investment plans and pensions. Deregulation and the removal of competitive barriers have allowed life companies to diversify

into other products and markets. The move into endowment-type mortgages has been significant, and recent legislation changes offer enormous
potential for developing the personal pensions business.

Investment companies

These are primarily concerned with investing their customers' funds
under a variety of schemes including annuities, pensions and savings
plans.

Building societies

Building societies as we know them today grew out of the Victorian
friendly societies based on the savings market, mostly around the Midlands
and the North. With the post-war housing boom and a rush of branch
openings, the building societies became a major street force. There are
currently (1986) 151 building societies in the UK controlling total assets
of £140bn. The sector is, however, highly concentrated, with the top five
societies controlling in excess of 60 per cent of total assets. The building
societies were, until recently, restricted to mortgage lending. The banks'
entry into the mortgage market has put greater pressure on the societies
and now the entry of the life companies can only make the situation
worse. Many societies see their only response as being in the broader
financial services market. It is considered by some observers that, by the
end of the decade, some societies will be indistinguishable from retail
banks.

Finance houses

These specialise in lending for major items such as car purchase and
consumer durables. Often subsidiaries of banks, finance houses have
suffered in the 'eighties from the arrival of credit card finance on a mass
scale. Hire purchase has now given way to 'plastic payment' for many
medium-value durables.

Credit card companies

These are owned by the major banks and generate card-linked credit
(Barclaycard, 8.5m cards; Access, 9.8m cards; and Trustcard, 2.5m cards).
Credit card lending has generally been the banks' fastest growing sector,
but recently competition in this sector is starting to grow and a price war
on interest rates is expected over the next few years.

Charge card companies

These companies offer card-linked credit as above but generally for larger amounts and shorter periods. The two major operators are American Express and Diners Club, but these have recently been joined by charge card equivalents of the Barclaycard and Access Card.

Retail credit

Retailers have become much more active over recent years in offering their own credit facilities linked to their own issued cards. Marks & Spencer launched its own credit card in 1985 and now has 2.5 million cards issued. Welbeck Finance operates the majority of independent retailer cards working for over forty retailers. In addition, House of Fraser has issued over 1.4 million cards and Dixons 500,000.

Insurance brokers/Independent Financial Advisors (IFAs)

These are intermediaries (or retailers) for financial services and sell services produced by the general and life assurance companies. The term 'broker' is popularly used to cover all intermediaries in this sector and not just those registered with the Insurance Brokers' Registration Council (IBRC). This whole distribution channel has already been directly affected by the Financial Services Act, and while there are many opinions as to the number and type of intermediaries that will be operating at the end of the decade, the current situation makes it difficult to forecast accurately the shape of this sector. Despite an active promotional campaign, large numbers of IFAs have already forsaken independent status and tied to major insurance companies.

Public sector

Through the 20,000+ main and sub-post offices in the UK the government also offers a range of financial services to the public. These include the National Savings Bank, National Savings Certificates, Premium Bonds and Girobank.

The above cover most of the UK financial services sector, although there exist a number of smaller and specialist organisations offering dedicated financial products to their customers. As can be readily appreciated, the sector is both wide-ranging in the products which it offers and the types of organisations which operate within it.

Beyond the sheer scale of the sector is the breadth of coverage of the UK population. There are very few people who do not use consumer financial services in some form. Eighty-seven per cent of the adult population hold at least one Bank or Building Society account and 81 per cent have at least one form of savings (see Table 3.1).

Table 3. 1 Consumer usage of financial services

Year 1987

Percentage of all adults (18+)		%
Life assurance:	protection	42
	endowment	28
	personal pension plan	5
General insurance:	house or flat	39
	home contents	52
	motor	40
	medical	5
At least 1 bank/building society account		87
At least 1 form of savings		81
Bank:	current A/c	67
	deposit A/c	30
	ATM card	38
Building society – any account		60
Premium bonds		20
Bank loan		7
Credit card		34
Retail store account		13
Mail order		23
At least one credit commitment		55
Mortgage to buy property		33

Source: Marketing Pocket Book, The Advertising Association, *from:* NOP Financial Research Services

Since in the British culture, money is always a sensitive subject, successive governments have taken it upon themselves to regulate the industry quite closely. The levels and details of governmental control are too complex to enumerate here, but the Department of Trade and Industry (DTI) closely monitors the financial and trading practices of all sectors broadly taking responsibility for security on behalf of the consuming and investing public.

Key issues facing the sector

The financial services sector is currently in a period of rapid and accelerating change. For decades the industry generally was spared the intense competition experienced by manufacturing and other services such as retailing. Now, for the first time, providers are faced with increasing turbulence and are having to re-examine the established business methods to which many have adhered for over a century. The key issues facing the sector in the 1990s are as follows.

Increased competition

For many decades the financial services sector has experienced a favoured position in British commerce – a well regulated business environment with known and understood competitors. Clearly defined lines separated banks from insurance companies and from the building societies. Each sub-sector kept to its patch and competed in a gentlemanly fashion with its peers.

Now competiton is starting to appear, although still not intense when compared to that in other industries. The first entrants from manufacturing are starting to be attracted by the high margins in the industry and have acquired companies bringing modern marketing techniques in their wake.

Also, the traditional barriers within the sector are starting to break down and banks are offering a wide range of services such as mortgages, investment and insurance and are thus competing with other firms in the sector. Building societies are now considering taking full banking status to compete, and the insurance companies are also broadening their range of services. This *convergence* is still in its early stages and it is unclear how far the process will develop. Most importantly, it is still unclear how the consumer will react to these full-range offerings. Generally, market research does not have a high profile in the financial services sector and many companies appear to be taking the market advantages of convergence on faith.

Increased competition is also apparent at retail level. Over recent years a number of retailers have started to offer their own credit facilities rather than pass the business on to the traditional credit organisations. For retailers, the benefits of operating their own systems are significant; not only do they access this high-margin business but credit cards offer an additional communication channel to their most regular customers. Despite this invasion by the major retailers the bulk of the business, unlike the USA and France, is still held by the two majors, Barclaycard and Access.

A visible sign of the increased competition is the explosive growth of advertising expenditure. Building society advertising rose from £8m in

1974 to over £80m in 1984, in the same year bank advertising reached £65m.

Legislation

Recent years have witnessed a wide-ranging change in legislation in the UK. In 1987 the Building Societies Act set up a new regulatory authority and for the first time allowed building societies to grant unsecured lending and to offer other non-mortgage related business. In 1988 they were also allowed to enter the life and pensions business with fewer controls. The Social Security Act and changes to SERPS (state earnings related pensions) has opened up the market for personal pensions. The impact of the Financial Services Act on the insurance industry has still to be fully measured, since its attempt to regulate the industry, its offerings and the commercial practices of its intermediaries may produce some unexpected side effects. These acts are all complicated pieces of legislation and cannot be examined in depth here. The main thrust of the legislation is aimed at increasing competition in the sector in the belief that a protected industry becomes inefficient, expensive and poor value.

Distribution

How financial products are distributed to the consumer has become a question of debate over recent years. The Financial Services Act has begun to set certain conditions for intermediaries of general and life assurance products which are expected to produce a severe reduction in the numbers of brokers and other financial intermediaries. The banks, who have long regarded their large numbers of branches as a barrier to competitive entry, are now reviewing their position faced with the use of automatic teller machines (ATM) which can be sited almost anywhere. Direct mail and direct sales forces are also offering competition to the traditional outlets.

Technology

Technology has long played a role in the financial services sector both in product development (life assurance) and in customer service (ATM's, credit cards etc). Technology has a difficult role to play in a service business where person-to-person contact should command a premium. Further developments in technology, especially EFTPOS (electronic funds transfer at point of sale), are available but are being held up by lack of agreement between the major banks and the retailers. As the UK moves closer towards a cashless society, the use of technology will increase. It depends upon the individual companies how well they are able to employ technology and still retain an image of personal caring.

The role of marketing

Traditionally, the companies in the sector have been technology- and process-led in their ability to produce financial services products. Until very recently marketing has been seen as solely responsible for designing the brochures. For example, the banks admit to two bad marketing mistakes in the 1960s and 1970s. The first was to install imposing security screening in the branches (union pressure), the second was the conscious decision to downgrade the calibre of the staff behind the counter. The thorny question of bank opening hours has still to be addressed. In the view of some, the antiquated opening hours of 10.00 am to 3.00 pm has been a significant factor in the steady decline of the banks' share of the personal savings market. With the increase in competition has come the realisation that the customer has a choice and that technical excellence alone is unlikely to guarantee continued growth into the 1990s. The move to market orientation is not an easy one for such a traditional industry but a number of companies are rising to the challenge.

These issues are not the only strategic questions facing the sector but they are generally seen as the most important. Adaptability, more than any other characteristic, is likely to separate the winners from the losers over the next decade.

Future developments

Given the changes now in train, industry reviewers have difficulty in forecasting accurately major future developments. There are, though, a number of points which can be made.

Industry concentration

Compared to most other sectors, both manufacturing and services, the general and life assurance sector supports a very large number of players. With increased competition a number of mergers can be expected and most commentators foresee a smaller number of very large organisations in competition with more smaller, specialist niche market players. The banking and credit sectors on the other hand have long preserved their domain with relatively few active companies. More new entrants can be expected here, although whether this entry comes from the building societies or from outside the financial services industry remains to be seen.

European harmonisation

The significance of 1992 is only now beginning to become clear to the sector and with a few exceptions, notably the banks, most organisations have little international business experience. Although the European situation differs from sub-sector to sub-sector, generally UK financial services industry is extremely well placed to make a significant impact. Europe generally has seen a rash of mergers and acquisitions as major players jostle for position, Barclays and Natwest have also bought small banks in Spain. Since most EC markets are even more heavily protected than the UK at present, the UK industry already begins with a healthy price advantage in most areas. The only question which remains is whether industry management is willing or able to take advantage of the significant opportunities offered by an enlarged domestic market.

The ageing population

Between now and the year 2000 a significant proportion of the nation's wealth will change hands. A higher percentage than ever before of today's pensioners own their own home. On death this wealth will transfer to the next generation who themselves will already own a home and will probably be at the peak earning level. The opportunity for the investment of surplus assets offers a major challenge to the sector.

Management attitude

More than any other factor the attitude of management to rapid and accelerating change will determine individual company success in the next decade. Changes in the financial services environment is already forcing management into decisions that have never before confronted them. Their ability to look outward to an increasingly sophisticated marketplace and offer service rather than technical solutions will tax all managers, but yesterday's thinking will not solve today's problems.

Already the life companies are recruiting managers from outside the industry who bring with them entrepreneurial and marketing expertise so far lacking in the financial services sector. In addition, the arrival of non-industry purchasers of business (such as BAT's acquisition of Eagle Star and Allied Dunbar) can be expected to change management thinking from within.

Banks and building societies have been slow buying in key expertise, but the trend has started and can be expected to grow.

Summary and conclusions

The financial services sector is undergoing a revolution partially stimulated by government action but mostly in response to consumer demand for better service and wider choice. Whatever the outcome there are bound to be some important, and well known, casualties before the process has run its course.

The single most important challenge facing the sector does not come from outside but from within. The challenge is that of changing management attitudes. If companies are to survive and prosper within the enlarged market offered by the EC, then management will have to adapt its thinking to the 1980s.

The future demands a pro-active, market-led leadership to face up to market changes and rapidly increasing competition. Although many bemoan the passing of the 'good old days' with their Victorian processing systems, protected and delimited market boundaries and competition which was both gentle and gentlemanly, those days will not reappear. The 1990s will be the time of the marketer and the entrepreneur – not the administrator.

It takes time to change and so far the marketplace has been overly generous. New people and new thinking are starting to appear. Once the new thinking demonstrates results, more will follow. As the Chinese proverb says, 'My friends, we live in exciting times'.

4 The retail sector

DR LEIGH SPARKS

Introduction

Retailing is one of the largest sectors of the UK economy and, indeed, is an important sector in the majority of countries of the world. The retail sector in the UK has in the past been characterised as being the domain of the small, owner-operated shop providing a commonplace mechanism for the distribution of goods. Classically, Britain was caricatured as a 'nation of shopkeepers'. The plethora of shops and shopkeepers produced an image of unimportance and inferiority for the retail sector. As McFadyen (1987) states 'successive British governments have treated the retail sector as of secondary importance ("they don't actually *produce* anything you understand old boy"); for years British retailers have suffered discrimination from government policies that favour manufacturing industry'.

Such an image does not do justice to modern-day retailing with its large, profitable and efficient companies, an emphasis on style, design and better facilities for the consumer and modern strategic outlook. Some of the largest companies, brightest minds and most effective and successful entrepreneurs and managers are to be found in the retail sector. A 'retail revolution' has occurred in recent decades that is claimed to be as dramatic and influential as was the industrial revolution.

This chapter explores this modern retail sector, building on the macro-economic and consumer analysis of Chapter 1. The aim is to understand the size and structure of the retail market and the forces that are changing retailing. This is undertaken via a brief statistical review of the sector followed by an analysis of the key trends in retailing. From these key trends it is possible to consider the likely future patterns in retailing and the special issues and problems that will be faced in the future. The focus of this chapter is the United Kingdom, but as Segal-Horn (1987) and Lusch (1987) and the various chapters in Davies and Rogers (1984) have shown, many of the trends operating in the UK are operable also in North America. It is also possible to see similarities with developments in western Europe (Dawson, 1982; Burt and Dawson, 1988).

Retail market size and structure

Retailing is a very large and important sector of the British economy. In terms of VAT registered businesses, retailing comprises 248,433 or 18.8 per cent of the total UK businesses (mid 1987). Estimates of employment in the distributive trades for mid 1988 indicate that they employ almost 3.3 million people or 15.2 per cent of the British total employees in employment. Of these 3.3 million employees, almost 2.1 million are employed in retailing as opposed to wholesaling or repairing. These figures exclude the self-employed. Estimates for Great Britain for 1985 suggest that there were 2.54 million self-employed people (with and without employees) of which 436,000 were in retailing (17 per cent). Retail sales were £95.155 billion in 1986 which is approximately 42 per cent of all consumer expenditure. Investment in physical resources in British retailing is over £2 billion per annum. The latest Retail Inquiry (1986) shows that there are 244,006 businesses in retailing, operating through 343,387 retail outlets. These businesses and outlets provided employment for 2.334 million people (employees plus self-employed) and had a turnover of £93,669 billion. The retail sector is indeed big business. The scale of change in retailing can be assessed by the evidence from the 1950 Census of Distribution which suggests that there were 583,000 shops in Great Britain. Somewhere in the region of 250,000 retail outlets and associated employment have been lost in this country since 1950. This net loss of outlets of course masks the true fluctuation in retail business numbers.

This massive change in retailing size has also been associated with considerable changes in structure and organisational type. The main categories of organisational type identified are owner-operated independent shops, multiple retailers and co-operative societies. Depending on sources used, however, department stores, mail order, voluntary groups and government chains can provide further axes of disaggregation.

Table 4.1 provides estimates of the change in organisational structure that has occurred between 1961 and 1980. Multiple retailers have expanded their market share at the expense of the traditional independent and co-operative retail sectors. The reasons for this change will be examined later. This process has not stopped at 1980. Due to data source problems the figures in Table 4.1 cannot directly be continued, but the Retail Inquiry data for 1980–86 indicate that outlet numbers have continued to decline, although the retail sector remains dominated in numerical terms by single outlet retailers. In terms of turnover, however, multiple retailers continue to gain market share at the expense of single outlet retailers and the co-operative societies.

Table 4.1 Retail sales by organisation type in the UK

	1961 (%)	1966 (%)	1971 (%)	1976 (%)	1978 (%)	1980 (%)
Multiples	28.2	33.0	36.4	40.1	42.2	42.8
Independents	53.9	49.9	48.1	43.0	41.0	40.7
Co-operative societies	9.5	7.7	5.8	6.2	6.0	5.8
Department stores (incl. Co-ops)	5.9	5.7	5.8	6.0	5.8	5.7
Mail order	2.5	3.7	3.9	4.7	5.0	5.0

Primary sources: Department of Industry, Business Monitor (SD Series); Economist Intelligence Unit, *Retail Business*, 1982 (April).
Secondary source: McGoldrick, P. J. (1984) Trends in retailing and consumer behaviour, pp. 29–54 of Davies, R. L. and Rogers, D. S. (eds) *Store Location and Store Assessment Research*, Wiley, Chichester.

Table 4.2 further demonstrates the increasing domination of retailing by large businesses and an increasing concentration of market power in the hands of fewer companies. This can be seen in terms of number of establishments, sales and capital expenditure. The retail sector is shrinking in terms of number of outlets and businesses, although not volume, but the sector as a whole is increasingly dominated and controlled by large

Table 4.2 General comparisons of retailing in the UK

All retailing	1961	1971	1980	1984	1986
Number of businesses					
Total '000	394	351	240	231	226
With single store '000	356	327	210	202	198
With over 10 stores	1900	1270	1260	950	
50 stores	430	330	300	284	
Number of establishments					
Total '000	540	480	362	343	339
in businesses with over 10 stores	96	79	74	68	65
50 stores	66	60	55	54	56
Percentage of sales					
in businesses with over 10 stores	40	44	55	58	60
50 stores	31	36	45	50	52
Percentage of capital expenditure					
in businesses with over 10 stores	63	73	70	70	71
50 stores	31	36	45	63	67

NB: Precise comparisons for 1961 and 1971 with later years are not possible but an attempt has been made to make the data as comparable as possible.
Primary sources: Business Monitors, Retail Inquiry 1986 figures based on IRS estimates of trends.
Secondary source: Dawson, J. A., Shaw, S. A. and Harris, D. G. (1987). *The Impact of Changes in Retailing and Wholesaling on Scottish Manufacturers*, 2 volumes, Institute for Retail Studies, Stirling.

Table 4.3 Retail trade by broad kind of business 1986

Kind of business	Number of businesses	Number of outlets	Average number of outlets per business	Persons engaged (000s)	Total turnover (inc VAT)	Capital expenditure £ million (net)
Food retailers	77,137	99,751	1.29	818	33,386	1,385
Drink, confectionery and tobacco retailers	44,344	56,511	1.27	268	9,704	135
Clothing, footwear and leather goods retailers	32,656	59,286	1.82	294	9,347	258
Household goods retailers	43,002	60,676	1.41	305	14,670	379
Other non-food retailers	39,110	50,915	1.75	234	7,882	142
Mixed retail businesses	4,921	10,395	2.11	380	17,356	540
Hire and repair businesses	2,839	5,853	2.06	34	1,323	76
Total retail trade	244,006	343,387	1.41	2,334	93,669	2,915

Source: Retail Inquiry 1986.

companies. The breadth of retailing and the importance of the retail sector as a whole is therefore well marked. The retail sector, however, is not an homogeneous one and can be disaggregated into a number of broad kinds of business.

Table 4.3 provides information on the structure of the retail sector. The largest kind of business is food retailing in terms of all the axes of evaluation. The process of concentration is well advanced in this sector (Akehurst, 1983; Davies, Gilligan and Sutton, 1985; Beaumont, 1987) and the main food retailers (Sainsbury, Tesco, Asda, Gateway and Safeway) claim over 70 per cent of the packaged groceries market in some regions of Great Britain. The second largest sector in turnover terms is that of mixed retail businesses, although this is one of the smallest sectors in terms of the other measures. The businesses in this sector are the large chain and variety stores such as Marks & Spencer and Littlewoods as well as the main department store groups. Again this sector is highly concentrated. The remaining sectors detailed in Table 4.3 all contain major household names in the form of big retailers, but the presence of many small retailers is also clearly indicated by the table.

Trends in retailing

Retailing is a highly dynamic sector (McFadyen, 1987; Bamfield, 1988). Currently, retail change is occurring at the same time as wider societal and industrial change, bringing retail change into a higher public and governmental awareness. The trends in retailing appear numerous, complex and in some cases controversial. Following Dawson and Sparks (1985) it is proposed here to divide the trends in retailing into changes in business organisation and changes in the operations of retailing. It has to be recognised, however, that both these sets of changes are themselves responses to, or attempts to change, trends in the wider environment of retailing. For example, retailers respond to, and direct, consumer behaviour and social change and are constrained or encouraged by the land-use planning system.

The relationship of retailers with consumers is central to retail change. A brief review of trends in consumer behaviour as they affect retailing is therefore required. Over a long period (30+ years) output from retailing as measured by sales volume has increased, although a distinction has to be made between food and non-food spending. Increases in retail spending have been directed mainly towards non-food, household-based or fashion products. This differential is caused by changes in the demographic and household structure, a rise in disposable incomes for those in employment, the advent of widespread consumer credit and the changing balance between food and non-food prices.

There are under way in the UK changes in consumer behaviour and consumption that are influencing retailers and to which retailers have to respond. First, there are economic changes associated with spending power, disposable income, credit and home ownership. Second, there are attitudinal changes through altered perceptions and consciousness (e.g. healthy eating) perhaps reaching an extreme in 'lifestyle'. Third are the behavioural changes in the use of time and perceived and actual mobility (retail as leisure). Finally, there are locational changes in terms of places of residence and work. All these changes are inter-linked and constitute a major factor underpinning retail change in terms of the segmentation of the market and the realisation of different requirements and needs from shopping at different times and places.

Changes in business organisation

As has been seen, within all sectors of retailing there has been a growth of large companies and an expansion of multiple retailers. In recent years, takeovers and mergers have been a way of life in retailing. Whilst the big takeover battles and mergers such as Asda–MFI, Burton–Debenhams, Dixons–Woolworths etc receive much publicity, many smaller and less controversial takeovers are occurring on a regular basis. Retailers such as Next, Harris Queensway or Ratners have engineered themselves a large share of retail markets through an ability to take over other companies and integrate them profitably with existing businesses. The largest firms in retailing are amongst the largest companies in Britain. Many retail sectors are dominated by large firms and have high concentration ratios. Typically, the grocery sector is highly concentrated, but other historically less concentrated sectors such as jewellery, toys and chemists have seen the emergence of large multiple groups such as Ratners, Early Learning Centre and Share Drug respectively. In some cases these are companies operating almost entirely within one sector (Ratners in jewellery) but in other cases are merely one arm of a corporation. For example, Woolworths have assembled a major drug store chain through the acquisitions of Superdrug, Tip Top Drugstores and Share Drug. This drugstore arm is merely one of their corporate branches with the others being the mainline business, the electrical sector (Comet), the DIY sector (B & Q) and the autocare sector (Charlie Browns) all traditionally low concentration sectors.

Table 4.4 demonstrates the size of the Sears Corporation retail arms which was put together after the Second World War in a series of major takeovers and has recently begun to develop new fascias and search for

Table 4.4 The Sears Corporation PLC (1987)

	Approximate number of outlets	
Footwear		
British Shoe Corporation	2200	
Freeman Hardy Willis	450	
Trueform	250	
Curtess	350	
Shoe City	5	
Dolcis	300	
Manfield	200	
Lilley and Skinner Saxone	700	
Department stores		
Selfridge's	1	
Lewis's	11	
Women's wear		
Miss Selfridge	82	
Wallis	112	
Children's wear		
Adams	102	
Sports goods		
Millets	170	
Olympus	100	
Jewellery		
Garrard	1	
Mappin and Webb	14	
Men's wear	*Number of outlets*	*Target customer*
Fosters	320	24–40, C1, C2, D
Your Price	110	16+, C2, D, E
Hornes	44	25–45, B, C
Esq	15	25–45, A, B, C1
Jargon	14	16–25, C1, C2
Zy	13	16–25, B, C
Bradleys	1	30+, C, D, E
Dormie	24	25+, A, B, C,

Note: Sears are also experimenting with a number of potential chains, including watches, and in February 1988 took over Freemans, the mail order company.

Sources: Retail Business, Retail Trade Reviews, September 1987, pp. 40–42.
  Retail, 5(2), 1987, pp. 20–23

takeover opportunities. The core business of the Sears Corporation has long been the footwear trade with the British Shoe Corporation, but the breadth of their business can be seen in Table 4.4 with developments coming from expansion into new sectors and takeovers.

The development and expansion of large retail companies is partly associated with an ability to raise finance on the Stock Exchange. Most large retailers are publicly quoted stock with the true ownership of these companies often difficult to ascertain. For the most part, retail companies are owned and controlled by those not in charge of their day-to-day operation and therefore a high share price is vital to maintaining profile and independence. Institutional change is also ensuring that there are fewer financial companies which are themselves growing larger. The effect is that the ownership of retailing is becoming more and more concentrated into a small number of institutions. Key decisions about the future of retail companies can be concentrated, as in the Dixons–Woolworths and Burton–Debenhams takeovers, in the hands of less than 20 major institutional investors.

It is usual to use the terms multiple, independent and co-operative retailers when considering change in retailing. Table 4.5, however, uses a slightly different taxonomy to explore in more detail the question of competition amongst organisational types. Although this fivefold distinction is a useful starting point, complications can occur in assigning companies to categories, as companies can operate outlets in several ways, e.g. the Body Shop which has both company shops and franchises. Changes in relative positions of these categories have seen consumer co-operatives and owner-operated independents lose market share to, in particular, the corporate chains (multiples) and the contractual chains. This is not only in the 'traditional' food sector where contractual chains such as Spar, Circle K etc are expanding, but in non-food sectors with the growth of specialist chains such as Apollo Window Blinds and Benetton, and in fast food with, for example, Wimpy and MacDonald's.

What is clear is that *chains* of stores are expanding at the expense of independent retailers and co-operatives. There are a number of reasons behind this rise of multiple retailers. In particular, multiple retailers can gain from economies of scale and economies of replication. As the companies have grown larger they have been able to gain from their size

Table 4.5 Organisational types in retailing

1 Corporate chain	– Public	e.g. Marks & Spencer
	– Private	e.g House of Fraser
2 Consumer co-operative chain		e.g. Normid
3 Contractual chain	– Voluntary group	e.g. Spar
	– Franchise	e.g. Sperrings
	– Buying group association	e.g. BIGA
4 Government chain		e.g. Post Office
5 Owner operated independent		

in terms of, for example, buying power from suppliers, administrative centralisation, specialist developments and wider market power. Expansion into new areas is also easier due to the size of the company. These benefits have also come from economies of replication in which a standard or relatively standard retail outlet or procedure can be duplicated over a large number of sites. This brings cost savings through speed of opening and conformity of operation, e.g. prices, systems etc. Both of these types of benefits are aided by the introduction of new technology. Such benefits are available to multiple retailers and also contractual chains and franchises. Owner-operated independents and the fragmented co-operatives are often unable to benefit in the same ways.

This move to centralised management and control is associated with the emergence of strategic planning and the adoption of a systems approach to retail operations. This can be seen in corporate chains (e.g. Tesco), contractual chains (e.g. Spar Eight Till Late) and through franchising (e.g. Tie Rack, Body Shop). One implication of these changes in management methods, enabled by new technology, is that it is now possible to operate efficiently chains of small units, as for example in Victoria Wine, Benetton or Next. These chains, it must be emphasised, are not operated by small businesses, but are branches of a corporate or contractual chain with centralised management control. The profitability of small units is a function of the control within large businesses, rather than as independent retailers.

Arising from the new management methods is the emergence of a clear corporate strategy (Knee and Walters, 1985; Johnson, 1987). Currently favoured strategies are segmentation often associated with multi-format development (e.g. Burton) on the one hand and diversification involving other service sector activities (e.g. Marks & Spencer's charge card and financial services) on the other. What is clear in the latter case is that there is an increasing 'blurring' of the distinction between services such as banks, fast food, travel agents and financial services and retailing.

Tables 4.6 and 4.7 demonstrate many of these changes in business organisation. Both Burton and Next have emerged during the 1980s from previous companies (Montague Burton and Hepworths respectively) which were struggling to come to terms with consumer and social trends. The Burton approach is to clearly identify a market and to tailor their retail offerings directly to the specified target market with each fascia having a distinct offering. Similarly, Next have segmented their business into small manageable chains and operate a large number of outlets across different sectors. The central, corporate strategy produces an emphasis throughout on Next style and design. A similar segmentation approach has emerged in the mail order market where the 1000 page agency catalogue has been

Table 4.6 NEXT PLC (1986/87)

	Outlets	Selling space ('000 sq. ft.)
NEXT (inc shops in shops) – Nov 1986		
Next Too	117	177
Collections	114	174
For Men	174	245
Lingerie	42	12
Accessories	8	10
Interiors	40	83
Cafe	10	23
Espresso Bar	8	5
Florist	8	2
Hairdressers	3	5
To Nothing	23	57
CES (acquired June 1987) – 1987		
Salisbury	150	
Collingwood	131	
Weir	107	
Zales	112	
Allens Chemists	100	
Biba	56	
Paige	205	
Dillons (acquired July 1987)	270	
Grattan (acquired July 1986)		
Look Again		
You & Yours		
Second Look		
Fashion Plus		
Streets of London		
Grattan		
Scotcade		
Kaleidoscope		
Manorgrove		

Note: Next are almost continually refining and adding to their offerings with, for example, a Next Jewellery chain set to begin trading. Next have also launched a radical mail order initiative, the Next Directory.

Source: Retail Business, Retail Trade Reviews, September 1987, pp. 35–39.

superseded by the direct mailing targeted 'specialogues'. These approaches demonstrate the clear growth of large companies, often operating small units, but controlling the business tightly and enjoying economies of scale and replication. Their approaches are instructed by changes in management methods, corporate philosophy and the clear emergence of a planned corporate strategy.

Table 4.7 The Burton Group PLC (August 1987)

Chain	Outlets	Outlet size range ('000 sq.ft.)	Target market Age group and gender	Target market People (millions)	Target market Value (£bn)
Burton Retail	502	1–15	20–44M	10.3	3.0
Top Man	239	1–27	11–30M	8.5	2.7
Champion Sport	72	0.5–3.5	15–35A	17.0	1.3
Principles for Men	81	0.8–3	25–45M	8.0	2.0
Principles for Women	154	1–5	25–45W	7.5	2.5
Dorothy Perkins	392	5–8.5	18–40W	9.5	3.5
Top Shop	268	0.7–32	11–30W	8.0	2.8
Evans	173	1–5	25–60W	12.6	1.6
Harvey Nichols	1	N/A	ALL	N/A	N/A
Debenhams	67	10–160	ALL	45.0	35.0
Experiments:					
Alias	5	N/A	25–40M	6.0	0.7
Radius	1	N/A	25–30M	N/A	N/A
Secrets	1	N/A	N/A W	12.4	1.7

Note: The total outlet figure here of 1956 includes all shops within shops and overseas outlets. Stand alone outlets at the same date (August 1987) totalled 1556.

Source: The Burton Group PLC 'Successfully Managing Change' Annual Report 1987.

Changes in retail operations

The changes in retail operations are dramatic and widespread. A shop of the 1950s bears little or no resemblance in many cases to the shops of the present day. The most basic change in retail operations is that the number of retail units has declined enormously. As a generalisation, there has been a considerable increase in the numbers of large units and a decrease in small units. It is, however, the traditional form of small retail units that has declined and those involving the retailing of goods rather than services. As the average size of retail unit has grown, it has become apparent that there is an emerging polarisation of retailing (Dawson, 1985).

This polarisation of retailing has developed as retailers have attempted to devise particular store formats. These attempts have been concentrated into developing small units and very large units. At the small-scale end of this polarisation growth has come from a number of particular store formats as is shown in Table 4.8. What is apparent from this table is that many of these growth strategies arise from multiple firms, whether of the traditional corporate variety or through franchising. In many instances growth in small-scale formats is occurring through the selection of a target market and the segmentation of the retail offering. In clothing, for

Table 4.8 The polarisation of retailing – growth formats

Small Stores	Examples
Discount food	Kwik Save/Lo-Cost
Convenience	Circle K/Eight Till Late
Small specialist	Holland and Barrett/Apollo Window Blinds
Brand concessions	Estee Lauder/Cacharel
Style	Jaeger/Country Casuals
Locality	National Trust
Service	Prontaprint/Klick
Large Stores	
Supermarkets	Presto/Safeway
General merchandise	
Food	Asda/Tesco
Non-food	C & A/Marks & Spencer
Specialist non-food	MFI/B & Q
Style	Habitat/Sears

example, the small specialists that are developing very rapidly include Sock Shop, Tie Rack, Shirt Factor and Knickerbox. Many such developments will be franchised as franchising offers a rapid growth route from independent retailer with a saleable product and format to major company. The growth history of the Body Shop provides a classic example. At the large-scale end of this polarisation, as Table 4.8 shows, growth is particularly concentrated in the corporate chains. In most cases this is because the entry costs to such store formats is very high. Again, however, whilst there are generalists in the large store market, growth has also come through segmentation as with developments such as Toys 'Я' Us, Grandstand, IKEA and Homebase.

Table 4.8 also indicates that the location of retailing is changing fundamentally. The large-scale growth formats have, through their size and their commitment to economies of scale, spearheaded a move out-of-town or to decentralised locations. A careful review of the small-scale growth sectors also reveals this move away from former high streets. For example, many convenience stores are away from town centres, reflecting the fact that such locations may no longer be the most convenient; service shops similarly are in secondary locations; specialist shops are in high consumer flow locations, which may be in high streets or in off-centre locations; discount food units are often in purpose-built precincts or district centres. From all viewpoints there has been a lessening of the role of the high streets and concern is now being heard about their future (Davies, 1987; Dawson, 1988)

Schiller (1986) has usefully characterised the decentralisation process as one of three waves. The first wave of decentralisation involved the move of food stores away from high streets in the form of superstores and hypermarkets (Dawson, 1984). Whilst commentators disagree over exact figures there are probably nearly 500 such units trading in Britain (Figure 4.1). The second wave, Schiller argues, is that of the 'retail warehouse' (Figure 4.2), which emerged after the superstore and development of which is probably currently close to its peak (Gibbs, 1987). Retail warehouses began as companies such as MFI, B & Q, Harris Queensway and Comet opened large stores off-centre. The sectors of DIY, carpets, electrical and furniture comprise the bulk of such retail warehouses. Recent figures suggest there are nearly 750 DIY stores of more than 15,000 sq. ft. trading in Britain with a further 200 with planning permission. Carpets, electrical and furniture stores probably double this total of trading retail warehouses. The process of developing such sites for both food superstores and non-food retail warehouses has not been a simple one, and planning authorities have in the past been reluctant to give permissions (Davies, 1984). In reality, however, town centres could not cope with the demand for new food stores of the size required or with the requirements of many of the emerging retail warehouse markets, and most town centres are now more pleasant and less congested without such outlets. The effect of such de-centralisation is probably more complementary than competitive with town centres.

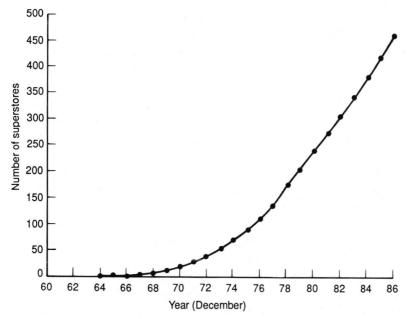

Figure 4.1 Number of trading superstores in Great Britain, 1960–86 (*Source:* Institute for Retail Studies Estimates)

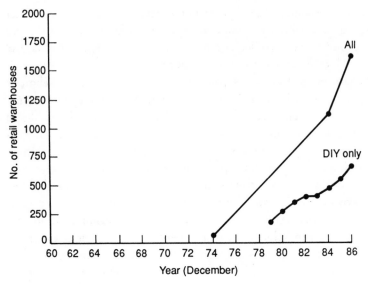

Figure 4.2   Number of trading retail warehouses in Great Britain, 1960–86
(*Source:* Institute for Retail Studies Estimates)

The third wave according to Schiller, however, is vastly different as it involves the movement to out-of-town locations by some of the very retailers around which town centres are built, e.g. Marks & Spencer, Halfords, Boots, Debenhams, John Lewis. In addition to these major retailers in 'traditional' outlet forms, many established companies are also experimenting out-of-town with new variants focused on specific markets, e.g. Boots Children's World, Courts Mammouth, Rumbelows Hometech, Terleys Texstyle World. Furthermore, the 'fashion' chains associated with smaller stores are also beginning to take an interest in some proposals, e.g. Next, Burton, Sears. Sears for example are operating a mini department store at the Metro Centre, Gateshead incorporating several of their fascias under the Sears banner.

This third wave probably has several components, although at this early stage it is unclear whether each component will be a major force in the future. On the one hand are the extensions to the retail warehouse style developments (DIY and carpets) which are growing into planned 'retail warehouse parks' (Bernard Thorpe and Partners, 1985) but incorporating not only retail warehouses but new-style outlets for example Children's World, World of Leather, Habitat, IKEA, Sharps Bedrooms etc, thus broadening their attraction. Recent developments proposed for off-centre retailing include a 'new generation' of smaller units at such locations retailing for example eyecare (Eyeland House), electrical goods (Hometech), household textiles (Atlantis) and even barbeques (Barbeques Galore).

The second component is the regional shopping centre which can prob-ably be disaggregated by size. Some proposed centres are c200,000 sq. ft. and are basically one or two magnet stores, e.g. a Tesco/Marks & Spencer combination. Other proposals, however, are for fully planned regional shopping centres ranging from 500,000 sq. ft. to over 2,000,000 sq. ft. Such centres (OXIRM 1987) have received a major boost by the Metro Centre at Gateshead and the recent agreement for development at Thur-rock near the M25. Centres such as the Metro Centre with its major anchor tenants including Frasers, Debenhams, C & A, Marks & Spencer, Carrefour, its leisure complex and the vast array of major multiple chains and independent specialist retailers including food courts and service retailers such as banks, hairdressers and travel agents are not complemen-tary to town centres, but rather compete fully with existing centres. Their strength and drawing power arise from the total management of the centre and a requirement for high standards of environment, facilities, cleaning, security and access.

Several 'pressure points' have emerged for these large centres with local authorities, in the main, being against their development. This has resulted in major public inquiries covering the applications in particular areas, as at Exeter, Manchester, and the Central Belt of Scotland. Figure 4.3 provides a register of proposals over 500,000 sq. ft. It is unclear at the moment how many of these large proposals will be permitted or will be developed. What is certain, however, is that such schemes which are effec-tively covered high streets and town centres change the locational pattern of retailing.

The reasons behind these locational changes revolve around the need for large sites for building, good car parking, limited pedestrian/vehicle congestion, and consumer and retailer desire for a better environment for retailing. In some cases planned shopping centres in-town can meet many requirements, e.g. Eldon Square, Newcastle, but often retailers cannot provide the facilities they require and consumers prefer the ease of access and environment provided out-of-town.

At the same time as this move to decentralise retailing there is a recog-nition that existing facilities often do not meet consumer needs. This has found expression in many cases in a greater emphasis on design and service. 'Customer care' is now a byword in retailing whether considered as new products, better products, greater range, more financial facilities, accessible location, more consumer information, better environment and so on. Service extension is being provided by the new regional shopping centres, by more convenient locations and by the resurgence of town centre schemes aimed at small-unit speciality retailing, e.g., Covent Garden, Waverly Market, Albert Docks etc. Consumer care extends into

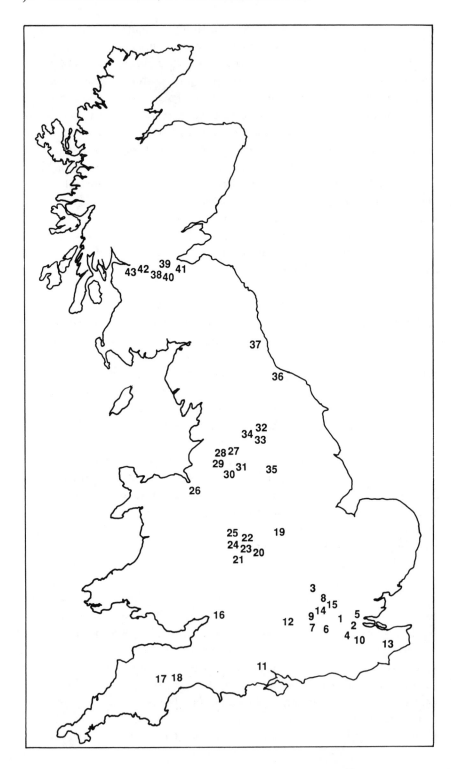

better pedestrianisation, the increasing use of food courts in towns and planned shopping centres, and the current high level of refurbishment of old shopping centre schemes. At the store level, design consultancies are being widely used to help retailers project an image and to improve performance.

The locational changes in retailing and in particular associated with the changing importance of small stores is in many cases enabled by new technology. One of the major factors enabling management control to remain effective in large stores and in chains of small units is the application of various new technologies in retailing (Dawson and Sparks, 1986). The most visible sign of the new technology is at the checkout where, as Figure 4.4 shows, the use of laser scanning is taking off. Laser scanning at the checkout, however, is merely one visible manifestation of major technological introductions throughout retailing. For example, EPOS (not laser scanning) tills are now common in many retailers, with the data polled overnight by head office for up-to-date sales information. Laser scanning and computer control are increasingly common in the warehouse and distribution centre with orders for stores received electronically.

Figure 4.3   Proposed out-of-town regional shopping centres
London and South East: 1 Docklands, Royal Albert Dock; 2 Dartford, Blue Water Park; 3 Luton, Sundon Springs; 4, Orpington, Hewitts Park; 5 Thurrock, Lakeside Centre; 6 Hook, Elmbridge Mall; 7 Wraysbury, Runnymede Centre; 8 Bricket Wood, Waterdale Park; 9 Colnbrook nr Slough, Tanhouse Pit; 10 Maidstone, Leybourne Grange; 11 Southampton, Adanac Park; 12 Reading, Great Lea; 13 Ashford, Big Scan Site; 14 Iver, Junction M4/M25; 15 Elstree, Aldenham Retail Park.
South West: 16 Bristol, Cribbs Causeway; 17 Exeter, Digby Hospital; 18 Exeter, Exeter Airport.
Midlands and Wales: 19 Leicester, Enderby Centre; 20 Birmingham, Fort Dunlop; 21 Bromsgrove, Barnsley Hall Hospital Site; 22 Walsall, Power Station; 23 West Bromwich, Sandwell Mall; 24 Dudley, Merry Hill; 25 Wolverhampton, Racecourse Site; 26 Shotton, Steelworks.
North West: 27 Rochdale, Milnrow Kingsway; 28 Salteye, Barton Locks; 29 Dumplington, Trafford Centre; 30 Carrington, Westside Park; 31 Stockport, Bramhall.
Yorkshire and Humberside: 32 Leeds, The White Rose Centre; 33 Leeds, University Site; 34 Pudsey, Mountleigh; 35 Sheffield, Meadowhall.
North and Scotland: 36 Middlesbrough, Metro Tees; 37 Gateshead, Metro Centre; 38 Motherwell, Junction M8/A73; 39 Bathgate, Landmark Centre; 40 Bathgate, Rover Group; 41 Edinburgh, Metro Scotland; 42 Glasgow Braehead Riverside; 43 Paisley, Linwood.
(© Hillier, Parker, May & Rowden, February 1988. *Reproduced by permission*)

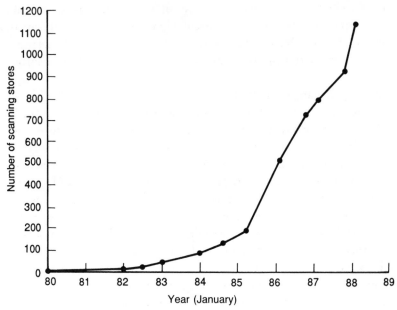

Figure 4.4   Number of scanning stores in the UK
(*Source*: Article Number Association Estimates)

Communications and payment between retailers and suppliers are increasingly via electronic data interchange such as TRADANET. At store and head offices increasing use is being made of decision support systems on microcomputers. Direct product profitability models may form a part of this. Despite a long gestation period some form of electronic funds transfer or credit card data capture (though often not real-time on-line) is now emerging in several retail trades. The important point to note in all this is the increase in control of all aspects of operation that is offered by technological data collection, transmission and interpretation.

Further changes in retail operations include the more complete management of labour use and costs. Retailing now has to be viewed as essentially an industry generating part-time, mainly female jobs, but with a core of full-time staff in each shop unit. The increasing desire for service may increase the need for staff and for training for staff, but increasingly sophisticated management will ensure that staff are brought in and out of the trading week when customers require, in a more close matching of customer flow and staffing levels. At the same time there is a greater reliance on sub-contracting for many tasks in stores and centres (Sparks, 1987).

The operational and organisational changes in retailing have also combined to make retailers aware of the importance of physical distribution within retailing (McKinnon, 1986; Sparks, 1986). In particular, retailers have begun to exert much greater control of the distribution channel by centralisation of regional distribution centres and the greater use of dedicated third-party carriers. This has been associated with, in the food trade, the rise of own-label products and the need to maximise selling space in the shop, and in non-food trades the requirements of maximising selling space and better matching the flow of goods to consumer desires. Examples abound, particularly in the fashion trade, of how technology is linking the store, the head office and the distribution system to ensure the retailer is stocking what is selling rather than what the retailer thinks will sell.

There are thus a substantial number of changes in retail operations. These changes are in the main aimed at tighter control of the business and a much better response to consumer desires and requirements. The ability of retailers to make these changes is in many cases a function of changes in business organisation. What is apparent, however, is that as this process of concentration increases and as retailers try to match their operations to perceived consumer changes, the consequences of an incorrect decision can be calamitous. The examples of the profits shortfall at Harris Queensway and the tarnishing of Sir Phil Harris's image, the problems in distribution of Mothercare and the difficulties this brought Sir Terence Conran, and the disastrous problems of the previously glittering Tip Top Drugstores which led to their agreed takeover by Woolworths, all bear testimony to the price of failure and the narrow line between retail success and retail failure.

Future developments in retailing

Retailing is undergoing a 'retail revolution'. Crystal-ball gazing during such a period of change is clearly a difficult proposition. Some trends can be developed, however. It would seem to be axiomatic now that the UK has moved from a distributive *trades* to a retail *industry*. This industry contains large firms, mass distribution components, is financed by major financial institutions, and has become increasingly sophisticated in its operations. Retailing has become a bastion of big business and there seems little reason for this to change. One threat would be the widespread development of professional and responsive independent retailers, particularly focussing on specialist trades, convenience and service. Indeed there is evidence that independents prosper when they emphasise their service and personal advantages. Through technology, however, large retailers are able to combine the benefits of size with the responsiveness of tailoring individual units to the characteristics of particular locations. This process is set to continue. This is not to decry the very considerable impact that new ideas, formats, products, entrepreneurs and companies can have in a short time as, for example, in The Body Shop, Laura Ashley, Sock Shop or even Next, and innovative entrepreneurs find retailing a welcoming sector.

It is also clear that the balance between central locations and decentralised retailing is changing. Developments in accessible off-centre locations remain set to expand whether via stand-alone units often replacing 'first generation' stores or through a number of regional shopping centres. Such decentralisation is, however, concentrating the minds of town centre retailers, local authorities and property fund managers. Out-of-town developments are provoking town centre reactions through new developments, theme centres, refurbishment, management and the better provision of ancillary facilities. In all cases it would seem that the trend is towards better managed retail environments, with the emphasis on management. The management of retail environments is set to become a key issue.

As the location and type of retailing changes, so voices of concern are raised over the problems that non-car owners or low-income customers inherit (Bowlby, 1985). The difficulties of shopping in rural areas, suburban estates and inner cities and provision for the old, car-less, disabled and poor are increasingly important areas of concern for the planning of retailing. Various schemes such as free buses, teleshopping, village shop support schemes, training for local shopkeepers and community shops are being tried, but mainly on a local, unco-ordinated level. Independent retailers, particularly in the food trade, continue to attribute their decline to unfair and discriminatory trade practices by multiples and suppliers which they argue are damaging to consumers in the long term.

If the management of the wider environment is set to become important then individual retailers are themselves having to consider the quality of their management at both the store and the head office level. Decisions at all levels are becoming more important and differentiation between retailers will increasingly be on the basis of store management quality and responsiveness and head office ability to interpret data and harness new technology. This differentiation will concern not only decisions about within-company issues and problems but also in terms of the wider network within which retailers work. For example the 'correct' choice of design consultants for a new design may prove vital to business success or failure. In price conscious markets the quality of management control of the business will prove crucial. It is true, however, that the design and customer care stances of many retailers are only as successful as the staff at the store level, and training at this level will become increasingly important. The highly central role of the stock market also ensures that institutional investors will switch resources to entrepreneurial and successful management teams.

Finally, the adoption and intelligent use of new technology will be vital. As noted above, it will be important in information systems terms within the company but technology may also play a part in consumer contact. For example, teleshopping whilst much tested has yet to really work in the UK. In-store interactive video systems and computer stock control linked to telephone ordering are further examples.

Summary and conclusions

Retailing is undergoing a revolution in association with wider societal trends. Retailing is no longer the preserve of the petit-bourgeoisie or the independent shopkeeper but is rather the territory of some of the largest firms in Britain. As Weir (1987) notes, 'the emergence of the retail sector as an important contributor to the creation of wealth and the enhancement of people's lives is now well established.' (p. vi). Major retail firms and new successful innovators have been responding to consumer changes in behaviour, tastes, finances and expectations and also directing consumer change. Retailing has moved up-market in design and style and is providing better facilities for many consumers. It is interesting to speculate whether this provides the opportunity for tightly controlled, low cost and low price retailers to re-emerge and to attract a significant share of the market. Retail formats such as warehouse clubs, off-price outlets and centres and full range discounters may find a market.

This maturing of the industry has seen many changes in business organisation in retailing and also an enormous range of developments in terms of retail operations. The land-use planning system has had difficulty in coping with these rapid retail developments which have come at the same time as other major societal changes. Retail management in responding to and directing retail change has had to be flexible and responsive. The changes now under way and those ahead suggest that the pressure on retail management is unlikely to abate. As retailing becomes yet more competitive and there is a greater need to persuade consumers to spend, so pressures will intensify. As Whitefield (1987) notes, successful retailers will be those who are precise in targeting consumers, provide superior merchandise and service, have clarity in ranging, differentiation in presentation and can integrate with product operations. Retail management is a challenging and dynamic sector that will need to attract the keenest minds if retailers are to continue to grasp their opportunities.

Bibliography

The references cited in this chapter have deliberately been kept relatively few. For further reading it is recommended that a useful starting bibliography of sources is:
Kirby, D. A. (1988) *Shopping in the Eighties*, British Library, London.

References

Akehurst, G. (1983) 'Concentration in Retail Distribution: measurement and significance', *Service Industries Journal*, 3(2), 161–79.

Bamfield, J. (1988) 'Competition and Change in British Retailing', *National Westminster Bank Quarterly Review*, February, pp. 15–29.

Beaumont, J. (1987) 'Trends in Food Retailing', pp. 52–61 of McFadyen, E. (ed) *The Changing Face of British Retailing*, Newman Books, London.

Bowlby, S. (1985) 'Shoppers' Needs: don't forget the old and the car-less, *Town and Country Planning*, 54(7), 219–21.

Burt, S. L. and Dawson, J. A. (1988) *The Evolution of European Retailing*, ICL, Slough.

Davies, K., Gilligan, C. and Sutton, C. (1985) 'Structural Changes in Grocery Retailing: the implications of competition', *International Journal of Physical Distribution and Materials Management*, 15(2), 1–48.

Davies, R. L. (1984) *Retail and Commercial Planning*, Croom Helm, London.

Davies, R. L. (1987) *Help for the High Street: some new approaches to revitalisation*, Tesco Stores, Waltham Cross.

Davies, R. L. and Rogers, D. S. (1984) *Store Location and Store Assessment Research*, Wiley, Chichester.

Dawson, J. A. (1982) *Commercial Distribution in Europe*, Croom Helm, London.

Dawson, J. A. (1984) 'Structural-spatial Relationships in the Spread of Hypermarket Retailing', pp. 156–182 of Kaynak, E. and Savitt, R. (eds) *Comparative Marketing Systems*, Praeger, New York.

Dawson, J. A. (1985) 'Structural Change in European Retailing: the polarisation of operating scale, pp. 211–229 of Kaynak, E. (ed) *Global Perspectives in Marketing*, Praeger, New York.

Dawson, J. A. (1988) 'Futures for the High Street', *The Geographical Journal*, 154(1), 1–22.

Dawson, J. A. and Sparks, L. (1985) *Issues in Retailing*, SDD, Edinburgh.

Dawson, J. A. and Sparks, L. (1986) 'New Technology in UK Retailing: issues and responses', *Journal of Marketing Management*, 2(1), 7–29.

Gibbs, A. (1987) 'Retail Innovation and Retail Planning', *Progress in Planning*, 27, 1–67.

Johnson, G. (ed) (1987) *Business Strategy and Retailing*, Wiley, Chichester.

Knee, D. and Walters, D. (1985) *Strategy in Retailing*, P. Allan, Oxford.

Lusch, R. F. (1987) 'A Commentary on the US Retail Environment', pp. 35–42 of Johnson, G. (ed) *Business Strategy and Retailing*, Wiley, Chichester.

McFadyen, E. (ed) (1987) *The Changing Face of British Retailing*, Newman Books, London.

McKinnon, A. C. (1986) 'The Physical Distribution Strategies of Multiple Retailers', *International Journal of Retailing*, 1(2), 49–63.

OXIRM (1987) *The New Regional Shopping Centre Phenomenon*, Authors, Oxford.

Schiller, R. (1986) 'The Coming of the Third Wave', *Estates Gazette*, 279, 648–651.

Segal-Horn, S. (1987) 'The Retail Environment in the UK', pp. 13–32 of Johnson, G. (ed) *Business Strategy and Retailing*, Wiley, Chichester.

Sparks, L. (1986) 'The Changing Structure of Distribution in Retail Companies: an example from the grocery trade', *Transactions of the Institute of British Geographers*, 11(2), 147–56.

Sparks, L. (1987) 'Employment in Retailing: trends and issues', pp. 239–256 of Johnson, G. (ed) *Business Strategy and Retailing*, Wiley, Chichester.

Thorpe, B. and Partners (1985) *Retail Warehouse Parks*, Authors, London.

Weir, R. (1987) Foreword in McFadyen, E. (ed) *The Changing Face of British Retailing*, Newman Books, London.

Whitefield, E. (1987) 'Retail Strategy: the requirement for professionalism', *Grocery Business*, March, pp. 7–18.

5 Tourism and hospitality

ANDREW LOCKWOOD

Introduction

There can be no doubt that tourism is a massive and a growing industry, both on a national and an international scale. There has been at least a fourfold increase in the annual level of international tourist arrivals since the early 1960s to its present level of around 355 million. Tourism receipts, which exclude payments for fares, have also shown substantial growth to around US$150,000 in 1987 (BTA/ETB, 1988), which represents around 5 per cent of the total value of international trade. In addition, domestic tourism within national boundaries is estimated to comprise around 3500 million trips (World Tourism Organisation, 1986). It is not surprising, therefore, that even when primarily concerned with tourism and hospitality within the UK that the scale and complexity of the industry presents considerable problems.

This chapter aims to provide a framework within which to analyse the size and structure of the tourism and hospitality industry within the UK. The analysis begins with a description of the overall structure of the linkages and interdependencies within the industry. This is followed by a summary of the statistics relating to tourism demand which leads to consideration of the nature of tourism supply. From here it is possible to identify the major trends shaping the current development of the industry and predict where these may lead in the near future.

The first problem to be overcome in this study is the need for a clear definition of what constitutes a tourist. The World Tourism Organisation base their definition of an international tourist on the concept of a visitor produced by the 1963 UN Conference on Travel and Tourism in Rome. A 'visitor' is any person visiting a country other than that in which they have their usual place of residence for any reason other than following an occupation remunerated from within the country visited. This is then further refined to describe a 'tourist' as a visitor remaining in the country for at least 24 hours and an 'excursionist' as any person staying less than 24 hours. Therefore, the term 'tourist' includes visitors on holiday, on business, visiting friends and relatives, for medical treatment or for education but would not include cruise passengers who spend the night back aboard their ship, transport crews or 'day-trippers'. Although developed largely for the purposes of international tourism, this distinction is easily applied to domestic tourism where the distinguishing feature once again would be the stay lasting for over 24 hours and so necessitating overnight accommodation. This definition is, however, not universally held. In international terms there is considerable discrepancy in the bases upon which tourism statistics are collected. Some countries use data based on international visitor arrivals, others data based on hotel registrations. The length of stay required to 'qualify' as a tourist for statistical purposes also varies between countries, even within Europe, from three nights in Austria, to four nights in Belgium, Great Britain, Ireland, Switzerland and the Netherlands and up to five days in West Germany. International comparisons are therefore difficult to make with any degree of reliability.

Even on a national basis there is a considerable variation in the perception of a tourist. A recently conducted survey of local councillors (Wanhill, 1987a) found that they strongly associated tourism with leisure activities such as being on holiday, visiting from other areas for the day, touring in caravans, walking, hiking and camping. People on business or on official visits were hardly mentioned, although they represent a very significant part of the total tourism demand.

The structure of the tourism and hospitality industry

Using the above definition of a tourist stresses the central role of accommodation, but the overall tourism product is made up of many additional components. These include transportation, attractions both natural and man-made, restaurants, retail outlets, entertainment and the general culture of the host community. The complexity of the interrelated nature of the industry is illustrated in Figure 5.1.

Tourism demand

Tourism demand can be analysed in a number of ways, but one of the most meaningful breakdowns is on the basis of the purpose of the visit. The World Tourism Organisation (WTO) recognises nine purposes of visit: holidays, business, health, study, mission/meeting/congress, family (visiting friends and relatives), religion, sports and others. In practice the main balance of tourism demand falls in the categories of holidays, busi-

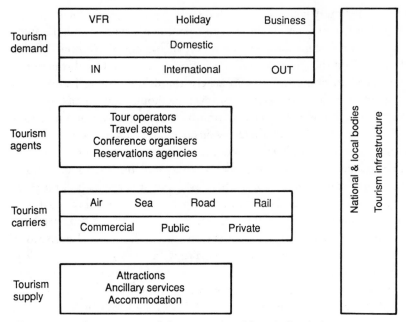

Figure 5.1   The structure of the tourism and hospitality industry

ness and VFR (visiting friends and relatives). For example, in 1986 out of the total of 150 million tourist trips by British residents, holidays accounted for 59 per cent, VFR for 20 per cent, business for 17 per cent and the other six categories for only 4 per cent. Tourism demand can be further subdivided into purely domestic tourism by residents within their country of origin and international tourism either incoming or outgoing. Domestic tourism in the UK in 1986 consisted of some 128 million trips generating an estimated spending of £7150 million. The UK is a major international tourism generator spending some US$8690 million in 1986, being third in the world behind West Germany and the USA. In terms of international tourism receipts, the UK received some US$7921 in 1986 which places it fifth behind the USA, Spain, Italy and France.

Tourism agents

The tourism demand must be converted into arrivals and this is partly achieved through the tourism agents. The tour operator puts together complete holiday packages which are prepared on a speculative basis before the demand actually appears. These packages are then sold either directly by the tour operator through their own sales offices or indirectly through tied or independent travel agents. Travel agents act as intermediaries between the customer and the supplier both for holiday demand and for business clients, selling either the tour operators pre-packaged products or making individual travel arrangements. Their income comes from a percentage commission on the sales they generate. Conference organisers concentrate on the business market helping firms to organise their local, national or international conferences and are also now becoming increasingly involved in incentive travel. Reservation agencies are primarily linked to the organisation of accommodation and ancillary services for groups but will also deal with individual requests. Although this complex structure of agents exists, it is still possible for individuals to make their own bookings at all stages of the process and organise their own 'package'. This is particularly the case with domestic tourism but less common on the international scene.

Tourism carriers

Tourism without transport is impossible. Tourism is about being elsewhere and transport is essential to bridge the gap between the starting point and the destination. This link is important for a number of reasons. First, tourism has developed hand in hand with developments in transport. Improvements in transport have stimulated tourism demand, for example, the arrival of the railways to seaside resorts in the UK such as Blackpool or Bournemouth, and in turn changes in tourism demand have prompted developments in transport, such as the growth of air charter services to cater for the increases in international holiday tourism. Second, transport is important because it makes tourist destinations accessible. Tourism depends on a destination being accessible; without accessibility a destination cannot hope to develop as a major tourism centre. Third, the transport network represents considerable private and public investment and is in turn an important generator of employment and revenue, revenue which is not normally included in figures of tourism expenditure.

The nature of the transportation system can be analysed in a number of ways. Faulks (1982) has identified four basic physical elements in any transport system: the way, the terminal, the carrying unit, and the motive power. The way is the medium of travel used and can be either natural, as in the case of the air or the sea, or man-made as is the case for road or rail systems. The nature of the way has obvious cost implications but also determines the need for and ease of implementation of control and management. For example, although the air as a way would seem to be available for free access, the nature of the way means that there is a constant need for the monitoring and control of traffic to ensure safety. There comes a point, as illustrated by long delays for holiday flights during the summer period, where the freedom of the air and the systems required to monitor it cannot cope with the expected traffic.

The terminal gives access to the transport system and allows an interchange between different modes of transport. The terminal is a major focus for the traveller, and its design and operation is a critical part of the total tourism product. The carrying unit is designed to cope with the distinctive demands of the particular way. The design of the carrying unit is also strongly influenced by motive power.

These four attributes combine to provide the specific characteristics of the four major transport modes. Road transport gives door-to-door flexibility within the total control of the driver but suffers from being able to carry only a small number of passengers at a relatively low speed, making it primarily suitable for medium or short journeys. A further problem for road transport is the need to share the road network with other users which leads to congestion at peak periods and in peak areas. The private car is, however, the dominant mode of transport for most types of tourism and accounted for up to 75 per cent of all international tourism journeys in 1980 (Boniface and Cooper, 1987).

Rail transport as the sole user of its own transport way can make the best possible use of scheduling to take account of demand patterns by increasing the frequency of services, adding or removing coaches or providing special services. For example, British Rail provides a special steam service between York and Scarborough during the height of the summer season which provides additional capacity to cope with peak traffic as well as being a tourist attraction in its own right. The major disadvantage of rail transport is the initial cost of investment in building the track and providing the rolling stock as well as the high cost of maintenance and replacement to maintain an up-to-date service. This heavy fixed cost requires the track to be used at a high level of efficiency. This can make services which are highly seasonal difficult to support.

Sea transport was once the major provider of long-haul traffic but, as aircraft can cross the Atlantic ocean 20 or more times for each return journey by ship, this traffic has been almost totally lost to the air. Ships do, however, use comparatively little power and due to their size can carry vehicles and give plenty of space for passengers at high standards of accommodation. They are therefore most suitable for short sea crossings, as in ferry services across the English Channel, or for ship travel for travel's sake as in the case of the cruise liner. Indeed, despite a rather uneven history, the cruise industry is at present going through a considerable resurgence of interest and there are optimistic expectations of the role that cruising will play in the 1990s (Page, 1987).

The most influential mode of transport for tourism purposes is air travel, where advances in technology have made all parts of the world accessible within a twenty-four hour flight. The main advantages of air transport are its ability to fly unimpeded by physical barriers that would deter other forms of transport and its speed. Air travel is therefore suited to applications both of short distance, such as the UK Shuttle services, or long haul flights to the Far East and Australia. The disadvantages of air travel are the high operational costs due to the high energy consumption and the need for rigid adherence to safety standards. The need to provide a large terminal area is also a problem, both in terms of the cost of providing the site and the social cost of noise pollution on local residents. Certain destinations are only accessible to mass tourism by air travel and this in itself can cause problems. For example, in April 1988 a dispute between British Airways and Air Mauritius resulted in the number of flights into the island provided by these carriers being reduced by a half. This not only caused considerable problems for the passengers who had booked to use these flights but meant that some tourists who had booked accommodation on the island were unable to arrive, so reducing the hotels' occupancy levels quite substantially.

Tourism supply

The tourism resources or tourism supply of a country can be divided into three main areas: attractions – both natural and man-made, accommodation provision and the availability of ancillary services such as restaurants, entertainment and shopping.

Attractions

For an area to develop a tourism industry of any kind there has to be a reason to attract the tourist. For holiday tourism this may be the attractions of beach tourism with the emphasis on climate and good beaches with plenty of water sport activities. On the other hand the attraction may be cultural with museums and historic buildings providing the drawing power. For business tourism in general the attractions are likely to be major commercial and population centres with good accessibility, whereas for a conference the availability of good meeting facilities with a range of complementary attractions would be paramount. Tourist attractions cannot simply be seen as the naturally existing physical environment but, due to the increased demand of tourism, there is a growing need for proper supervision and management if the tourism resource base is to be preserved.

One useful method of classification for the resource base of an area was devised by Clawson (1966). This classification describes a continuum of attractions from intensive user-oriented developments to areas based simply on the natural resources of the area. At the user-oriented end of the scale, the developments will often be man-made, such as parks, zoos or marinas, with a high intensity of use probably close to major population centres. The focus of these areas would be activity based on either sport or culture. At the resource-based end of the continuum, the emphasis is on the natural quality of the physical resources with man-made facilities at a minimum. These areas are likely to be some distance from the user and the activity would be based on the particular resource of the area. Examples might include birdwatching in the Falkland Islands, mountain climbing or visiting areas of particular scientific or historic interest. In the UK these areas may exist within very short distances. For example, the area of Tenby in South Pembrokeshire represents high user-oriented development with many facilities for entertainment and activity provided in the resort and on its beaches. *The Pembrokeshire Guide* describes Tenby North beach as offering 'all facilities – accommodation, playground, bowls, golf, deckchairs, cafés, ice cream, aqualung lessons, sailing and windsurfing lessons . . .' (John, 1986). Not more than ten miles away is Barafundle Bay with a beautiful beach flanked by limestone cliffs. There is no road access and the nearest car park is approximately a mile away over the headland. The guide description simply states 'no amenities'.

The provision of man-made attractions in the UK is undertaken both by the public sector, which controls a large proportion of the historic and

Table 5.1 Visits to tourist attractions 1986

Top ten tourist attractions for which an admission charge is made

	1985 '000	1986 '000
Madame Tussaud's, London	2313	2391
Alton Towers	1915	2250
Tower of London	2430	2020
Magnum Leisure Centre, Irvine	1114	1326
London Zoo	1254	1190
Kew Gardens	1112	1147
Thorpe Park, Surrey	1100	1060
Drayton Manor Park, Staffordshire	910	962
Jorvik Viking Centre, York	897	868
Edinburgh Castle	923	832

Source: Britain's Tourism, BTA/ETB, 1987

cultural attractions of the country, and by the private sector. Table 5.1 gives the numbers of visitors to the top ten tourist attractions in the country for which an admission charge is made, in which it is possible to see this split of public and private involvement.

Other popular attractions include the Roman Bath and Pump Room at Bath, Royal Windsor Safari Park, the London Planetarium, Windsor Castle, the Royal Academy in London, Wisley Gardens and Beaulieu in Hampshire. This list gives an interesting picture of the types of activities which visitors, both tourists and day trippers enjoy.

Accommodation

The supply of accommodation in a country can be broken down into many different types ranging from private accommodation, such as staying with friends or relatives, or staying in a second or holiday home and including pleasure boats, yachts or mobile homes, through to the commercial provision of furnished apartments or holiday flats, hotels of various types, holiday villages and condominiums as well as camp sites, static caravan parks and cruise liners. Additional accommodation is also provided by non-profit organisations such as the Youth Hostels Association and the YMCA. Table 5.2 provides an estimate of the accommodation provision in England divided into serviced accommodation, self-catering accommodation and holiday centres.

Accurate information on the supply of accommodation in England is quite difficult to obtain as the UK does not operate a compulsory regis-

Table 5.2   Accommodation in England

Serviced accommodation						
Bedroom breakdown	Hotels, Inns Guest Houses		Bed and Breakfast		Farmhouses	
	Estab.	Beds	Estab.	Beds	Estab.	Beds
>101	422	158,092	3	523		
51–100	757	99,295	48	5,893	1	106
11– 50	7,883	306,462	875	32,343	11	295
1– 10	15,481	184,258	9,972	65,067	3,170	21,317

Self-catering accommodation						
	Groups and Young People		Self-catering		Caravans and Camp sites	
	Estab.	Beds	Estab.	Beds	Estab.	Beds
Totals	621	89,991	13,664	59,498	2,898	342,100

Holiday Centres/Camps			
	Establishments	Serviced Units	Self-catering Units
Totals	102	16,672	21,296

Source: Britain's Tourism, BTA/ETB, 1987

Table 5.3 Comparison of hotel stock 1971–1981

Size of unit	Rooms 1971	Rooms 1981	Rooms % change	Units 1971	Units 1981	Units % change	Average unit size 1971	Average unit size 1981	Average unit size % change
<15 rooms	191,800	96,100	−49.90	20,700	9,500	−54.11	9.27	10.12	9.17
15–50 rooms	223,600	200,000	−10.55	9,600	8,400	−12.50	23.29	23.81	2.22
50–200 rooms	124,200	141,000	13.53	1,550	1,650	6.45	80.13	85.45	6.65
>200 rooms	39,200	70,900	80.87	115	190	65.22	340.87	373.16	9.47
TOTAL	578,800	508,000	−12.23	31,965	19,740	−38.24	18.11	25.73	42.12

Source: Census of Population 1971/1981

tration scheme. The figures shown in Table 5.2 are based on those properties whose capacity is known to the ETB. It is likely, however, that the properties which are missing will be the smaller ones and therefore the total picture should not be too seriously affected. A more comprehensive assessment of the supply of serviced accommodation can be found through the Census of Population. These figures are shown in Table 5.3.

These figures indicate that there have been significant changes in the stock of accommodation since 1970. The number of hotel units has fallen dramatically by over 38 per cent where the number of rooms available has fallen by only 12.2 per cent. The average size of a hotel has increased from 18 rooms to nearly 26 rooms. These changes have been brought about by the closure or change of use of large numbers of the smallest hotels over this period with a reduction of one-half of the room stock in establishments of less than 15 rooms. The number of larger hotels particularly with over 200 rooms has, however, increased by two-thirds giving an 80 per cent increase in the room stock at this size.

These changes have not been spread evenly throughout the country. The most significant reductions in the number of bedrooms available has occurred in Northumberland, the North West and the South East and increases have shown in Yorkshire and Humberside, the East Midlands and Greater London. This trend can be explained by the decreasing popularity of the traditional seaside resorts as a venue for domestic tourism and the growing importance of business and short break tourism in industrial centres and the countryside. The South West continues to be the UK's main domestic holiday destination and has therefore maintained its accommodation stock as has Wales and to a lesser extent Scotland. The hotel sector, then, continues to be typified by a large number of small units but with an increasing concentration in large units, with a spatial restructuring away from traditional holiday areas toward rural and industrial areas.

Ancillary services

The size and scope of the ancillary services supporting tourism and hospitality are very difficult to determine as they are by their nature an established part of the infrastructure of the country and distinguishing between 'normal' use, 'leisure' use and 'tourism' use is impracticable. However, figures collected by the British Tourism Survey give an indication of the breakdown of spending by British tourists in Britain.

Approximately one-third of the total expenditure by British residents is accounted for by the cost of the accommodation. Accommodation is particularly important in business and holiday tourism but obviously not of great importance when visiting friends and relatives. Travel costs make

Table 5.4   Breakdown of British tourist spending in Britain

Total spending (£ million)	All trips 7150	Holiday trips 4250	Business trips 2150	VFR 550	Other 175
	(%)	(%)	(%)	(%)	(%)
Accommodation	31	32	38	7	21
Travel	26	18	36	26	20
Eating/drinking	25	23	18	50	39
Buying clothes	3	6	0	3	3
Other shopping	7	10	2	10	8
Entertainment	4	10	1	3	6
Services/advice	1	0	2	0	0
Other	2	3	2	2	3

Source: British Tourism Survey 1986

up a quarter of the expenditure with business trips having a higher than average proportion due to the longer distances travelled and the shorter average duration of stay. The remaining 40 per cent of the expenditure goes on eating and drinking, shopping, entertainment and other ancillary services. A higher proportion of holiday expenditure is given over to shopping and entertainment whereas the majority of spending when visiting friends and relations goes on eating and drinking. Business travellers spend proportionally less on eating and drinking but it is likely that part of that expenditure is included with the cost of the primarily hotel accommodation. It can be seen from these figures that the economic benefits of tourism are not limited to the suppliers of accommodation and travel but 'leak' into most other sectors of the economy, including retailing, financial and public sectors, through the provision of these ancillary services. A discussion of these sectors is to be found elsewhere in this book.

Tourism infrastructure

If the tourism resources of any country are to be fully developed, some organisation either public or private needs to take action. The public sector, due to the scale of the development, normally takes responsibility for the development of the initial tourism infrastructure such as roads, parking areas, railway lines, harbours, airports and runways, as well as providing the public utilities including water supply and drainage. This development is obviously closely linked with the normal provision for the resident population. The private sector then typically takes responsibility for the development of the tourism superstructure of hotels, restaurants, entertainment and so on.

Under the Development of Tourism Act 1969, the Government established four tourist organisations: the British Tourist Authority, the English Tourist Board, the Scottish Tourist Board and the Wales Tourist Board. Each board is an independent statutory body and is mainly financed by direct grant-in-aid from the Government.

The British Tourist Authority is responsible for the promotion of tourism to Britain from overseas, advising the Government on matters affecting tourism to Britain as a whole and encouraging the provision and improvement of tourism facilities and amenities in Britain.

The English, Scottish and Wales Tourist Boards' role is to encourage British residents to holiday in Britain and to encourage the development and improvement of attractions and facilities for domestic and overseas tourists. To encourage the development of facilities, the Boards administer the Government scheme of financial assistance for tourist projects. In the three years up to 31 March 1986, the English Tourist Board alone approved grant assistance of around £34 million to investment projects totalling over £250 million. It has been estimated (Trippier, 1987) that this aid directly created nearly 6000 full- and part-time jobs. This aspect of job creation has led to plans for a revised scheme which will give more emphasis to larger, innovative projects attracting substantial numbers of visitors, as these have been found to be more cost effective in generating employment than smaller projects.

England is, in turn, split into twelve regional tourist boards, sponsored and grant-aided by the English Tourist Board. These regional boards are responsible for the planning, development and marketing of tourism in their own particular area working in partnership with the ETB, local government and trade interests in the regions.

The implementation of tourism strategy, however, lies firmly with the tiers of local government who formulate the area structure plans and have powers to promote or stop developments. The Tourist Boards are only advisory in these matters and have no power to overrule local planning. Local government is, not surprisingly, sensitive to the views of the local resident population and has tended to respond to tourism mainly in areas of decline as a way of returning some employment and prosperity to the area. Wanhill (1987b) suggests that '. . . tourism has been seen as an industry of last resort which reaches those parts of the economy that others cannot.' He further argues that as neither the industry nor the tourist boards have control over all the factors which make up the attractiveness of a destination that the development of tourism must be considered at the highest level of government and that public administrators should have or should develop expertise in tourism. There is however little evidence of a comprehensive government approach to tourism strategy which led the

House of Commons Trade and Industry Committee (1985) to report that: 'The Government minimises the appearance of involvement by reducing policy aims to statements of the obvious but maintains the fact of involvement in the tourist boards and the grants provided through them. The trouble is that this financial commitment is then left without there being any clear specific strategy to guide its use'.

Employment in tourism and hospitality

As indicated above the structure of the tourism and hospitality industry is complex and employment patterns are similarly complex. The industry is typified by large numbers of small establishments operated either independently or as a branch of a larger company. The industry is also made up of a wide diversity of types of business each of which will experience different patterns of customer demand, will need different levels of employee skills and will be organised differently. There are also likely to be different regional patterns as each area will have its own business mix, for example, between holiday and business tourism, and will operate in different labour market conditions.

Estimates of employment in the tourism and hospitality field vary between 1 and 2 million depending on the classification used. The DoE Quarterly estimates break the industry into three principal sectors: hotel and catering (but excluding institutional catering), travel and transport services and leisure and related services. This breakdown does not include jobs in related areas such as retailing, public utilities or industries supplying goods and services to tourism and hospitality. It does, however, include some jobs which cannot be directly attributed to tourism and hospitality as the breakdown in Table 5.5 illustrates.

Over 900,000 people are employed in the hotel and catering sector, not including the self-employed and working proprietors who are estimated by the annual Labour Force Survey to number around 185,000. It must also be noted that this figure does not include the institutional sector of the industry, notably those employed in industrial and contract catering, schools and hospitals. The total including these sectors has been estimated by the Hotel and Catering Training Board at over 2.1 million (HCITB, 1978). The hotel sector and public houses account for over half the total employment, with 28 per cent each. Nearly two-thirds of the workforce is female but only one-third of that total is employed on a full-time basis, with female part-time employees being particularly important in the public house sector.

On the other hand, women constitute a very small part of the workforce

Table 5.5 The structure of employment in tourism and hospitality

Number of employees (000s)	Male F/T	Female P/T	Female F/T	Total
Hotel and catering				
Hotel Trade	90.8	72.0	99.4	262.2
Restaurants and Cafés	74.7	34.0	83.2	191.9
Public Houses and Bars	76.7	16.4	164.4	257.6
Clubs	62.6	10.6	81.8	155.0
Other tourist accommodation	25.7	13.7	14.6	53.9
Total	330.5	146.7	433.4	920.6
Travel and transport				
Railways	135.9	8.8	0.6	145.3
Other inland transport	173.4	10.7	6.6	190.7
Sea transport	31.8	3.5	0.3	35.5
Air transport	29.5	13.4	0.6	43.5
Transport support	75.5	11.7	2.4	89.7
Total	446.1	48.1	10.5	504.7
Tourism and leisure				
Theatres, radio and TV	40.7	23.0	8.4	72.1
Tourist and other services	15.6	6.2	12.8	34.6
Museums, Art Galleries etc.	19.8	25.7	20.4	65.9
Sport and other leisure	123.0	46.0	92.7	261.7
Total	199.1	100.9	134.3	434.3

Source: DoE Quarterly Estimates (June 1985)

in travel and transport with the majority to be found in air transport or transport support services, usually in clerical or personal service jobs and with a very small number of part-time jobs. This sector includes a large number of employees not directly related to tourism and hospitality who are employed in freight movement or in travel to work. Overall it has been estimated that tourism only accounts for 10 per cent of the direct employment in this sector.

The tourism, leisure and related services sector includes employment in radio, theatre and television which might not be considered directly part of the other sectors which include tourism, museums and art galleries, sports and related leisure services. It has been estimated (Morrell, 1985) that of the 434,000 people employed in these sectors only 23 per cent of employment is directly attributable to tourism and leisure. As in hotel and catering there is a high density of part-time female employees, particularly in the tourism, museums and sport sectors which have to cope with daily peaks of demand and consequent fluctuations in work loads.

The tourism and hospitality industry has been accused of providing only 'candy floss' jobs due to the seasonal patterns of demand and its volatility. Recent evidence (Parsons, 1986) suggests that, on the contrary, employment in the sector has increased steadily by more than 300,000 since the mid 1970s to represent nearly one in ten of those in work. Most of the growth has been in the hotel and catering sector with 41 per cent growth between 1975 and 1985. This combined with a similar growth in tourism and leisure has offset the decline in the travel sector. In fact, following the recession of the early 1980s it has been the hotel and catering sector in particular that has recovered quickly with an 11 per cent increase of some 92,000 jobs between 1982 and 1985 alone.

Evidence also suggests that seasonality is no longer a feature of employment in this sector as it once was. The hotel and catering sector shows the largest seasonal variations, but from peak to trough this amounts to less than 9 per cent of the total workforce. Much of this seasonal variation can be accounted for by natural wastage in an industry with a traditionally high rate of labour turnover, so that seasonal lay-offs amount to only a very small figure. This reduction in seasonality has been brought about by the stretching and generation of demand to fill shoulder and off season periods, through developments such as the short break holiday. There has also been a considerable increase in the use of part-time and sub-contracted workers who provide the necessary numerical flexibility without the need to lay off full-time staff (Lockwood and Guerrier, 1988). The majority of seasonal employment is now restricted to school and college students who only require work for the holiday periods anyway. Many of these students are also retained to act as casual staff, employed for a few hours, for occasional off season work.

Trends in the tourism and hospitality industry

Trends in tourism demand

World international tourist arrivals have increased by some 20 per cent since 1980 to reach 340 million in 1986, while receipts from international tourism, excluding fare payments, have increased to US$115 billion. Long-haul travel, particularly to the Far East, has seen considerable growth in recent years but still accounts for a relatively small proportion of the total. Over 80 per cent of all international arrivals in 1986 were accounted for by Europe and the Americas. This is despite the volatility of the US market which was strongly affected by world events such as Chernobyl and the threat of terrorism in 1986 or Black Monday and the stock market crash in October 1987, but which also seems to respond well to promotional effort.

In fact it is Europe which dominates the international travel scene, simply because distances and costs are low and much travel between neigh-

Table 5.6   International tourism league tables

International tourism receipts (1986)

	1986 rank	1976 rank	Tourism receipts (US$ million)
USA	1	1	12,913
Spain	2	4	11,945
Italy	3	7	9,853
France	4	2	9,580
United Kingdom	5	6	7,921
West Germany	6	3	7,826
Austria	7	5	6,928
Switzerland	8	8	4,240
Canada	9	9	3,853
Belgium/Luxembourg	10	–	2,269

Only OECD member countries are included

Tourism generating countries (1986)

	Tourism spending (US$ billions)	Spending in UK (US$ millions)
West Germany	20.67	500
USA	17.63	1,834
United Kingdom	8.69	–
Japan	7.14	148
France	6.38	411
Netherlands	4.43	182
Canada	4.30	315
Austria	4.22	47
Switzerland	3.38	178
Belgium/Luxembourg	2.88	128
Sweden	2.81	192
Italy	2.76	260

Source: OECD Blue Book

bouring countries can be by surface transport. This factor, combined with a well developed industry and a wide variety of resorts, attractions and amenities, explains why Europe alone accounts for around two-thirds of world tourist arrivals. Table 5.6 shows the importance of Europe both as a tourist destination in terms of international tourism receipts and as a tourism generator spending money abroad. Europe provides eight of the top ten international tourist destinations. All are well-established host countries with Spain leading the way, helped by large numbers of inclusive tours from the UK. Europe also provides the top tourism generator in the world – West Germany closely followed by the USA with the UK in third position. Japan features strongly as a generator of tourism, but its strong currency has deterred high volumes from going to Japan in return.

Tourism to the UK showed an overall fall of 5 per cent in numbers of arrivals in 1986 from the total of nearly 14.5 million in 1985. Estimates

Table 5.7   Overseas tourist visits to the UK

1985 Country of origin	Trips (000s)	Duration (nights)	Spending (£ million)
USA	3170	10	1500
France	1620	8	250
West Germany	1480	10	240
Ireland	1000	8	250
Netherlands	760	7	110
Canada	630	14	230
Middle East	590	18	650
Belgium/Luxembourg	500	4	80
Italy	490	14	160
Australia	470	25	260

Source: BTA/ETB, National Facts of Tourism, 1987

for 1987 show a recovery to around 15.6 million and the BTA set a target for 1988 of some 16.4 million. The BTA also suggests that of those visits around 27–28 per cent should come from North America, 40–42 per cent from Europe and 31–32 per cent from the rest of the world. Spending, which reached a total of £5400 million in 1985 and 1986, should rise to £6300 million in 1987, £6900 million in 1988 and £7600 million in 1989 (MacArdie, 1988).

In 1986 overseas visitors spent an average of 11 nights in the UK spending £5400 million and a further £1300 million on fare payments to UK carriers. They came for a variety of purposes including holidays (43%), visiting friends and relatives (21%) and business (23%). Table 5.7 shows a breakdown of tourist visits to the UK by country of origin.

In comparison, the numbers of British residents travelling abroad in 1986 rose to 22 million representing 235 million bednights and spending £7075 million. Holidays abroad alone accounted for around 80 per cent of these trips generating 210 million bednights and spending £5325 million. France and Spain are the most popular destinations but they attract different types of tourist. France tends to attract the independent traveller, where Spain is dominated by package holidays. Other popular destinations are Ireland, Greece, West Germany and Italy, closely followed by Portugal and the USA.

Not everybody in the UK goes abroad, however, and domestic tourism in 1986 was made up of 128 million trips, 510 million bednights and an expenditure of £7150 million. Of these trips only 55 per cent were holidays, 23 per cent were visits to friends and relatives and 17 per cent were business trips. Table 5.8 provides a breakdown of tourism in Britain and abroad by British residents.

Looking at tourism by British residents in the UK it can be seen that,

TOURISM AND HOSPITALITY 83

Table 5.8 Tourism in Britain and abroad by British residents

(Millions)	Trips			Nights			Spend		
	Total	Britain	Abroad	Total	Britain	Abroad	Total	Britain	Abroad
1980	146	130	16	720	550	170	7,700	4,550	3,150
1981	143	126	18	705	520	180	8,475	4,600	3,875
1982	140	123	18	695	505	190	8,725	4,500	4,225
1983	150	131	19	735	545	190	9,775	5,350	4,425
1984 (old)	154	135	19	750	550	200	10,950	5,650	5,300
1984 (new)	159	140	20	765	565	200	11,525	5,975	5,550
1985	144	126	19	695	500	200	11,675	6,325	5,350
1986	150	128	22	745	510	235	14,225	7,150	7,075
Purpose of visit									
On holiday	69	55	80	76	70	89	67	59	76
VFR	20	23	2	11	15	2	5	8	2
Business	17	17	17	10	11	8	26	30	22
Other	4	4	2	2	3	1	2	2	1

Source: *The British Tourist Market*, 1986, BTA/ETB/WTB

although holidays make up 55 per cent of the total trips, they make up 70 per cent of the nights spent away from home but only 59 per cent of the total expenditure. Visits to friends and relatives may account for nearly a quarter of all trips but, in terms of revenue generation, it only provides 8 per cent of spending. The business traveller on the other hand accounts for 17 per cent of the trips but only 11 per cent of the nights suggesting a much shorter average length of stay. At the same time the business traveller spends 30 per cent of all revenue meaning a much higher average spend per night than the holiday traveller. It must be remembered, however, that although the business traveller is an increasingly important part of the market, particularly in certain areas and in certain types of hotels, in revenue terms the holiday market is still by far the largest part of the total UK tourism market, although it is spread much more widely across different types of accommodation.

A comparison of domestic and overseas tourism shows that, although the total amount spent was roughly the same, the number of domestic trips was more than five times greater suggesting a much lower average cost per trip. The number of domestic bednights, however, was only double those spent abroad suggesting a much shorter average length of stay. In fact, domestic long holidays of four nights or more fell to 31.5 million trips in 1986, decreasing by 13.5 per cent from 1980 as more holiday-takers decide to take their main holiday abroad. In contrast, short holidays increased to 32 million trips in 1986 as more people take advantage of weekend breaks and similar holiday packages and more people consider taking a second domestic holiday. The length of a domestic holiday has declined to an average of five days. Long holidays continue to show a high degree of seasonality with 45 per cent of these trips in July and August, but short holidays are reasonably evenly spread across the year. The move to short break holidays which are usually taken in a hotel has also slowed down the move to self-catering accommodation which accounts for around 60 per cent of the holiday market.

The implications of these trends for the traditional seaside resort are manifestly obvious and are reflected in the changes to the pattern of hotel units mentioned earlier. More and more people are taking their long holiday abroad so reducing the demand for domestic resorts. This fall in demand has encouraged many businesses to change originally from serviced accommodation to self catering, but as even this market now seems threatened the current move is into care homes for the elderly. This still leaves seaside resorts struggling to find accommodation for the peaks of the season particularly during August. The move towards more short break holidays does not help the seaside resorts as most of these are taken either in the countryside or in major cultural or historical centres. The South

West of England still remains the most popular domestic destination in terms of volume – 11 million trips; bednights – 71 million; and spending – £925 million. It is interesting to note that this one region accounts for almost as many tourist trips as the total number of trips by overseas visitors to the UK. Domestic holiday tourism still represents large movements of people.

Trends in tour operations

It has been estimated that 80 per cent of travel abroad is for holiday purposes, making some 17 million trips. Of these trips in 1987 11.5 million were as part of an inclusive tour or package holiday put together by tour operators. These ITs generated some £3000 million revenue. However it has been estimated (Heape, 1987) that only one in six of the UK population take an inclusive tour in any one year and that 50 per cent have never been on one. This provides a large market for increased penetration in future years as does the trend to taking multiple holidays with increasing numbers of people taking two or even three packages in a year. The price of package holidays is one factor which encourages increasing demand as the price of a holiday in 1986 was in fact less than a similar package in 1981 despite a 30 per cent increase in the retail price index over the same period. The market for inclusive tours looks very buoyant both currently and for the future, with some estimates suggesting that the market will reach 20 million trips by the 1990s.

However, the picture for the tour operators does not look quite so good with very narrow profit margins of only one or two pounds per holiday and a fiercely competitive market place. The severe price competition in 1987 left the top 30 tour operators with a loss for the year of around £25 million pounds and 15 companies going out of business (Williams, 1988). This struggle for market share has led to increasing economic concentration in the industry. In 1985 the top ten operators shared 50 per cent of the business, in 1986 the top two operators shared that same 50 per cent and forecasts suggest this will rise as high as 60 per cent. The actual share of holidays in 1987 put the Thomson group in first place with 31.5 per cent and the International Leisure Group, which includes Intasun, in second place with 18 per cent. The Civil Aviation Authority licenses tour operators to sell inclusive tours, and in 1988 licensed a total of 679 operators, but the top 40 account for 84 per cent of the business. The top licensed companies are shown in Table 5.9. The trend for increasing concentration is still continuing as Bass, who own Horizon, had recently bought Wings and OSL from Rank, and BA Holidays and Sunmed Holidays have combined to form Redwing Holidays.

Table 5.9   Tour operators licensed market share 1988

Company	Percentage
Thomson Group incl. Portland and Skytours	28
International Leisure Group incl. Intasun, Club 18–30	17
Horizon (bought by Thomson 18/8/88)	8
Redwing incl. Sunmed and BA Holidays	5
Owners Abroad Group	4
Airtours	3
Best Travel	3
Yugotours	2
Granada Group incl. Neilson, Pilgrim, Grosvenor Hall	2
Cosmos	2

Source: Civil Aviation Authority

Although the companies are facing difficult economic circumstances, there seems to be little change to the destinations that are and will be popular. Greece, Yugoslavia and Portugal have virtually doubled their numbers between 1981 and 1986, but Spain still remains the dominant destination, although small falls have been noted as tourists move from Greece and Spain into Turkey. There is little evidence, however, that mass tourism will move to other destinations despite the current interest in long-haul, exotic destinations.

There are, however, substantial changes occurring in the type of holidays on offer. Self-catering holidays have a strong presence in the UK domestic holiday market and this trend seems to be moving abroad with 20 per cent of all packages being self-catering or apartment holidays in 1986 and forecasts suggesting it rising to 50 per cent in the 1990s. There is also a growing trend to multiple branding by the large companies specialising in particular market segments. For example, the International Leisure Group includes Club 18–30 which is focussed at the youth market; Intasun which offers Golden Days packages aimed at senior citizens; and Lancaster has a special family brochure linked with Mothercare. Thomson Holidays offers a total of 24 different brochures aimed at different groups. Current interest in 'lifestyle' has also allowed the operators to offer more specialist products such as sports holidays for the fitness-conscious, long-haul trips to exotic locations and an increasing number of seat-only deals where the operator provides the flight only and allows the traveller to arrange his or her own accommodation. In fact this market which was virtually unknown two or three years ago has now reached some 2 million trips per year.

The tour operations field is increasingly dominated by large companies who may well have interests outside the industry. Thomson for example have interests in oil and publishing, where Horizon until the middle of

1988 were owned by the brewing group Bass. These large companies are able to weather the current low profitability of tour operations through their parent companies and through the fact that they also operate the charter airlines which carry the passengers on holiday, this being a more profitable business. Companies in the middle of the market, however, are unlikely to be able to continue in operation and will be squeezed out of the market. Smaller specialist companies are likely to remain successful as they are able to tailor their packages to particular client groups, resorts, countries or activities. The increasing brand segmentation by the larger companies suggest that they, too, are looking for more specialist markets to take advantage of what should be a boom time in inclusive tours abroad.

Trends in travel agencies

The fortunes of the travel agents are closely linked to the business of the tour operators whose products the agents sell. The traditional character of the travel agency business has been one of mutual co-operation and support between primarily small independents. The largest multiple agency has only 8 per cent of the total market. This image of the small local agent giving independent advice to potential travellers and then executing their requirements is likely to change dramatically in the 1990s as the five largest companies gain control of 50 to 60 per cent of travel retailing.

The actions of the large tour operators in cutting prices to try to gain market share has resulted in increased demand but has also worn away the profit margins for the travel agent, and those independents who are not protected by the umbrella of a parent company have suffered. The parent companies themselves are very diverse – Thomas Cook and American Express are owned by financial institutions, Hogg Robinson by an insurance broker, Pickfords by National Freight, Lunn Poly by the Thomson Group and W. H. Smith. They do have a common need to see their investments prosper and take an aggressive approach to profit generation, particularly in the very competitive high street retailing environment where holidays have to compete with videos, clothes and other luxury goods for disposable income. A recent ruling by the UK Monopolies and Mergers Committee has stated that travel agents should be actively encouraged to compete.

This need to compete has also affected the relationship between the agent and the tour operator. Traditionally, the tour operator has had the upper hand giving out merchandising material to the agent for display with no input from the agent to the products on offer. The multiple agents have now gained enough control of the high street to be able to challenge the operators and ask for additional commissions, special offers and extra advertising. Agents such as W. H. Smith are already going one step further and acting as their own tour operator to set up their own branded product.

The future for the travel agent is challenging as they strive to make the best use of expensive high street locations. The technology is constantly developing and will now allow easier direct selling which could undermine the agent, but it will also allow the agent to operate in new sites such as inside other stores such as Thomas Cook's experiments in Tesco supermarkets and Top Shop. Perhaps the most important development will be the agent taking more of a responsibility for putting packages together on behalf of the customer and adopting the Marks & Spencer approach of instructing the operator what products to provide and what standards to achieve.

Trends in hotel operations

The experience of London hotels in 1986 when occupancy levels dropped from 81 per cent in 1985 to 74 per cent in 1986 largely due to the fall-off in American tourists from 42 per cent to 36 per cent of guests, highlights the vulnerability of the hotel industry to trends in tourism. This was especially felt by the luxury end of the market where room occupancy dropped by 14 percentage points to under 70 per cent, the lowest for a number of years. Tourism prospects, as mentioned earlier, look reasonably promising over the next few years, as does the growth in domestic short break holidays and the development of business travel. This has combined with the ability of all hotels over recent years to increase their achieved average room rates in excess of the rate of inflation to give the hotel companies confidence in the future and invest heavily in new developments, acquisitions and renovations.

A recent survey by the building group Mansell (Caterer and Hotel-keeper, 1988) estimates that the total UK market for leisure construction projects has increased by at least 50 per cent in the past two years and is running currently at about £2000 million per year. Out of this total some £928 million is accounted for by the hotel market with £371 million in London alone. The top ten hotel groups accounted for 58 per cent of this market. The English Tourist Board's own figures, given in Table 5.10, show that in the latter half of 1987 £357 million went into programmes of building and refurbishment in hotels. This expenditure has been spent not only on new building but also on extensions to existing properties incorporating the provision of leisure facilities and the refurbishment and reconstruction of older properties. The Ramada Renaissance in Manchester was in fact converted from an old office building at a total cost of some £9 million for the luxury 200-bedroom hotel.

Table 5.10   Tourism and leisure investment July–December 1987

| | Opened | | Under construction | |
	(£m)	(No)	(£m)	(No)
New hotels	48.7	18	153.3	37
Hotel extensions	30.1	11	41.3	26
Hotel refurbishment	25.1	9	58.8	19
Totals	103.9	38	253.4	82

Source: English Tourist Board

Perhaps the most significant development of 1988 for the hotel industry has been the takeover by UK companies of international hotel chains. The takeover by Bass of Holiday Inn International and franchising rights outside America and the purchase of Hilton International by Ladbrokes now places the control of four of the world's most significant hotel operations under UK control. Trust House Forte (THF) now have control through ownership and associates of 824 hotels worldwide with 79,000 rooms. Bass, through Holiday Inn, control the operation of 1971 hotels with 365,700 rooms. Ladbrokes with Hilton International and the newly created domestic chain of Hilton National represent 569 hotels with 159,600 rooms. The fourth major international chain is Intercontinental Hotels with 112 units and 42,369 rooms. This chain was, in August 1988, still part of Grand Metropolitan, although it had officially been placed on the market for sale.

There has been a continued growth in domestic hotel groups in the last two years. Crest Hotels now firmly a UK chain following the Bass acquisition of Holiday Inn to front its international expansion has put forward plans to build new hotels in the Leeds/Bradford area. Swallow Hotels have opened three new hotels as well as splitting the tied houses from the parent company Vaux breweries to form a separate Inns division. Similar expansions have occurred with Queens Moat, Thistle and Whitbread not to mention the acquisition by THF of Anchor Hotels and Kennedy Brookes hotels and restaurants.

Many UK groups are showing a greater international focus particularly THF who are now building hotels in Europe for the first time in their history and Queens Moat Houses who have made significant acquisitions in Germany. The UK has also become the focus for a number of international groups notably Accor, the largest French hotel company through their Novotel, Ibis and Formule 1 chains, Aer Lingus and Tara hotels who have bought the Copthorne hotel group from British Caledonian Airlines prior to their merger with British Airways, and Ramada who now have a substantial presence in all of their three brands of Ramada Inns, Hotels and Renaissance properties.

Table 5.11 Brand segmentation in 3 UK hotel companies

	UK Bass	UK Ladbroke	UK THF	Rest of the World Bass	Rest of the World Ladbroke	Rest of the World THF
5*	Holiday Inn Crowne Plaza	Royal Berkshire	Exclusive	Holiday Inn Crowne Plaza		Exclusive
4/5*		Hilton International			Hilton International	
4*	Holiday Inn		Forte Classic	Holiday Inn		Forte
3/4*	Crest	Hilton National	Post Houses		Hilton Inn	
1/2*	Holiday Inn Garden Court Toby Hotels Osprey Hotels		Travelodge Little Chef Lodges	Holiday Inn Garden Court		Travelodge

Another significant trend has been the emergence of market segmentation within the industry. A number of companies have now rationalised their portfolios of hotels to present a multi-branded organisation to the market place. Ramada have three tiers with their budget Inns, their middle of the range Hotels and their up-market Renaissance Hotels. Even THF with their very diverse portfolio of hotels have attempted a brand rationalisation. Table 5.11 shows the portfolios of THF, Bass and Ladbroke's broken down by brand both in the UK and in the rest of the world.

A further benefit of multiple branding has been the freedom for companies to develop new product concepts without damaging established brands. The two main product developments have been in the budget hotels market and the country house hotel market.

The budget hotel market has long been dominated by French and American chains who have not until recently made any inroads into the UK. The lodge concept seems to have caught on, however, with new developments from THF's Little Chef Lodges and Travelodge, Beefeater Travel Inns, Rank and Granada. It is interesting to note that these developments have come from the restaurant divisions of major companies and not their hotel divisions. Also joining the battle for the budget market are Friendly Hotels a UK company, French companies Accor, in the guise of Ibis and Formule 1, and Campanile, with the American influence of Marriott and Holiday Inn Garden Court supervised by Bass. The lodge is aimed primarily at the businessman travelling by car on a restricted budget and also at families who can all share one room at a very reasonable cost. The standard of facilities offered varies between groups but aims at a good 2 to 3 star standard of room but with minimum personal service and a limited availability of food.

At the opposite end of the market the country house hotel is coming in for a lot of attention. Traditionally these hotels have been run by independent owner-operators, but now the groups have realised the potential of the enhanced levels of service and the enhanced room rates. Thistle Hotels have opened Cannizaro House in Wimbledon and have plans to add further country house hotels including a completely new hotel with a comprehensive leisure spa to be built very close to Haydock Park race course. Norfolk Capital has acquired Celebrated Country Hotels and now has four country properties including Eastwell Manor in Kent and the Oakley Court near Windsor.

There is also renewed interest in opening hotels in London as the local boroughs relax somewhat their strict planning regulations. For example, Edwardian Hotels have converted the old Dental Hospital in Leicester Square into a prestigious deluxe hotel and plans have been announced to convert the old GLC buildings south of the Thames into a new hotel development.

It is apparent that the hotel industry is in a buoyant situation and is likely to continue to prosper as long as the world economy remains reasonably stable. Current consolidation of the major hotel groups will benefit the UK industry as a whole as this country is able to control more of the international hotel industry. New product development continues at a rapid rate with considerable investment in new building and in the addition of the health, fitness and leisure centres that the business traveller seems to demand. The industry is also well placed to generate employment, indeed one estimate suggests that 200,000 new jobs could be created in London alone by the mid-1990s (Bodlender, 1987). There is, however, a problem with this expansion – even now hotels in central London are experiencing extreme difficulty in finding, recruiting and keeping staff at almost every level and as demographic trends reduce the number of young people entering the labour market, the situation can only get worse. It is also likely that this shortage of labour will hit hotels in other parts of the country by the end of the decade.

Future developments in tourism and hospitality

The development of the tourism and hospitality industry is heavily dependent on the trends in the marketplace. Prospects for world tourism look encouraging. The World Tourism Organisation (WTO) has forecast that visitor arrivals will rise to 380 million by 1990 representing an annual growth rate of 4 per cent. The WTO also expects domestic tourism to grow faster than international tourism with total worldwide movements reaching between 4700 and 5300 million over the same period. Other forecasters have predicted that tourism will be the world's largest industry by the year 2000.

This growth in tourism will not be spread evenly. Particular growth markets can be identified. Worldwide demographic trends will result in an increasing number of senior citizens – by the year 2000, every fourth person in Europe will be over 55. The retired population often has a large amount of leisure time and, if money is not a problem, represents a large potential market.

Business travel will continue to grow and women business travellers will increase as will combined business and vacation trips. Another growth sector in the business field is that of incentive travel, where travel is given as a reward for employee performance. This sector of the market is growing at an annual rate of some 15 per cent and is a particularly profitable sector as companies look further afield for newer and more exotic locations able to provide fun, recreation and sightseeing.

Mini-holidays or short break holidays will also continue to increase as more and more people take a second or third holiday. These short breaks may well be special interest holidays offering a package of activities related to a particular hobby or sport. Active holidays will also become increasingly important for main holidays as typified by the growth of the Dutch company Sporthuis Centrum and their chain of eleven Center Parcs in the Netherlands, Belgium, France and the UK. This concept offers a comprehensive range of sporting activities in a forested village setting of self-catering villa accommodation around a dome housing a sophisticated leisure swimming pool.

Increasing sophistication of the customer will have an impact on all product development throughout the industry. There will be an increased requirement for high standards of product design, efficiency and safety. This will be achieved through strong branding and tailoring the product more closely to the needs of specific market segments. There will be a need for multiple options rather than a simple take it or leave it. An example of this development can be seen in the provision of executive rooms and female executive rooms in hotels geared to appeal specifically to the business traveller.

Although not all market segments will require high levels of personal attention, there will be a need for more personnel in all sectors of the industry capable of delivering customer service. The current demographic trends and problems recruiting certain types of staff suggest that there will be a severe labour shortage and that tourism will have to compete with many other industries for its staff. This will increase the labour cost element of all services and will give rise to a need either to cover these costs through increasing the charges paid by the customer or reducing labour costs through reduced staffing levels or the replacement of labour with capital as in the fully automatic check-in provided by Formule 1. To make best use of all staff resources training will be important as will the skills of managers in handling employees. Managers will also need to improve their general business skills and become more technology-oriented.

Technology will play a major role in the industry. All major companies in the industry either in hotels, travel agents or tour operations rely heavily on computers for day-to-day administration and increasingly for help with management decision making. Computers are used extensively for handling reservations, processing and transmission of accounting information, property management systems keeping track of the usage of a building and making fuel savings possible, as well as point of sale terminals and electronic payment systems linked either directly to banks or to credit card companies. Technology may lead to increasing integration between the different sectors of the industry as all the processes of a customer making an airline reservation, booking hotel rooms, checking in and being given a key, paying the bill and even completing a guest satisfaction questionnaire could be linked through the same technology. Already the major airline reservation systems which are linked to hotel chains and car hire have had a significant impact.

It has in fact been suggested that technology would encourage the growth of mega-corporations covering all aspects of the present industry as part of a new 'transpitality' industry (Palmer, 1984). This combination of airlines and hotel companies has not really become established, although considerable vertical and horizontal integration does exist. For example, the Thomson group owns Britannia Airlines and Orion, two of the largest charter airlines. It is likely that further consolidation of companies in all sectors will continue with increasing economic concentration in a small number of large companies, although it seems unlikely at this point that these companies will combine across sectors. For example, Bass have recently sold their tour company Horizon to Thomson but have also bought extensively into the hotel market with Holiday Inn.

Summary and conclusions

The tourism and hospitality industry is a collection of many diverse sectors all centred around providing service to customers away from home for whatever reason. This diversity means that the operation of each sector is quite distinct and that few managers transfer freely between them.

Despite this diversity, however, the industry is facing a common set of challenges. An increasingly discerning travelling customer is looking for the best value for money product and expects that product to meet their expected standards for both physical facilities and service. This highly competitive market has led to the growth of the large company which can operate effectively on an international basis. At the same time, the need for wide geographical coverage coupled with relatively easy entry to the industry and customers who are always on the look out for something different ensures the continuation of the small independent operator. The larger companies, also realising the need for catering to the needs of specific market segments, have responded by increasing brand segmentation and developing new products to suit.

The operations side of the industry will be hampered by the shortage of skilled and semi-skilled staff but will realise the importance of staff to providing service quality or will attempt to replace staff with new technology and increasing customer involvement in the service delivery process.

To be successful the industry must continue to be customer-centred.

References

Bodlender, J. A. (1987) *United Kingdom Hotel Industry 1987*, Horwath and Horwath Ltd, London.

Boniface, B. G. and Cooper, C. P. (1987) *The Geography of Travel and Tourism*, Heinemann, London, p. 35.

BTA/ETS Tourism Intelligence Quarterly, Vol. 10, No. 1, May 1988.

Caterer and Hotelkeeper, 9 June, 1988, p. 6.

Clawson, M. and Knetsch, J. (1966) *The Economics of Outdoor Recreation*, The Johns Hopkins University Press, Baltimore.

Faulks, R. W. (1982) *Principles of Transport*, Ian Allan, Weybridge, Surrey.

HCITB (1978) *Manpower in the Hotel and Catering Industry*, HCITB, London.

Heape, R. (1987) 'Inclusive tours – an untapped market', *Tourism Management*, Vol. 8, No. 2, pp. 169–70.

John, B. (1986) *The Pembrokeshire Guide*, Greencroft Books, Newport, Dyfed.

Lockwood, A. J. and Guerrier, Y. (1988) 'Work flexibility in hotels', in: Johnston, R. (ed) *The Management of Service Operations*, IFS (Publications) Ltd, Bedford.

MacArdle, M. (1988) 'Realistic targets', *British Travel Brief*, BTA, London, No. 5, pp. 22–3.

Morrell, J. (1985) *Employment in Tourism*, BTA, London

Page, K. (1987) 'The future of cruise shipping', *Tourism Management*, Vol. 8, No. 2, pp. 166–8.

Palmer, J. (1984) 'The transpitality industry', *International Journal of Hospitality Management*, Vol. 3, No. 1, pp. 19–23.

Parsons, D. (1986) *Jobs in Tourism and Leisure – an Occupational Review*, English Tourist Board, London.

Trade and Industry Committee (1985) *Tourism in the UK*, Vol. 1, Para. 73, HMSO, London.

Trippier, D. (1987) 'Tourism in the 1990s – UK government view', *Tourism Management*, Vol. 8, No. 2, pp. 79–82.

Wanhill, S. R. C. (1987a) 'UK – politics and tourism', *Tourism Management*, Vol. 8, No. 1, pp. 54–8.

Wanhill, S. R. C. (1987b) 'Making Tourism Work', Inaugural lecture given at The University of Surrey, 18th March 1987.

Williams, I. (1988) 'Profits take a holiday', *Sunday Times*, 31st July, p. 7.

World Tourism Organisation (1986) *Yearbook of Tourism Statistics*, WTO, Madrid.

6 Public sector services

NORMAN FLYNN

Introduction

This chapter looks at issues and trends relating to the provision of public services. Public services are a significant part of the economy, and are mainly in the business of producing infrastructure, essential services and various measures to relieve distress. They are organised in a variety of ways which mean that management in public sector services is different from management in the private sector. There are major changes facing managers. The present government is keen to reduce the scope of the public sector and increase the involvement of the private sector. Managerial accountability is being enhanced and organisations are being broken up into smaller accountable units, whose performance is coming under increasing scrutiny.

Scale and scope

There are about 5.6 million people employed in the public sector in the United Kingdom. Table 6.1 shows the areas in which these people worked in 1986/7. Not all of these employees are working in what we would normally define as 'service industries'. But even if we exclude the armed forces (330,000) and the civil servants working in defence (160,000) and the manufacturing nationalised industries (steel and coal employ about 180,000) there are still over 5 million people.

If we exclude defence and support for nationalised industries, expenditure on public services in 1987/8 was about £128 billion, including the income support services of Social Security, which cost £42.6 billion. Table 6.2 shows where this money was spent in 1987/8.

Table 6.2 shows that the social security service is by far the biggest central government application of resources, followed (again excluding defence) by health and personal social services. The £40.9 billion spent by local authorities are predominantly spent on education, law and order and

Table 6.1 Public sector employment

Thousands, whole time equivalents – 1986–87 actual

Central government deparments	
Defence	167.4
Foreign and Commonwealth Office	8.0
Overseas Development Administration	1.5
Ministry of Agriculture, Fisheries and Food	10.7
Intervention Board for Agricultural Produce	0.8
Trade and Industry	11.5
Export Credits Guarantee Department	1.7
Energy	1.0
Employment	58.0
Transport	11.1
Department of the Environment	6.5
Home Office	37.6
Lord Chancellor's Department	10.2
Education and Science	2.4
Arts and Libraries	0.1
Department of Health and Social Security	94.7
Scotland	12.0
Wales	2.3
Northern Ireland Office	0.2
Customs and Excise	25.3
Inland Revenue	68.8
Chancellor's other departments	12.1
Property Services Agency	23.1
Other departments	12.3
Total Civil Service manpower in running costs	**579.2**
Trading funds	6.3
Other Civil Service manpower	12.0
Civil Service manpower totals	**597.5**
Armed Forces	331.1
National Health Service	981.0
Northern Ireland Departments (NI Civil Service)	25.2
Northern Ireland Office (NI Civil Service Group and Prison Service)	4.4
Other NI Government Service	119.3
Research Councils	11.0
Other central government	42.0
Local authorities community programme	66.0
Local authorities (other non-trading)	2054.0
Manpower in planning total (excluding trading funds)	**4225.0**
Nationalised industries	1049.0
Other public corporations	112.0
Local authorities (trading)	232.0
Total public sector	**5625.0**

Source: The Government's Expenditure Plans 1988–89 to 1990–91, HM Treasury, January 1988, Volume I.

social security (housing benefit is administered by local authorities). Table 6.3 gives the breakdown of local government current expenditure in England for 1987/8.

Table 6.2 Expenditure by spending authority and department, 1987–88

1987–88 estimated outturn

Central government*	**109.7**
Of which:	
Defence	18.8
Foreign and Commonwealth Office	2.0
European Communities	1.4
Ministry of Agriculture, Fisheries and Food	1.9
Trade and Industry	1.2
Energy	0.6
Employment	3.8
Transport	1.4
DOE – Housing	1.3
DOE – Other environmental services	0.4
Home Office	1.9
Education and Science	2.7
Arts and Libraries	0.4
DHSS – Health and Personal Social Services	16.5
DHSS – Social Security	42.6
Scotland, Wales and Northern Ireland	8.9
Chancellor's departments	2.3
Other departments	1.5
Local Authorities*	**40.9**
Public corporations	**1.1**
Of which:	
Nationalised industries	0.5
Other public corporations	0.6
Privatisation proceeds	−5.0
Adjustment	0.6
Total	**147.3**

* Excludes finance for public corporations
Source: The Government's Expenditure Plans 1988–89 to 1990–91, HM Treasury, January 1988, Volume I.

Table 6.3 Local authority public expenditure in England by function

Percentage of 1987–88 estimated outturn

Current expenditure in England	
Agriculture, fisheries, food and forestry	.5
Industry, trade and employment	.6
Arts and libraries	1.5
Roads and transport	6.1
Housing	2.1
Other environmental services	9.9
Law, order and protective services	14.1
Education and Science	45.4
Health and Personal Social Services	9.5
Social Security	10.3
Total current expenditure	**100**

Source: The Government's Expenditure Plans 1988–89 to 1990–91, HM Treasury, January 1988, Volume I.

What sort of services?

Services may be categorised in many different ways. Three useful distinctions are:

1   Those services which people use because they enjoy them and they enhance their lives. These include travel, entertainment and some aspects of education. The main features of these services are that they need to be targeted carefully and that people have a lot of choice.

2   Those which people are forced to use, in order to be able to keep living and working. Car insurance is compulsory if you want to own a car. Bank accounts are necessary if you are paid directly. These services need to be accessible and reliable, and the dependency which they imply needs to be softened by an emphasis on quality.

3   Other services relieve pain or distress. Sometimes plumbers, car mechanics and doctors provide services like this. The emphasis in these services is on speed of response and caring behaviour towards the customers. Within each category, there can be a further distinction based on how the services are supplied – whether by a monopoly or by a variety of providers, thus giving the customer a choice. An important starting point for all service management is to identify exactly what kind of service the organisation provides and arrange the elements of the service accordingly.

The growth parts of the service economy are mainly in the first two categories: entertainment, catering and tourism in the first, and insurance, banking and finance in the second. A large proportion of public sector services are in the third category. The police service, most of the health service and personal social services are examples of the public services which people generally use when they are in unfortunate circumstances. Other public services are in the second category: infrastructure and public transport are examples of services which are essential but which are not noticeably life-enhancing or fun to use. Life without them would be much less comfortable, but their existence is taken for granted. In addition, many public services are *de facto* monopolies for many of their customers.

The consequence of this is that as more people get used to receiving private sector services and dealing with service providers who are in competition with each other, they encounter public sector services which are often inherently unpopular (nobody likes to be in a position to require pain relief) and provided by people who know they have a monopoly. This puts public service managers at an immediate disadvantage in relation to most of their private sector counterparts in the area of customer attitude and perception of the services.

This management problem is compounded by the fact that the users of many of the services are not 'customers' at all. Their relationship with the organisation is not one in which they can exert pressure by threatening to go elsewhere or not use the service at all. Nor is the relationship always one between a willing service receiver and service producer. Education is compulsory between the ages of 5 and 16 and many pupils would rather not be customers at all. Some of the services provided by social services departments involve removing children from their parents or detaining mentally ill people against their will.

In these cases it is a strained use of language to call the service recipients 'customers'. 'Clients' or even 'victims' would be more appropriate. And if this is the sort of relationship that is implied, then management practice which is concerned to foster good 'customer relations' needs to be greatly adapted before it is applied in particular public sector cases.

The other impact of the particular service/recipient relationship in parts of the public sector is on the use of marketing. If marketing consists of identifying the needs, desires, wants, preferences and therefore demands of customers and potential customers, it implies that the organisation is geared to meeting those demands in such a way and at such a price as to produce a mutually beneficial exchange with the customer. In the case of some public services, this is not the case. Social Security officers are acutely aware of the desires of their clients. The management task is to ration the provision of service, not generate extra demand. The same is true of the Health Service, in which marketing efforts are occasionally made to ascertain the preferences of consumers, but where the principal strategic task is rationing supply.

It is simply not the case that 'demand' (the willingness and ability of the customer to pay) brings forth the supply, except by a very roundabout route through the political process. Marketing often has to be replaced by 'demarketing', where resource constraints make a priority of suppressing demand.

Because of this it is not possible simply to transpose good service management practice from the private sector to the public. Listening to the customer may simply reveal demands which cannot be met. Good communications may reveal customers for whom there is no service available. Good customer care may create unrealistic expectations. The managerial solution to this problem in the Health Service is to produce an effective rationing system for hospital services by channelling demand through the general practitioner service, and then to provide the best standard of care for those to whom the service is provided.

Organisation and accountability

Public services are organised in a variety of ways: some are provided by civil servants directly employed by central government (such as the Foreign and Commonwealth Office, the Ministry of Agriculture, Forestry and Food), some through nationalised industries (e.g. The Post Office, the British Railways Board), some through public corporations (e.g. the British Broadcasting Corporation, the Royal Mint), through local authorities (e.g. primary and secondary education, personal social services, public housing) or through health authorities (e.g. hospital services).

Because of this diversity of organisational form, managers of public services operate within a diverse range of structures and arrangements for accountability. Managers in local authorities are accountable to directly elected local councillors. These councillors, operating within statutory and financial constraints, make the policy within which managers have to operate. Civil servants manage within a hierarchy which has a Minister at the top. Nationalised industries have Boards which are accountable to a sponsoring department of central government.

In all these cases the accountability and control structures make managers' jobs different from those of managers of private services. For example, a district health authority manager may be instructed to do all s/he can to keep a hospital open. The Regional Health Authority may have different ideas and wish the hospital to close, as might the Minister. Such ambiguous accountability has no parallel in the private sector, where managers are ultimately accountable to shareholders. For more detail on the different forms of accountability in the public sector see Day and Klein (1987).

Because of this ambiguity, an important part of managerial work in the public sector involves managing the relationship between the organisation and the political process. Simple models, in which the paid managers have a very clearly defined role which consists of implementing policy, rarely work out in practice. This is for three main reasons:

1   The services are in many cases run by managers who are also professionals, who have a legitimacy which arises from their professional status as much as their organisational position. As professionals they expect to be able to exert a good deal of autonomy.

2   Policies are often introduced onto the political agenda by managers, officials or professionals.

3   Politicians like to get involved in management, whether a Minister of Defence who feels the need to have detailed involvement in the procedure for defence equipment procurement or a local councillor who

feels that the nature of the management process in a local authority is an important part of politics.

Managerial work in public services therefore involves an important and complicated interface with the political process. In the United Kingdom, the top civil servants or local authority managers are not traditionally replaced when there is a change in political control, as happens in other countries. There is, however, a tendency for appointments to be influenced by the question 'Is s/he one of us?' or 'Is s/he "sound"?'. Managers who do not fit with the basic values of their political employers find life uncomfortable.

The skills of managers in a political environment include the ability to present choices so that politicians can make decisions. One of the reasons for the demand for *output measures* in documents such as the Public Expenditure White Paper is that politicians want to know what they are *buying* for the public funds they are voting.

Inevitably, senior managers' jobs also involve advising on policy and saving their political employers from embarrassment. Advice on policy and on tactics inevitably involves making political judgements about what is likely to be acceptable.

Whenever managers get involved in policy work, therefore, it is difficult to draw a very clear distinction between what politicians do and what employees do. Managers need to have good awareness of the political consequences of their advice and actions. Increasingly, politicians are becoming aware of the managerial consequences of their actions.

One solution is to try to separate policy from operational management. *Improving Management in Government: the Next Steps* (Efficiency Unit, 1987) recommended the establishment of 'agencies' or executive units which deliver services for government. These agencies would have their outputs and objectives determined for them but would have a high degree of managerial autonomy about the way they achieve their objectives. Management would be more separate from politics and managers would be free from day-to-day political control. The report also recommends an alternative accountability structure: 'What is needed is the establishment of a convention that heads of executive agencies would have delegated authority from their Ministers for operations of the agencies . . . Heads of agencies would be accountable to Ministers . . . but could be called . . . to give evidence to Select Committees as to the manner in which their delegated authority had been used . . .' (p. 17). This approach is a variant on contracting out which also separates operational management from policy making.

Major trends

There are four main issues affecting public services in the UK. These are decentralisation, the shift to the private sector, contracting out and performance measurement. A common approach in many parts of the public sector has been to devolve managerial responsibility to accountable units within the large bureaucracies. This approach has been led by two motivations: first, to increase control on spending, and second, to make the organisations more responsive to their 'customers'. These two motivations may lead in different directions: a more responsive organisation may well spend more as it identifies more demand for its services. Where supply is limited by public expenditure controls, managers find themselves in a contradictory position.

In the Health Service, for example, a system of management has been installed in which General Managers have been appointed to run Districts, and within the Districts, Unit General Managers have the responsibility for aspects of the service, such as a hospital, or care of the mentally ill. The operational management of the units is devolved from the District, but resource allocation is left at District level. In the Civil Service, the Financial Management Initiative has established Cost Centres which have managers responsible for budgets. The emphasis in the Civil Service is on accountability for keeping budgets under control, rather than responding to the 'market' for services (see Metcalfe and Richards, 1987). Likewise, proposals for management in education devolve budgets to schools in which Governors and Headteachers will be responsible for the use of the resources allocated to the schools (Coopers and Lybrand, 1988).

Many social services departments in local authorities have attempted to devolve budgets and responsibility to operational managers (Flynn, 1988). In this case there has been the same mixture of motives: the need to keep overall expenditure under control and the desire to make the organisations more responsive to needs.

In all these cases, managers find themselves with more responsibility for the operational management of their units, but not necessarily with sufficient authority to make strategic changes in direction which might be required. Nor do they find themselves empowered to break up the rigid hierarchies above them, and the rules which prevent change from happening. These experiments in decentralisation have a long way to go before they really turn the organisation upside down in the way that, for example, Peters is advocating for in *Thriving on Chaos* (1988). One reason for this is that public services are not in fact able to be fully responsive to the customers, because one of the main tasks is to *limit supply*, rather than *generate demand*. Another is that the public sector bureaucracies are still controlled by powerful managers whose position would be threatened if their organisations really were turned upside down.

The second major trend is the shift to the private sector. A superficial look at public services suggests that they are separate from the private sector. More detailed examination shows that the public, private and voluntary sectors are closely linked together. Health care in Britain has a private sector component, but many of the doctors who work in private hospitals are also employed within the National Health Service (NHS). And in the NHS, drugs and materials are all purchased from the private sector. Educational supplies (including this book you are reading) are produced and sold by private companies.

One ambition of the Conservative government in the UK and many others is to change the boundary between the public and private sectors. Ultimately, the desire is to have as many services and activities as possible in the private sector, and as little as possible in the public. So, for example, Nicholas Ridley (Secretary of State for the Environment) argued that 'we should always question whether it is right for the public sector to do a job when private individuals or companies could and would compete to do the job themselves' (1988).

This ambition has led to different approaches in different parts of the public sector. In housing, for example, the first approach to reducing the scope of public provision was to limit the resources available for new building, then to give tenants the right to buy at a large discount below market value, and then to give those people who wish to remain tenants the right to choose a landlord other than the local authority, meanwhile introducing rules which will lead to a further great reduction in rent subsidies. As the White Paper ('Housing: The Government's Proposals' September 1987) put it: '. . . there will no longer be the same presumption that the local authority itself should take direct action to meet new or increasing demands' (para 5.1). In other sectors the approach has been less swift. Care of the elderly has always been dealt with by families and a mixture of private, public and voluntary provision. Since 1980 there has been a great increase in the provision of private accommodation for elderly people, following a regulation which allowed DHSS payments for private homes to increase. More recent proposals emphasise the need for the public sector to act as an enabler rather than a provider in the field of community care. In health care there has been less progress, although there has been a growth of private health insurance and private hospital provision in recent years.

Faced with such a set of policies, managers have a dilemma. They could either change their whole approach from one of being service managers of directly provided services, and act in such a way that eventually they have a new role as 'enablers not providers', or they could persist in their mission to make public services so attractive that they win in competition with private and voluntary providers. Either way, they are likely to have a diminished and different job in future.

Another major trend and one aspect of the reduction of the role of public services as direct service providers is the use of competitive tendering and contracting out of service provision to private companies. The 1988 Local Government Act requires local authorities to put out to competitive tendering many of the services previously provided by directly employed labour, extending the provisions of the 1980 Local Government Planning and Land Act which required competitive tendering for building, maintenance and highways work.

Health authorities have been required since 1981 to engage in competitive tendering for 'hotel' services in hospitals, particularly catering and cleaning. Experiments have been made in central government to contract out building maintenance.

This approach changes the method of service management. Services provided by directly employed people are managed directly. The managerial task is similar to that in the private sector services: the management of a workforce in such a way that their behaviour fits with the intentions of the organisation. Contracting out requires managers to specify in great detail the requirements of the 'buyer', in terms of quantity and quality of service. The day-to-day management then becomes a separate function which may be carried out by the public sector workforce (if they win the tender) or by the company which wins it. In either case there is a very clear separation of the functions of specifying and carrying out the work. This separation demands new skills for both the buyer and the provider: the buyer needs to know how to run contracts, from writing specifications, through designing watertight contracts to dealing with defaults and performance payments; the contractor needs to be profit-conscious (especially if the in-house workforce has to make a surplus).

The impacts of contracting-out and competitive tendering are:

- costs are reduced, mainly because wages are reduced as a result of the competitive process;
- the contractors (whether in-house or private) become detached from the rest of the organisation;
- the 'buying' side of the organisation is an identifiable function, rather than part of the general management arrangements.

In the longer term, contracting out will result in very different public sector organisations, concentrating on organising services rather than providing them directly.

Contracting-out also provides a sort of solution to the problem of measuring performance in public services. Contracts have to specify levels of performance and service quality. They also have to be clear about the consequences of good or bad performance.

Measuring public service performance has been a concern of managers for many years. With no 'bottom line' of profitability, how can managers know whether they are doing well? Some progress has been made in various parts of the public sector. The Civil Service publish several hundred performance measures in the public expenditure White Paper. In Health and Local Government, league tables are produced, with measures of unit costs, throughputs and quantity of activity. These provide some broad indications on a narrow range of criteria about how individual organisations are performing. However, most of these measures have been devised to help scrutiny by auditors, select committees and other people outside the organisations.

Managers of public services need different measures to help them assess their own performance. They need to know whether they are achieving what their organisations were set up to do, and whether they could be doing better. They also need performance measures which tell them how well they are fulfilling their service obligations to their clients/customers. Measures of customer satisfaction, as well as matters such as equitable treatment need to be built into performance assessments (Pollitt, 1986).

What is measured also needs to be susceptible to influence by managers. If the relative performance of schools is determined mainly by the social composition of the population of the schools' catchment areas, then the publication of examination league tables for schools will be of no help at all to headteachers or teachers seeking to improve their schools' performance. What is interesting for managers are measures which help rearrange the inputs to the service in such a way that the outputs can be improved. Outputs themselves need to be very carefully specified, so that quality is included in the measurements as well as quantity. For example, increasing the number of operations performed is only an achievement if the success rate of those operations is maintained.

Conclusion

Managers in the public sector have never had an easy life. The recent developments in the public services have made life even more difficult. If the public services are to continue to change in the directions we have identified, managers will be involved in significant changes:

1 There will probably be a shrinkage of the relative size of the public sector as more private sector participation in service delivery develops.

2 For managers whose job is concerned with dealing with contractors (whether within or outside the public bodies) the skills required will be different from those involved in managing workforces.

3 As decentralisation proceeds, and independent agencies are established, managerial responsibility will be pushed further down the various organisations. This will require greater managerial skills among a larger number of people. It also implies that those at the top of the organisations will have different functions. Both middle and top management need to change.

4 The middle managers will both be more powerful and more exposed as their performance is subject to greater scrutiny through published performance measurement.

References

Coopers and Lybrand Associates (1988) *Devolved Financial Mangement for Schools*.

Day, P. and Klein, R. (1987) *Accountabilities – Five Public Services*, Tavistock Publications, London.

Efficiency Unit (1988) 'Improving Management in Government: the Next Steps: Report to the Prime Minister' by Kate Jenkins, Karen Caines and Andrew Jackson, HMSO.

Flynn, N. (1988) *Decentralised Management in Social Services*, DHSS, Social Services Inspectorate

Metcalfe, L. and Richards, S. (1987) *Improving Public Management*, Sage, London.

Peters, T. (1988) *Thriving on Chaos*, Macmillan, London.

Pollitt, C. (1986) 'Beyond the Managerial Model: The Case for Broadening Performance Assessment in Government and the Public Services', *Financial Accountability and Management*, 2(3) Autumn.

Ridley, N. (1988) *The Local Right: enabling not providing*, Centre for Policy Studies, Policy Study No. 92.

Part II
Strategic and organisational issues in service industries

It is clear from the detailed discussion in Part I that most service organisations are rapidly developing new strategies to cope with the major shifts in the environment they are facing and are also restructuring to a greater or lesser extent. Strategy and structure have for some time been recognised as fundamental to successful business performance, and it is these two issues that are explored in Part II.

Robert Johnston, in Chapter 7, explores the process of strategy formulation in service organisations and illustrates this through three case studies representative of the full range of different types of service provision. Once again, some of the themes highlighted in Part I are clearly evident – the importance of knowing and understanding the consumer and of effectively responding to changing circumstances; a tendency to segment the market or at least have a clear market focus; and the role of information technology in contributing to developing new service delivery systems. These and other recurrent themes are also explored by Sue Segal-Horn in Chapter 8, when she examines the trend of service firm globalisation. In particular she explodes the myth of 'fragmented' service industries, particularly the consumer service sectors which are the principal focus of this book.

As one of the essential elements in a successful global service strategy, Sue Segal-Horn identifies corporate culture. David Rea, in Chapter 9, also talks of culture but in the context of public sector service organisations. He questions the accepted view of strategy formulation and makes a critique of the assumption that managers always behave on a rational basis. The nature of public services, the role that elected representatives at national and local levels, and the delivery of these to sometimes reluctant consumers make public sector strategy formulation and execution in some respects more complex.

One of the major current trends in the public sector is the introduction of competitive tendering for many of the services provided by local government, with the subsequent introduction of many private sector firms into this area. In Chapter 11, Michael Brooke discusses the concept of management contracts. A feature of service industries is that ownership, management and delivery can be separated from each other. Contracting is only one way in which this can be achieved. As John Stanworth, in Chapter 12, explains, franchising is another. In fact, both contracting and franchising are to be found in services far more than in the manufacturing sector of the economy.

Although consumer service organisations may not always own, manage and deliver the services they are concerned with, it is the case that most service firms do so. In Chapter 10, Sue Ricks and I examine the nature of service firm organisations and how these may be different from manufacturing firms. The characteristics of services have a significant impact on structure. In particular, to be near the customers, firms must have many relatively small service delivery points and employ a very large number of staff to carry out that delivery.

Part II focusses on strategy and structure and some major issues of specific relevance to service organisations. In Part III, we go on to look in more detail at some of the implications of these for the different functional management responsibilities within the organisation.

7 Developing competitive strategies in service industries

ROBERT JOHNSTON

Introduction

The purpose of this chapter is to provide a framework that describes the development of competitive strategies in service organisations from an operations management perspective. This aims to identify the interface between the service operation and corporate strategy. The framework is then applied to three case studies to illustrate the development and implementation of service strategies.

The key to success in service industries, both nationally and internationally, is in recognising competitive strengths and then capitalising on those strengths. 'Successful service firms separate themselves from "the pack" to achieve a distinctive position in relation to the competition' (Heskett, 1986). Success is based on differentiation, that is developing distinguishing features. Most authors in the past have discussed the elements that can create a distinction, for example Mills (1986) and Fitzsimmons (1982), but few have demonstrated how these elements need to be integrated to create a competitive strategy. One notable exception to this is Heskett (1986).

A service strategy is a company's plan to achieve an advantage over its competitors. There are three stages in the development of a competitive service strategy. First, the key elements of service strategy have to be identified and understood. Second, there has to be an understanding of the need for change that is driving the development of the strategy. And, third, there is the integration of the key elements into a complete and consistent strategic plan. These three stages will now be considered in more detail.

Key elements of service strategy

A service strategy can be considered to consist of five key elements; the company itself, its service concept and its delivery systems and there is the environment in which it operates, comprising the competition and the customers. These elements are represented in Figure 7.1.

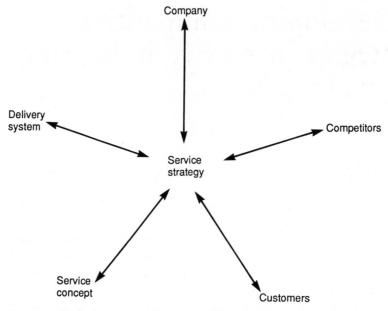

Figure 7.1   The elements of a service strategy

The company

The service company includes the tangible elements such as the people, processes, financial investments and equipment, and the intangible elements such as the requirements of the shareholders and the needs and aspirations of the workforce.

Service concept

'A service concept describes the way . . . (the company) . . . would like to have its service perceived by its customers and employees and its shareholders' (Heskett, 1986). It defines the business in which the company is involved and describes the service(s) to be provided. The service concept is the basis for the company's market image and the design of the service system.

Competition

The competition comprises all the companies who have similar service concepts and/or are competing for the same customers.

Customers

The customers are those who select the service organisation instead of a competing organisation. Customers choose, consciously or unconsciously, by comparing competitors' market images or service offerings or as a result of their own or others' previous experiences (Johnston, 1987). The customers, therefore, have needs and expectations, implicit or explicit, that they require to be fulfilled by the service operation. In order to satisfy the needs and expectations of the group or segment of customers that are attracted to the organisation, its market image must be compatible with its ability to satisfy the needs and expectations of that market segment.

Service operation

The operation is the service providing part of the service system and attempts to match the customers' expectations of service with their perceptions of the provision of that service (Johnston, 1987).

The need for change

A strategy is a set of plans to bring about change and its development is driven by the need for change. The need for change may be as a result of the changing demands of the shareholders of the company for a greater return on assets or for expansion, for example. It could be in response to,

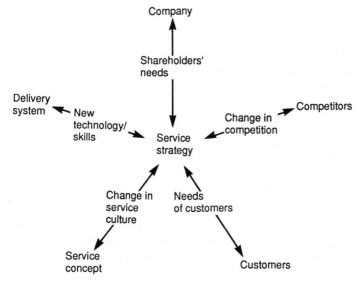

Figure 7.2   Sources and types of needs for change

or in anticipation of, changes in its external environment. This could include new competitors entering the marketplace, or the strategic developments of competitors through different positioning or service developments, or the changing needs of customers as a result of the activities of the competition, or the loss of customers because their needs are not being met. Opportunities for change may come from developments within the company, such as an ability to change the operation as a result of the availability of new technology or new skills, or the development of new service concepts as a result of developments in the service culture leading to new service requirements. Figure 7.2 summarises the sources and types of the needs for change.

Integrative elements

As a result of the needs for change, or the opportunities for change, a company must harness all the five key elements of the operation into a clear strategic plan that ensures that all the elements are supporting each other and are consistent with the need for change.

There are five stages that integrate the key elements. These stages involve the development of: revised corporate objectives, a clear market orientation, differentiation criteria, the service concept and the operation.

Corporate objectives

The development of clear corporate objectives is based on the new needs for change or the opportunities that are facing the company, such as, the needs of the shareholders, the activities of the competition, changing customer tastes or expectations, or the ability to provide new concepts using new delivery systems. These objectives need to be clearly stated and will provide the means of measuring the success or otherwise of the service strategy.

Market orientation

In order to ensure that those objectives will or can be achieved, there is a need to develop a clearer market orientation requiring increased awareness of the size and nature of the competition and of the market segmentation to assess the likely reaction of the competition and to focus the strategy on a defined set of customer needs and expectations.

Differentiation criteria

From a greater understanding of the market, a service strategy needs to provide the means of differentiating that company from the competition. There are five main ways in which companies can do this (Heskett, 1986; Hill, 1985; Knee and Walters, 1985; Riddle, 1986; Voss et al 1985):

Range of the services: a company can provide a greater range of services than the competition.

Price: a company can charge lower prices than those charged for competing services.

Availability: a company can provide services that are more easily available to the customer than those of the competition.

Quality: a company can provide services that have a higher level of service quality than those of the competition.

Uniqueness: a company can provide a unique service that is not offered by any of its competitors.

Service concept

A service concept incorporating the requirements of the new service needs to be developed in order to create a service differential, based on increased understanding of the market and potential customer needs and expectations. There are three major dimensions on which a service concept is based (Chase, 1978; Heskett, 1986; Johnston and Morris, 1985; Maister, 1983):

Generalist v *specialist:* one strategic shift that can occur in the focus of the service concept is the move from a generalist service provision to a specialised service provision or vice versa.

Standardised v *customised:* a second strategic decision is the degree of customisation of the service. Whether the service is to be highly customer orientated and created for each individual customer or standardised using more impersonal routines and standardised products. The choice of these has significant implications for the customer–service relationship.

Product v *process:* a significant element of the service concept is the degree of product or process focus. On one hand is a product orientation, the provision of goods with less emphasis on how they are served, to a process orientation with more emphasis on the way the service is provided and less on the products themselves.

Service operation

The final stage is the development of a service operation to support the new service concept. This is the identification of the way in which the operation is to create the new service concept to provide service differentiation in order to meet corporate objectives. The operation is the part of the system that interacts with the customer or his/her order and provides the services and products. This detailed plan has then to be checked against the corporate objectives to ensure that the total strategy is consistent and will achieve the objectives that have been set.

The traditional mechanisms for implementing changes in delivery systems (Chase, 1978; Knee and Walters, 1985; Voss et al, 1985; Wild, 1977) are:

Capacity planning – chase demand *v* level capacity
Manpower management – high contact *v* low contact
Location – single site *v* multi site
Operations control – centralised *v* decentralised
Technology – high technology *v* low technology

Service strategy development

It is the function of the integrating elements; the development of corporate objectives, the development of a clearer market orientation, the identification of differentiation criteria, concept development and operation development, driven by the needs for change, to bring together the five key elements; the company, the competition, the customers, the concept and the operation, to form a complete and consistent plan for implementation. This process is summarised by the framework in Figure 7.3.

The process of developing and implementing a service strategy is now examined with reference to the integrating stages of service strategy development using three case studies of companies that successfully developed and implemented change strategies. The three brief case examples outlined below will be analysed in terms of the service strategy framework.

Case studies

Company A

In the UK most breweries either own public houses, and employ managers to run them, and/or have trade agreements with independently owned and

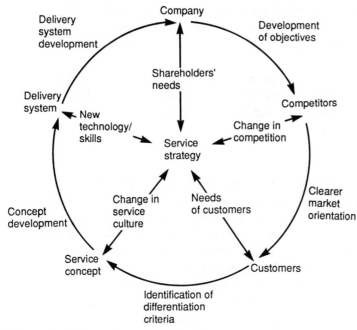

Figure 7.3 The service strategy development framework

run pubs limiting them to the sale of the brewery's own products. Company A is a large UK brewery which owns over 1000 public houses. This company was having to come to terms with the fact that the public are spending less and less in public houses. It was finding it difficult just to maintain its market share. The company decided that it needed to differentiate itself from the competition if it was to survive. Some breweries had tried to compete on product range, though in the long term this had afforded little success as all products are relatively reproducible at similar prices. Others had made attempts to change their market offering and had turned pubs into restaurants or developed theme pubs, neither of these, in the opinion of Company A, had been particularly successful and did not seem to be worth pursuing.

This company decided that a competitive edge could be sought through development of the quality of service in its outlets. A number of surveys were commissioned which reported that 'good service', including the friendliness of the manager and the bar staff, was a significant factor in the customer's choice of pub. A project team was set up to try to define what was meant by 'good service' and to decide how it could be improved using its current resources. The project team made many recommendations including the provision of better and different staff training, an improvement in some of the pub's facilities, in particular the decor and the rest rooms, the development of an appropriate reward and motivation system for the staff, and a change in company control systems and company culture.

The Company set up a pilot scheme involving a small number of pubs and tried to implement some of the recommendations. Within six months the revenues of those pubs had increased by a small but significant amount.

Company B

A well known high street travel agency, which had been in business since the 1950s, had slowly grown through acquisition, and had acquired a strong team of directors and senior management. It devised a strategy whose objective was to be the number one seller of inclusive package tour holidays within four years. The Company felt that it could not differentiate itself in terms of quality as most products were available to all of its competitors. The Company believed that the market was price-sensitive so it devised a strategy to differentiate itself from the competition in terms of price. This strategy could only be successful provided that the Company rapidly increased its volume of sales to a level that would gain higher than normal commissions from the tour operators, by selling its own insurance on every holiday and by ensuring that overheads were as low as possible and that the whole Company was focussed totally on this objective.

To this end the Company sold off its business travel department. This created capital with which it financed an increase in the number of its retail outlets. This sale also created spare capacity at head office to cope with the expected increase in volume of sales and at the same time improved the return on commissions, as commissions on business travel were poor. The Company also mounted a large scale and aggressive marketing campaign. But by far the most significant step in its strategy was the total re-orientation of its travel agencies into holiday shops that would only sell and support the sale of inclusive tour packages. This created spare capacity at the retail outlets to cope with the expected increase in volume of trade, reduced the need for specialised training and improved return on commissions at a stroke.

The company became the largest seller of the top brands of inclusive tour packages one year ahead of schedule and has witnessed few attempts at retaliation by its competitors.

Company C

A firm of solicitors in the south of England with a determination to expand found that it was difficult to do so on the returns from 'normal' practice work as there were plenty of alternative firms available who were offering the same services in the same way at similar prices. The partners agreed that it was time that they tried to influence the type of work they did rather than wait for a customer to come through their door. Their strategy was to concentrate on the commercial sector, where the returns were significantly higher than for personal work, and to differentiate themselves in terms of availability. It was soon apparent that this was going to require them to operate quite differently than they had done before, indeed quite differently from most other firms of solicitors.

Because they were based in a small market town where there were not enough industries to provide sufficient work for them, the firm had now to think in terms of a larger geographical market. They decided to consider all major conurbations within a hundred-mile radius, including London some 150 miles away, as being in their market. Their main advantage over city firms was that their overheads were low. However, their skills and abilities were little different. The key to success was to appear to be easily available and be able to provide a fast response to clients, this would create a significant service differential.

To do this they set up associations with other companies in the key locations to provide local bases for their activities. They then backed this up with telex and facsimile links, and bought in a radiopaging service to allow them to instantly respond to client enquiries wherever they happened to be. Now the task was to attend the client, speedily, on request. As a result, the 'home' office became largely redundant and was sold, further reducing overheads. The partners worked from their homes and the secretarial staff were replaced by a nearby business support service, which also supplied the communications equipment and manned the telephone.

By identifying a major criterion that could give it a significant competitive edge and restructuring the organisation to focus on it, the company has now not only more work than ever before, but work that promises higher returns that is enabling the company to look for expansion in the near future.

Illustrating strategy development in the three cases

All of these companies developed strategic plans which integrated the five key elements of a service strategy with the needs for change; the company and the needs of the shareholders, the competition over which it was trying to gain an advantage, the customers whom they were trying to satisfy, and the service concept that underpinned the operation. This was achieved by undertaking the five distinct integrating stages. These will now be used to illustrate the development of the change strategies in the three case examples.

Corporate objectives

Each company set itself new and clear corporate objectives as a result of threats and opportunities which presented themselves, and measured against these objectives each firm can be seen to have been successful. Company A wanted to improve its market share in a declining market. Company B set itself the objective of becoming the number one retailer of package holidays in Britain. Company C wanted to provide substantially greater returns for the partners that would improve their own financial position and also facilitate growth.

Each of the three companies was also facing a threat. They felt threatened by stagnant or declining markets. This forced the companies to search for new opportunities in the marketplace. The realisation of these needs was only as a result of developing a clearer market orientation which helped them to define the market segments and consider the risk associated with them. The type of risk that would be acceptable was also implicitly defined as the corporate goals pushed organisations either towards entre-preneurialism; using the drive of the entrepreneur to change systems and develop new service opportunities as in Companies B and C, or towards intrapreneurialism; a more conservative approach to developing new opportunities from established products and management structures (Riddle, 1986) as used by Company A.

By stating clear corporate goals and making their intentions known in the companies, the three companies not only provided their employees with clear signals that change was about to occur but that the companies were going to take positive action to develop their activities and implicitly secure their jobs.

Market orientation

The need for change and resultant corporate objectives had to be matched to a market and a particular market segment. All the companies constrained their strategies by restricting themselves to operating in the same markets, though in more carefully defined segments. Clearer market understanding came from a positive attempt to look at what the competition were doing, which ranged from nothing in the case of Company C's competitors to diversification in the case of Company A. The emergent market segments that were to be supported became clear, and in the case of Company C, involved focussing on a particular and more specialised market segment. Having identified opportunities in the market by which they could achieve the objectives they had set, the companies had to decide the means by which they could qualify to compete in those markets and, more importantly, how they could win customers (Hill, 1985).

Differentiation criteria

Each company had to achieve a certain level in each of the first four of the differentiating criteria; range, price, quality and availability; just to qualify to be in the marketplace. All the companies selected one of the five criteria to differentiate themselves from the competition. The three cases provide examples of differentiation in terms of quality, price and availability.

Company A decided to differentiate itself in terms of its quality of service. This the Company saw as something that would be difficult for the competition to reproduce. In the beer, wine and spirits trade, products were relatively easy to reproduce at similar prices. However, quality of service was seen to be more difficult to reproduce, thus creating a barrier to entry into that particular segment for the competition, not only because of the provision of a highly differentiated product but also because of the high cost requirements of its implementation. The Company recognised that in order to be able to provide a higher level of service it would have to considerably increase, improve and re-orientate its training programmes. Also it would have to change its control systems which were particularly oppressive and totally financially based and provided little or no scope for individual initiative and flair in the provision of its products. It would involve a lengthy process of culture change at the pub level to change the vision of the role of staff from beer providers and money takers to service givers, and at headquarters level from financial controllers to limit the seepage from the trade to hand-holders who could help the licensed house manager develop and improve the business using his/her skills and understanding of consumer needs and expectations.

Company B chose to compete on price believing that the market was price-sensitive. This was only going to be successful as long as the competition did not enter the price war before the company had secured its larger share of the market and established an enlarged retail network to maintain that share of the market. The sale of its business travel division gave Company B the cash to expand its distribution channels and the limited product focus provided it with the means to gain economies of scale in a traditionally diverse product-orientated market. Having firmly established itself in the market, Company B then moved away from its price differentiation strategy to one that tried to differentiate it in terms of quality of service.

Company C re-orientated its product focus to provide higher returns by investing in a new technological infrastructure, expanding its distribution channels and predominantly by providing a more available service than that of the competition. Using the technology and the distribution channels, and by moving away from traditional methods of operation, the partners were able to appear to be more accessible to a different and much larger market segment than they had been operating in before.

Service concept

Having developed a clearer market orientation and determined how they could differentiate themselves from the competition, each company was now able to devise its new service concept. This stage involved the focussing of the service package on the identified market segment by identifying the major elements of service to be provided and how the company would like it to be perceived by its customers.

Generalist v specialist

Company B chose a concept that would focus its operations on a specialist service provision in complete contrast to that of the competition, who were providing all the normal trappings of travel agencies; British Rail timetable information, foreign currency, coach tickets and round-the-world tours. The Company limited its offerings to the sale of inclusive tour packages. It recommended other specialists to its customers to deal with any other requirements. Company C also made a move towards specialisation as it reduced the amount of personal work it undertook and started to move into the more lucrative commercial market. The Company took the risk of reducing its service for personal customers despite the fact that some of the commercial work was generated as a result of undertaking personal work.

Standardised v customised

Company A based its strategy on the improvement of the customer–service relationship, realising that the customer would like an improved and more personal service, it could only be achieved by providing improved staffing, control systems and company culture to provide the level of customer recognition and diagnosis that would now be required to provide the enhanced service.

Product *v* process

Company A traditionally operated in a product-orientated way and was now attempting to provide a greater process orientation, concentrating on the way it dealt with its customers rather than acting as a beer provider and money taker. This too was going to have a significant effect upon its customer–service relationship which would have to be carefully designed and controlled in ways that were largely unfamiliar to the organisation.

Service operation

From a clear understanding of the service concept the companies were able to plan in detail how their operations were going to support those concepts and provide the distinctive competence through service differentiation to meet corporate objectives.

For all the companies their change strategies involved a restructuring of the organisation or a part of it, in order to provide the new service concept. In all cases, the new service concepts required far reaching changes to their delivery systems.

Capacity planning

Company A operated a chase demand strategy. This was not to change, however, the intention was to try to increase overall demand for the products. This could easily be managed as few operations ever operated at peak and flexible part-time labour was easily available. Company B created spare capacity in its retail outlets by reducing the services that it provided. This also reduced the need for support activities at head office so more capacity was available to support the growth that was planned.

Manpower management

The change strategies employed by all the companies had significant effects on the manpower. The improved quality of service that was sought by Company A could only be achieved through the activities of the front-of-house staff, the bar staff. The problem was that most bar staff did not see their work in the pub as a 'real' job. It was an opportunity in most cases, to either supplement the family income or save up for a summer holiday. The situation was made even more difficult as the bar staff stayed on average six months in a job. This meant that the bar staff changed more often than the customers. The issue was to be dealt with through the pub managers, whose job it was to select and train their own bar staff. The first activity was to get the managers to recognise that there was a problem and a product called 'customer service', then develop a feeling of ownership of that problem by the managers. The second step was to provide support for the managers to help them deal with the problem by improved and more focussed training, and head office support through changes in culture and control systems.

In Company B, the need for training reduced as the company specialised on a smaller and more limited range of products. This made it easier to recruit and train staff and also provided the Company with more time to train in 'selling' as less time was needed to train in product knowledge.

In Company C, the partners no longer operated from their desks, but were much more mobile. It took them some time to settle to this new way of working. It also had far reaching consequences for the secretarial staff who were replaced by a sub-contract business service.

Location

Companies A and B are multi-site operations. The number and location of their outlets were important to them. In all cases, as a result of the change strategies, they were able to expand the number of sites. Company C, however, changed from a single-site operation towards a multi-site operation as the partners developed access to other markets through associate offices. It is likely that future growth may lead to the takeover of the other firms involved.

Operations control

Company A recognised that its formal financial control systems had to be made less oppressive and had to be operated in parallel with a system that would reward the managers not only for meeting financial targets but also for providing good service. The company defined what was meant by good service and started to audit the pubs on that basis. They have not, as yet, found any adequate means of directly rewarding financially the provision of good service, but because of the increase in trade, which was assumed to be as a result of more attention given to service, higher rewards followed through the normal bonus scheme.

Technology

The use of technology seems to underpin many change strategies in service organisations (Quinn and Gagnon, 1986). In the case of Company C, they could not have adopted their new service strategy without it. The use of communications technology, facsimile and radiopaging equipment, provided them with the means to provide a fast response to their clients.

Conclusion

These cases have illustrated how the three companies integrated the five key elements of a service operation with the needs for change by using the integrating stages of strategy development.

Each company recognised the need to change and as a result identified the reasons for change and through that set itself clear objectives against which it could measure its success. In order to meet these objectives the companies had to achieve an advantage over their competitors. To do this they developed clear market orientations that helped them understand their position and the segmentation of the markets. Having identified a new or enhanced market segment, the companies considered how they not only could provide a service to customers in that segment but also how they could differentiate themselves from the competition and so identified their own order winning criteria. From this they were able to develop new service concepts which defined how the services were to be provided in order to provide their distinction and thus support the market and, hopefully, achieve their objectives. From a clear service concept all the companies developed and changed their delivery systems to support the new service concept. The final stage was the checking of their results of changes against the objectives that had been set.

The development of service strategies was broadly in the order as indicated by the arrows in Figure 7.3, though at each stage there was a checking-out through the strategic plans that each stage was possible and supported all the other stages. As such, it was an iterative process. For all the three companies, the development of strategy started with the company recognising the need for change. It is possible that the impetus for change may come from another part of the system, for example, the availability of new technology that presents an opportunity in the operation, or a significant market change that forces a review of the services provided. Wherever the impetus may come from, the same elements have to be dealt with and combined to provide a consistent and coherent service strategy.

References

Central Statistical Office (1986) *Annual Abstract of Statistics*, HMSO, London.
Chase, R. B. (1978) 'Where does the customer fit in a service operation', *Harvard Business Review*, Vol. 56, No. 6, November–December, pp. 137–142.

Fitzsimmons, J. A. and Sullivan, R. S. (1982) *Service Operations Management*, McGraw-Hill, New York.

Heskett, J. L. (1986) *Managing in the Service Economy*, Harvard Business School Press, Boston.

Hill, T. (1985) *Manufacturing Strategy*, Macmillan, London.

Johnston, R. (1987) 'A framework for developing a quality strategy in a customer processing operation', *International Journal of Quality and Reliability Management*, Vol. 4, No. 4, pp. 3–46.

Johnston, R. and Morris, B. (1985) 'Monitoring and control in service operations', *International Journal of Operations and Production Management*, Vol. 5, No. 1, pp. 32–38.

Knee, D. and Walters, D. (1985) *Strategy in Retailing*, Philip Allan, Oxford.

Maister, D. (1983) 'Some implications of factory *v* professional service', *Current Research in Production/Operations Management*, C. A. Voss (ed), London Business School, January.

Mills, P. (1986) *Managing Service Industries*, Ballinger, Massachusetts.

Porter, M. E. (1980) *Competitive Strategy*, Free Press, New York.

Quinn, J. B. and Gagnon, C. E. (1986) 'Will services follow manufacturing into decline?' *Harvard Business Review*, Vol. 64, No. 6, November-December, pp. 95–103.

Riddle, D. I. (1986) *Service-Led Growth*, Praeger, New York.

Voss, C., Armistead, C., Johnston, R. and Morris, B. (1985) *Operations Management in Service Industries and the Public Sector*, Wiley, Chichester.

Wild, R. (1977) *Concepts for Operations Management*, Wiley, Chichester.

8 The globalisation of service firms

SUSAN SEGAL-HORN

Introduction

Global industries are those which are obliged to compete on a worldwide co-ordinated basis or face competitive disadvantage. It is not a definition commonly thought appropriate to service industries, which are most often conceived as 'fragmented' industries, lacking powerful market leaders (Porter, 1980). This is because service industries were conceived as characterised by low entry barriers, diseconomies of scale, close local control, high personal service and 'image' content, where service delivery is at the point of sale to the customer (Normann, 1984; Daniels, 1985; Heskett, 1986). This chapter addresses the changing nature of international competition in the service industries. It is argued that maturity of markets, developments in communications and information technology, changing notions of service, economic and cultural homogenisation of markets, have combined to change the competitive environment for service industries. It is now possible for world market leaders to emerge and reshape the sources of competitive advantage in their sector.

Many of the central themes commonly discussed in relation to globalisation and global strategic management (e.g. relations between global companies and host governments, operational economies of scale, supply chain issues) are absent from this analysis. The aim, however, has been to distinguish issues of particular relevance in globalisation of the service industries, rather than to discuss the strategic management of globalisation in general.

Why globalisation?

The factors underlying the changing pattern of international competition in the service industries are familiar and well documented (Levitt, 1983; Porter, 1985; Ohmae, 1985). The process is predicated on the convergence of markets. There are economic and cultural interdependencies between a growing number of economically strong countries. Whether we call it 'a global economic village' (Naisbitt, 1982) or what Levitt (1986) speaks of as 'this growing flattening of the competitive terrain', recurrent efforts to erect artificial trade barriers (tariffs, voluntary restraints, quotas) are not 'barriers to the intensification of global competition – rather they are symptoms of it'.

There is no single force pushing for globalisation. Instead, a combination of technological/microelectronic development, cultural homogenisation and the removal of industry barriers via deregulation, have permanently changed the international business environment. The speed and scope of technological innovation has affected service industries at least as much as manufacturing. It now makes more sense to minimise the gap between the launch of new products and services in international markets, since lead times for securing markets become shorter and shorter. For example, the recent USA launch by American Express of its 'Optima' credit card, followed shortly on its testing of credit facilities in the UK in the form of personal reserves at the Amex Bank. 'As global competition grows, so does the need for rapid worldwide rollouts of new products' (Quelch and Hoff, 1986).

Global oligopolies are developing in which successful firms are able to achieve economies of scope in international information systems and product policy. Sheth (1987) recently discussed such oligopolistic growth in terms of three major players for any industry. 'If you are not number one, number two or number three, chances are that you will have to merge or consolidate with someone else.' At least one each of the top three in each industry is likely to be a Japanese company and an American company. The third may sometimes be a European company. Such views echo those of Ohmae's (1985) 'triad'. The principal participants (Japan, USA, Western Europe) are also the principal markets and the principal companies compete everywhere. Managing multidomestic markets independently becomes more difficult as more firms find ways of gaining advantage from working globally and forcing others to do the same, or risk being relegated to small niches which may themselves become indefensible.

Environmental trends relevant to globalisation

The forces behind the growing globalisation in the service industries may be summarised under four main headings:

1 the inexorable shift from labour to capital-intensive industries;
2 the accelerated technology life-cycle;

3 the emergence of global markets and the 'global consumer';
4 deregulation and protectionism: political and economic pressures.

The inexorable shift from labour to capital-intensive industries

Labour has become a much less significant element of cost because of what Ohmae (1983) calls 'the mirage of low-cost labour'. Based on Organisation for Economic Cooperation and Development (OECD) figures Ohmae has calculated that total labour costs in OECD nations amount to at least 14–15 per cent of total costs. Although labour costs in the non-developed countries (NDCs) are only half that, the gap of 7–8 per cent is not even large enough to cover insurance and transportation, which normally account for 10–15 per cent of costs. Companies are therefore locating nearer their markets and investing in flexible computer-aided design (CAD) and manufacturing systems (FMS) that give cheap, short, variable production runs, so that economies of scale and scope become even larger than before.

For the service industries the labour/capital issues are rather different and more finely balanced. As Porter and Millar (1985) show, the information intensity of the value chain in service industries is always high and the information content of the product frequently so. Service industries are highly technology-dependent for the creation and delivery of its offerings. However, they are equally people-dependent. Although the service industries are busy shedding low-level labour like everybody else, they are acquiring an ever higher proportion of technical and professional staff to develop and manage their sophisticated operations. Financial, 'creative', retail and professional service organisations, e.g. consultancies, are heavily dependent on their technical and professional staff, whilst often lacking effective skills and procedures either for managing them or for developing their managerial, as opposed to their technical, skills in order to make them effective as managers (Segal-Horn, 1987a). The labour/capital relationship is a particularly delicate one in the service industries. Capital-intensive industries require capital-intensive people to develop and run them. The management issue for the service industries is greater still because direct contact is usually required with the consumer and the staff themselves control the quality of that experience.

The accelerated technology life-cycle

- The cost of R&D is soaring.
- Monopoly of any technology for any period of time is very hard to sustain.
- Diffusion rates for new technologies are extremely rapid.

For these three reasons technological advantage is increasingly hard to gain or sustain. FMS and CAD have increased the threat of substitution by making substitutes quicker, easier and cheaper to design and develop. As a result of the combined effect of these factors, companies are having to launch new products or services simultaneously into all the main world markets (Ohmae, 1985). This means that global companies are designing products to be global from the start, thereby significantly cutting development time (Lorenz, 1986). These are also the main reasons behind the large number of joint ventures (Harrigan, 1984; Perlmutter and Heenan, 1986; Hout, Porter and Rudden, 1982; Lorange, 1985). Joint ventures are not just about sharing the huge development costs involved, but also to avoid leaving markets unguarded during periods of new product development. The inability to hold on to proprietary technology makes immediate global launch the more compelling strategy.

The emergence of global markets and the 'global consumer'

There has been a lengthy and vigorous debate surrounding the validity of global markets, triggered by Levitt (1983). He argued that the new communications technologies are a key influence in the growing 'homogenisation' of markets, reducing social, economic and cultural differences, including old-established differences in national tastes or preferences. This process has meant that companies need to examine the growing similarities between consumer preferences. Market segmentation based on lifestyle has been around for a long time (Sheth, 1983). However, the argument for global markets 'does not mean the end of choice or market segments. It means the beginning of price competition for quality products aimed at fewer but larger global market segments' (Levitt, 1983) which are themselves discrete and heterogeneous. This view receives strong support from Hamel and Prahalad (1984) who argue that future competitive advantage will be variety at low cost: 'we must disabuse ourselves of the notion that product variety always comes at the expense of a cost penalty'. The price/quality/variety trade-off, implicit in Porter's (1980) generic strategies of cost leadership or differentiation, is increasingly based on outmoded assumptions, particularly with regard to the effect of CAD/CAM and FMS.

Thus, 'globalisation does not mean the end of market segments, it means that they expand to worldwide proportions' (Levitt, 1986). Ohmae (1985) speaks of the 'Californianisation' of the young within the Triad, forming a massive lifestyle-related segment. Global marketing also does not necessarily mean providing the same product in all countries, but offering local adaptations around a standardised core. 'The big issue today is not whether to go global but how to tailor the global marketing concept to fit each business' (Quelch and Hoff, 1986). As Stopford and Turner (1985) conclude: 'even if the case for global brands is somewhat oversold, there is an obvious case that consumer-oriented companies can internationalise general marketing strategies'.

Even though service industries are mainly growth industries, many are competing in mature markets where competition is fierce and demand is at replacement level only, or rising only in a few segments (e.g. retailing and especially food retailing; airlines in general compared to the business travel segment; even financial services as a growth industry is heavily oversupplied). Redefining your target markets as global markets provides a way out of mature markets once industry restructuring, via mergers and acquisitions, has been taken as far as it can.

Global marketing is a strategy that is consumer-oriented and as such reflects the close-to-the-consumer bias of the service industries. In contrast to manufacturing industry, in service industries globalisation is not about yielding high production economies, but about high efficiency in using scarce new ideas. It also provides a route out of mature markets.

Deregulation and protectionism: political and economic pressures

Despite the social, cultural and technological changes behind the development of global market segments, there are additional economic and political pressures on governments to create barriers to this increasing transnational flow of goods. Deregulation promotes international investment and global competition (Citicorp/Citibank, 1986). Protectionist policies, such as quotas or tariff barriers, create constraints on global competition. Such government protection is most likely to occur in industries that are 'salient', i.e. that affect government policies or objectives, e.g. defence, regional development, employment. However, they may also occur as a response to severe imbalance in volume of international trade between nations (as between Japan and the USA in the 1980s). As mentioned above, the very need for artificial trade barriers is evidence of the strength of international demand by consumers for international goods and services.

Deregulation is a deliberate attempt to improve the efficiency of markets by opening them up to increased competition. It has been most visible in the world financial markets, where the removal by governments of fixed commissions has shifted competition from service to price and triggered mass exits from the industry either through mergers or even business failure. The same process occurred earlier in the 1970s in the USA when

President Carter deregulated the airlines in order to encourage competition. The short-term effect was to encourage many new entrants. The longer-term effect was a massive shakeout in the industry; leaving a few internationally competitive 'supercarriers' and higher entry barriers.

The two policies exist in relation to each other. Fierce international competition and the changed economic structures of many industries, lead to the devastation of many firms or indeed entire sectors in their home markets (Hamel and Prahalad, 1985), leading to political pressure for protection. Under this continuing cycle of events, global companies have to operate as what Ohmae (1985) calls 'true insiders', honorary citizens perceived as direct investors in the home market.

The service industries are relatively new to the influences of deregulation and protection (the unique regulatory structure of the international airline industry being the exception). They have been less generally visible and their effect on jobs and the balance of trade less well publicly understood. By and large they have also constituted growth industries, where jobs were being created rather than lost and where no dependent, historically long-established constituency of communities existed. In addition, jobs that have been lost in the services in any great numbers (e.g. in banking, retailing, medical support services) have been largely (though not always, e.g. bank middle management) low-level, female and often part-time (Rajan, 1987).
To summarise:

- the service industries are information-intensive and therefore well-positioned for operating in all major markets;
- rapid IT substitutability and imitability lend great pressure for global offerings;
- global market segments populated by global consumers are highly receptive to global products;
- political and economic policies (such as deregulation) intensify international competition, for both aggressive and defensive reasons.

The importance of the service sector

This section considers the growing importance of the service sector in advanced economies, together with some of the reasons for its continued rise. Although the UK is taken as the example, the trends discussed and the reasons behind them are mirrored throughout the developed economies (Riddle, 1986). The point of making such an assessment is simple. The service industries are significant to the developed economies in terms of output and, with continued growth expected, they represent the new strengths of the developed (and particularly of the Western) economies. Opportunities for globalisation of the service industries must be clearly understood and grasped by Western companies, before yet another position of competitive strength is eroded. 'Many US markets for services are no safer from foreign competition than were domestic markets for manufactured goods. Indeed, foreign direct investment in the US service sector has exploded since the mid-1970s.' (Quinn and Gagnon, 1986).

Service output has begun to overtake non-service output in recent years (see Fig. 8.1). This performance has been viewed as the almost inevitable outcome of the 'second industrial revolution' mirroring in investment and 'takeoff' the first industrial revolution in production. This growth in services has been influenced by three factors (Rajan, 1987):

1   demand for new services;
2   legislative changes;
3   'externalisation'.

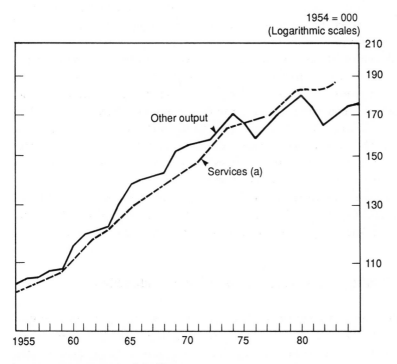

(a) Excluding ownership of dwellings

Figure 8.1   UK growth in output, 1955–85
(*Source: Economic Trends*, 1986. Reproduced with the permission of the Controller of Her Majesty's Stationery Office.)

Emergent social groups such as the affluent middle classes, dual-income families, financially sophisticated consumers, single-person households, etc. have created a demand for new types and configurations of services. (See Segal-Horn, 1987b, for a detailed breakdown of the demographic, social and economic trends behind these changes in consumer markets.) The kinds of 'new services' referred to can be illustrated by the number of credit card holders in the UK having tripled since 1975; as also has expenditure on insurance services. Demand for services has secondly been stimulated by change in the prevailing legislative framework. Mortgage interest relief, government policies for competition, privatisation of nationalised industries and deregulation of financial markets, have led directly to an increase in all kinds of advertising and consultancy services. 'Externalisation' is defined as the contracting-out of services previously carried out in-house. There have been some extremely well-publicised examples of this trend, such as Rank-Xerox's 'homeworkers'. Less well known would include firms of architects involved not just in design but in day-to-day management of construction projects, work previously performed in the construction industry. This forms part of the progressive industry restructuring already mentioned as arising from the increased capital-intensiveness of both manufacturing and service industry. Much of the shakeout of labour from the manufacturing industries as a result of this process thus becomes part of the build-up of the service sector.

Demand growth will begin to flatten out as market penetration increases and industry concentration and rationalisation take their course. This process is already well-advanced in retailing and all sectors of financial services. The next stage following domestic industry restructuring must then be expansion into world markets. At present, the services constitute only 18 per cent of world trade. But worldwide service trade is growing at 19 per cent per year, as opposed to 14 per cent for world production (Quinn and Gagnon, 1986). It is notable that the UK's share of this has already declined from 12 per cent in 1968 to 7 per cent in 1983.

Globalisation as a strategy for service industries

Globalisation as a concept has been developed with a focus on manufacturing. Most of the current literature of global strategies is based on evidence from the manufacturing sector, favourites being automobiles, motorcycles, construction and farm machinery, watches, textiles and consumer electronics (Altshuler, 1984; Doz, 1986; Hamel and Prahalad, 1984; Kotler, Fahey and Jatusripitak, 1985). The best documented global market development for a service industry is that of the financial services sector. Attention has been given to deregulation and the effect of the 24-hour financial marketplace on international banking and financial services (Arthur Andersen, 1985; Pecchioli, 1983; Stelzer, 1986; Channon, 1986; McGee, 1986; Hamilton, 1986). Yet little real analysis has yet occurred of the routes to creating global strategic capability or the common denominators in such capability which are emerging more generally for service industries.

Distinctiveness of service industries

1 Bringing the customer to the service.
2 Reproducing the service concept.
3 Controlling the quality of the offering.
4 New usage patterns.

Service industries are those whose output is not a physical good or product and where added-value is derived from such factors as concept, image, quality of service delivery, security, convenience, flexibility. This underpins an essential difference in the significance of globalisation in services as opposed to manufacturing. For manufacturing industries the sources of global advantage come mainly from: comparative advantage, e.g. in factor costs; economies of scale in production, marketing, distribution, logistics and purchasing; mobility of production; or any combination thereof (Porter, 1980). This means that manufacturing is concerned with the most effective ways of moving the product to the market.

In service industries, globalisation means that a mobile customer base (often literally mobile, e.g. the tourist, the business traveller) experiences an identical product wherever they go, at each access point or transaction. Service delivery is about controlling the quality of the offering at the point of sale to the customer. In service industries the customer can move to the product. It is for this reason that American Express labels its core charge card (and travellers' cheque and travel shop) business: 'Travel Related Services' (TRS). The TRS market is the international traveller for whom the TRS core concept – the 'global servicing concept' – has been developed. The aim is to provide a standard quality service to the customer, wherever that service is taken up (American Express, 1983, 1985, 1986). This approach is a common one in the service industries. It is highly visible in the airline industry whose travel offices and staff uniforms are identical worldwide and with the international hotel chains (Hilton, Sheraton, Intercontinental) which undertake to make the traveller's experience of Hong Kong, London, Rome and Bali, similar in all respects.

In some very real ways, services travel and can be recreated globally much more easily than products, since what is being recreated is the concept and the quality of its delivery. One aspect from which service industries benefit is what van Mesdag (1987) calls 'the age symptom', of acculturation and usage. Some products are associated with long-established national usage patterns, which makes them less amenable to international adaptation. However, fewer predetermined assumptions exist for newer service offerings (e.g. credit cards, ATMs). Usage patterns are less firmly established. It can be argued that for this reason services generally need fewer adaptations for global markets than do manufactured products.

The 'fragmented' service industries?

Service industries are usually defined as 'fragmented' industries (Porter, 1980). By this is meant an environment in which many firms compete, but in which there are no clear market leaders with significant market share. It is this absence of market leaders with power to shape the industry which Porter stresses as being the most important feature of the competitive environment for fragmented industries. Services, retailing, distribution and 'creative' businesses are commonly considered to conform to the fragmentation stereotype. The reason for this is that these industries possess many of the characteristics by which fragmented industries are defined including:

- high personal service content (service must be experienced as individualised and responsive);
- high labour content;
- hard to routinise;
- high 'transportation' costs (defined as high for services because the product cannot be transported, but is either produced at the customer's premises or the customer must come to the service, i.e. service delivery at the point of sale to the customer);
- low entry barriers;
- diseconomies of scale (e.g. where rapid response is required to changes in demand);
- heavy creative content (difficult to maintain in a large operation);
- close local control;
- product differentiation based on image.

While most or all of these characteristics applied to service industries in the past, and some such as personal service or high 'image' content still do, to a very large extent consolidation has occurred as a result of fundamental changes in many of the key factors listed above. The following points should be considered in relation to the 'fragmented' stereotype of the service industries:

Industry restructuring and concentration

Although gaining momentum over the last 5–10 years, service industries have been undergoing a long process of concentration and rationalisation for the last 20–30 years, as witness the emergence of very large firms in insurance, the banks and building societies, as well as distribution, consultancy and business services, fast food, leisure companies, and retailing, where 80 per cent of food retailing is in the hands of multiples and 50 per cent in the hands of 5 large firms. Even very traditional professional services such as law and accountancy (e.g. Arthur Andersen) increasingly consist of international firms of great size, marketing a global brand of quality and service delivery (*The Economist* 9/1/88). Consultancy firms such as McKinsey have been doing so for some time. Merger and acquisition have been commonplace across all these groups but they have not noticeably experienced difficulty in recreating the image and the service delivery package. Service concepts can and do 'travel'.

Vertical integration

Also of relevance to the general trend towards increased scale, is the vertical integration occurring in the service industries. The takeover of brokerage firms by banks (Hamilton, 1986), and the acquisition of chains of estate agencies by building societies and insurance companies are among the more recent examples. The absolute size of the leading firms in the service industries is increasing. This has begun to change the structure of the service industries. PIMS (Profit Impact of Marketing Strategy) data suggests that concentration in the service sector is comparable to that in manufacturing.

The effect of new technology

The effect of deregulation and legislative change on industry restructuring in the service industries, has already been discussed. The other major driving force for restructuring has been new technology. Information technology (IT) increases a company's ability to co-ordinate its activities nationally and internationally. It can provide powerful opportunities to boost service performance and help develop switching and entry barriers that shut out foreign competitors (the airline reservation system provides a classic example of such system bias).

Quinn and Gagnon (1986) showed for every service industry 'important new economies of scale driven by the application of new technologies'. But IT also creates opportunities to take advantage of new competitive scope, since companies can deliver better and more varied services with no significant cost penalties. They can simultaneously achieve a high degree of segmentation in their activities and lower their costs. For example, bar code scanners in retailing or computerised reservation systems in airlines or travel agencies give instant feedback on sales and hence opportunities for greater control over margins, operating costs and patterns of demand. Costs can actually be lowered as hardware and software development are allocated over a broader base of applications, or as entirely new services utilise established networks for little additional cost. Large-scale network effects are very important in service industries, more so than in manufacturing, since additional links increase attractiveness to the consumer (e.g. in how many places can I use my credit card?).

IT has increased capital requirements, thus raising entry barriers. For example, without electronic support systems it is now impossible to compete effectively in many markets, the money markets being only the most obvious. IT has also affected competition in these service industries by breaking down many of the traditional boundaries. IT is at the core of the growing interrelationships in financial services, where the banking, insurance and brokerage industries are merging, and the boundary between financial services and retailing is becoming increasingly fuzzy.

Internationalisation of services

A final point to be made in refuting the 'fragmented' stereotype of the service industries concerns the view that services cannot be exported. It has already been argued that service concepts and service delivery systems do travel. Although obvious problems of quality control do exist (and will be returned to below), positive benefits can be derived by service companies operating internationally. The company may be able to serve its clients better; indeed it may be the customer who internationalises first, with the service company following to keep important clients (Normann, 1984). In tackling new markets quality in general may be improved, including the quality of people in the company. The image of the company may be enhanced, not only in the eyes of its customers but also in the eyes of its staff and potential staff it might wish to attract. This is an important element in the service industry's 'quality wheel' (Heskett, 1986), with high level employee motivation contributing to high level customer satisfaction.

For all the reasons discussed above, the current structure of the service industries no longer fits the pattern of 'fragmented' industries. They have become significantly concentrated and capital-intensive with increased barriers to entry.

The global decision

The preceding sections have been concerned to demonstrate changes in the structure and environment of the service industries, such as to create potential for globalisation strategies to be adopted more widely by service companies. However, creation of the potential climate is one thing and the decision to act quite another.

There appears to be widespread agreement that one of the most significant differences between Japanese and Western companies is the willingness and the ability of the former to make long-term commitments. Successful pursuit of a global strategy depends on such commitments. Trevor (1986) describes Mitsui's Global Industrial System Constellation (GISC). When company research predicted 80 per cent of free world production would be dominated by 200–300 global enterprises by the mid-1980s, Mitsui reorganised into four 'quadripolars' to promote its own global aims. By contrast, the management survey reported by Brooke and Remmers (1978) showed less than half the respondents regarding the development of global strategies for resources and markets, as a reason for international expansion. Defensive strategies scored much more highly than aggressive ones. As has been repeatedly emphasised (Doz, 1986; Hamel and Prahalad, 1985), globalisation is an aggressive strategy, where significant advantage may be obtained from pre-emptive strikes. The success of many Japanese firms in global industries can be largely attributed to their early adoption of a global perspective aimed at long-term competitive objectives. Doz (1986) argues that 'leading globalisation through early integration may have tremendous pay-offs in many industries . . . (may) enable the first firm to integrate to take a permanent market leadership'.

Gilbert and Strebel (1985) use the concept of 'outpacing strategies' to differentiate between highly successful companies and the rest. They argue that 'the message is clear: sustained success requires well timed and substantial shifts in strategic focus as the industry passes from one phase of its development to another'. Well-known worldwide service companies such as American Express, Benetton and Saatchi & Saatchi have made the global decision – large-scale commitments of resources to long-term strategic objectives. Each has thus understood the implications of the restructuring and concentration of the service sectors described above and demonstrated the main ingredients of an outpacing strategy:

- a thorough understanding of the industry, enabling anticipation of shifts in the pattern of its evolution;
- sharp focus in initial building of competitive advantage (either perceived product/service value or process cost and increasingly, both);
- reinvestment of cashflow in switching strategic emphasis to pre-empt the competition.

The 'new game': global brand dominance in the service industries

Sources of competitive advantage within service industries are changing. The service industries are going through a period of rapid evolution in which the ability to focus and switch is at a premium. In financial services, retailing, professional service firms, leisure, travel and 'creative' businesses (e.g. advertising) substantial developments may be observed in the strategies adopted to cope with the structural, environmental, technological and competitive shifts. Merger and acquisition activity has created rapid concentration. The redefined boundaries of the industry have provided scope for careful repositioning. Individual companies within each sector are demonstrating global strategic intent.

New game strategies are not about playing the same game better, but about changing the rules 'to challenge the conventional wisdom about product and market head-on' (Ohmae, 1983). The focus is on identifying the objective function of the offering for the customer, rather than on existing approaches to satisfying customer needs. With the core concept in place, it is possible to plan global expansion. Table 8.1 illustrates this change in approach made by some well-known service companies. Each of the companies illustrated has a clear, business concept on which their global strategy is based.

Table 8.1   The new games – changing the approach to the customer

Company	Objective function	Existing approach
American Express	Integrated travel related services	Individual product offerings
Benetton	One 'united' product	Fashion ranges
Saatchi & Saatchi	International business services	Media-based advertising

The American Express strategy is specific: world leader in integrated financial and travel-related services (American Express, 1985/86/87). American Express has particularly used the scope of its information technology network to differentiate its financial and travel services for corporate customers. For Benetton the global strategy puts fashion on an industrial level. 'When speaking of the "second generation" Benetton, I am speaking of a new business reality which is extra-European in scope' . . . 'we have kept the same strategy all along to put fashion on an industrial level' (Luciano Benetton, quoted in Labich, 1983). They have developed one product line of sufficient breadth to accommodate the needs of all their markets and stores, 'the united colours of Benetton' (Heskett, 1986). The Saatchi & Saatchi strategy to provide global business services for global client corporations was based on '. . . their intention to build a global business services conglomerate . . . and set about positioning the agency as a brand' (O'Reilly, 1986b). So far, the combination of size and creativity has been successful.

Appreciation of the possibilities inherent in global brand dominance for service companies goes beyond the advantages arising from detailed knowledge of the acceptability of a world-standardised offering within a worldwide market segment. Hamel and Prahalad (1984) have demonstrated how global companies can capitalise on their brand franchise by rapidly expanding across product categories. The American Express 'Blue Box' logo gives brand acceptability to financial planning programmes, travel agencies, travel management services, banking and credit facilities, all derived from the global brand dominance of its charge card and travel cheques. New products and service offerings use the existing distribution and marketing infrastructure either to fill existing segments or for horizontal expansion into adjoining ones.

Implementing a strategy to establish strong, quality, global brand names in any industry will require:

- a focus on customer needs;
- multiple distribution channels;
- ability to introduce product offerings quickly;
- careful selection of clear, profitable, target markets;
  ('only the most prestigious but also the most valuable' (AmEx, 1986));
- entry of market segments with market share leadership potential;
- sophisticated global marketing and global systems networks.

However, the distinctive character of service industries creates further special demands:

- global marketing must be backed up by global service delivery;
- uniform quality at outlets worldwide;
- uniform level of customer service at outlets.

The critical feature of the service industries rests on control of the offering at the transaction point with the customer or client. It is this quality of customer experience by which service quality is measured ('the moment of truth' (Normann, 1984; Carlzon, 1987). Successful globalisation for service companies rests on the management of service delivery on a global basis and across a diffuse corporate environment. For service companies operating globally, the ability to sustain a corporate culture across units thus has operational significance.

The 'new game' and corporate culture

Recent research (Heskett, 1986) suggests that the internal strategic service vision, quality control of service delivery and commercial success, are interconnected. Hence the importance of absorbing and integrating staff worldwide. The strongest mechanism for achieving such integration is corporate culture. All airlines make the strongest possible use of corporate identity flags, from the colour of the planes to the uniforms of the cabin crew and ground staff. This is not done simply for differentiation purposes, but as with all corporate identity programmes, to provide internal focus for the staff (Bernstein, 1985).

Integration for a global service company is critical, since its business depends on consistency of service delivery at the point of sale. The central importance of welding together a real company identity can be illustrated by the problems of Citicorp. Despite investing heavily in such activities as the Management Orientation Programme to orient staff to company strategy and practice: 'selling Citicorp around the world . . . as a beneficial presence . . . in the integrating global economy' (The Communications Unit, Citicorp, 1985), it has suffered some very public setbacks, e.g. in its European offices, resulting in loss of teams of senior staff. By contrast, American Express, Saatchi & Saatchi and Benetton have been successful in achieving consistency in corporate identity. In these examples are found both formal (Amex 'Blue Box' and 'Put People First' programmes) and informal mechanisms (the Saatchi & Saatchi and Benetton 'family' figureheads and the personal leadership characteristics commonly found in very young, rapid growth businesses). American Express has achieved a high degree of internal consistency with the soft but pervasive sell of its 'Blue Box' culture to its staff. Saatchi & Saatchi adopt a soft, hands-off approach to the creative (although not the financial) side of acquired companies, usually retaining company names and keeping creative staffs intact. As for Benetton, both the contracting system (in which the owners of the knitwear contracting companies are in most cases also Benetton managers) and the 'Benetton mentality' by which managers and shopowners 'had to have the right spirit to work in Benetton' (Labich, 1983), are combined with personal loyalty exhibited towards the Benetton family and to

Luciano Benetton (Chairman/padrone) in particular. Benetton's 'high-touch' merchandising concept is reflected in an equally high-touch, open-door senior management approach. Of course, rapid, large-scale expansion has brought with it the usual problems of moving from an entrepreneurial to a professional senior management, but the cohesiveness and centrality to all operations of the controlling family group, now itself enlarging to the second generation, has sustained the unique character and loyalties of the company.

The management of service delivery on a global basis is viewed as fundamental to successful implementation of a global servicing strategy (Segal-Horn, 1988). The issue is to secure, in the diffuse corporate environment of a global company, control of the service offering at the transaction point with the customer or client.

Conclusion: the service industries and global strategic intent

The sources of competitive advantage in service industries have shifted as a result of recent environmental, structural, market and technological changes. This has provided a major shift in the potential for globalisation as a competitive strategy available to service industries. There exists now some evidence that, as has already occurred in sizeable segments of manufacturing industry, those companies with clear strategic intent to leverage existing competitive advantages in support of long-term global brand dominance, can establish identifiable worldwide market presence.

The growth and performance of individual service companies is of wider competitive importance, for as Hamel and Prahalad (1985) argue: 'if no-one challenges a global competitor in its home market . . . its profitability rises and the day when it can attack the home markets of its rivals is hastened.' The strategic intent of companies like American Express, Benetton and Saatchi & Saatchi is significant, since their expansion of market share worldwide is the strongest protection of their core businesses.

Finally, it is appropriate to place these issues in context. The service industries are strong in the developed economies. They are significant in terms of output, wealth and jobs. Many of them still offer considerable growth potential. However, they could too easily find themselves following the path of many manufacturing industries (which were themselves also in equally strong positions) if their existing financial resources, brand strengths, distribution networks and skill base are not utilised as a platform for building world market share. The effect will be lost market opportunities abroad and a gradual erosion of the domestic base.

References

Altshuler, A et al (1984) *The Future of the Automobile*, Allen & Unwin, London.

American Express Annual Reports, 1983, 1985, 1986, 1987

Andersen, Arthur, & Co. (1985) *The Decade of Change: Banking in Europe – the next 10 years*, London.

Bartlett, C. A. and Ghoshal, S. (1986) 'Tap your subsidiaries for global reach', *Harvard Business Review*, November–December, pp. 87–94.

Bernstein, D. (1985) *Company Image and Reality*, Holt, Rinehart & Winston, Eastbourne.

Brooke, M. and Remmers, H. (1978) *The Strategy of Multinational Enterprise*, Pitman, London.

Carlzon, J. (1987) *Moments of Truth*, Ballinger Publishing Co., Cambridge, Mass.

Channon, D. F. (1986) *Bank Strategic Management and Marketing*, Wiley, Chichester.

Citicorp/Citibank (1986) *Sector Review*, March.

Daniels, P. (1985) *Service Industries – a Geographical Appraisal*, Methuen, London.

Doz, Y. (1986) *Strategic Management in Multinational Companies*, Pergamon Press, Oxford.

Gilbert, X. and Strebel, P. (1985) 'Outpacing strategies', *IMEDE Perspectives for Managers*, No. 2, September.

Hamel, G. and Prahalad, C. K. (1984) 'Creating global strategic capability', Discussion Paper, London Business School.

Hamel, G. and Prahalad, C. K. (1985) 'Do you really have a global strategy', *Harvard Business Review*, July–August, pp. 139–48.

Hamilton, A. (1986) *The Financial Revolution*, Viking/Penguin, Harmondsworth.

Harrigan, K. (1984) 'Joint ventures and global strategies', *Columbia Journal of World Business*, Summer, pp. 7–16.

Heskett, J. L. (1986) *Managing in the Service Economy*, Harvard Business School Press, Boston.

Hout, T., Porter, M. and Rudden, E. (1982) 'How global companies win out', *Harvard Business Review*, September–October, pp. 98–108.

Kotler, P., Fahey, L. and Jatusripitak, S. (1985) *The New Competition*, Prentice-Hall International, Englewood Cliffs.

Labich, K. (1983) 'Benetton takes on the world', *Fortune*, 13th June.

Levitt, T. (1983) 'The globalisation of markets', *Harvard Business Review*, May–June.

Levitt, T. (1986) *The Marketing Imagination*, The Free Press, New York.

Lorange, P. (1985) 'Comparative ventures in multinational settings: a framework', INSEAD Strategic Management Seminar, November.

Lorenz, C. (1986) *The Design Dimension*, Basil Blackwell, Oxford.

McGee, J. (1986) 'Do financial services need a management revolution?' Templeton College, Oxford: Mimeo.

Naisbitt, J. (1982) *Megatrends*, Warner Books, New York.

Normann, R. (1984) *Service Management: Strategy and Leadership in Service Businesses*, Wiley, Chichester.

Ohmae, K. (1983) *The Mind of the Strategist*, Penguin Books, Harmondsworth.

Ohmae, K. (1985) *Triad Power – the Coming Shape of Global Competition*, The Free Press, New York.

O'Reilly, D. (1986a) 'Advertising's doublespeak', *Management Today*, November.

O'Reilly, D. (1986b) 'The Brothers Saatchi', *Business*, May.

Pecchioli, R. (1983) *The Internationalisation of Banking: the Policy Issues*, OECD, Paris.

Perlmutter, H. V. and Heenan, D. A. (1986) 'Cooperate to compete globally', *Harvard Business Review*, March–April, pp. 136–52.

Porter, M. (1980) *Competitive Strategy*, The Free Press, New York.

Porter, M. (1985) *Competitive Advantage*, The Free Press, New York.

Porter, M. and Millar, V. (1985) 'How information gives you competitive advantage', *Harvard Business Review*, July–August, pp. 149–60.

Quelch, J. A. and Hoff, E. J. (1986) 'Customising global marketing', *Harvard Business Review*, May–June, pp. 59–68.

Quinn, J. B. and Gagnon, C. E. (1986) 'Will services follow manufacturing into decline?' *Harvard Business Review*, November–December, pp. 95–103.

Rajan, A. (1987) *Services – the Second Industrial Revolution?*, Butterworths, London.

Riddle, D. I. (1986) *Service-led Growth: the Role of the Service Sector in World Development*, Praeger, New York.

Segal-Horn, S. (1987a) 'Managing professionals in organisations', *International Journal of Manpower*, Vol. 8 No. 2.

Segal-Horn, S. (1987b) 'The retail environment in the UK', in: Johnson, G. (ed) *Business Strategy and Retailing*, Wiley, Chichester.

Segal-Horn, S. (1988) 'Global service delivery – managing the critical interdependencies', in: Johnston, R. (ed) *The Management of Service Operations – Proceedings of the Operations Management Association Annual International Conference*, IFS Publications, London.

Sheth, J. (1983) 'Marketing megatrends', *Journal of Consumer Marketing*, No. 1, Summer, pp. 5–13.

Sheth, J. (1987) quoted in *The Times*, 19th February.

Stelzer, I. (1986) 'City sets off global echo', *The Sunday Times*, 22nd June.

Stopford, J. M. and Turner, L. (1985) *Britain and the Multinationals*, John Wiley/IRM, Chichester.

The Economist (1988) 'Not only exciting but risky too', 9th January.

Trevor, M. (1986) 'Japanese decision-making and global strategy', in: McGee and Thomas (eds) *Strategic Management Research*, Wiley, Chichester.

Van Mesdag, M (1987) 'Winging it in foreign markets', *Harvard Business Review*, January–February, pp. 71–4.

9 Strategy in public sector service organisations

DR DAVID M REA

Introduction

Organisations, both public and private, are predominantly understood to be systems for transforming human irrationalities into rational behaviours. The conventional wisdom, once almost universally imparted to management and public adminstration students by business schools, and teaching departments in colleges and universities, is that organisations are 'rationally conceived means for the achievement of collective ends which, potentially at least, facilitated the institutionalisation of group values and norms to which individual ends and action could be initially subordinated and eventually assimilated.' (Reed, 1985, p. 6). Bob Johnston's chapter, earlier in this book, presents a model of organisational behaviour which is a typical product of modern business and management schools and so serves as a convenient example. The model presented conforms to what is called the 'rational' model and takes its inspiration from Simon (1957).

It may appear odd to be critical of rationality as a model of human behaviour but, in fact, there is a wealth of criticism on which to draw. Criticisms usually take Charles Lindblom's classic article 'The science of muddling through' (1959) as their starting point. The model of rational organisational behaviour makes several central, but questionable, assumptions. First, it assumes that what happens can be attributed to a decision-maker. It then makes two further assumptions about this person or body of people: that it wants to act on a rational basis and that it is capable of doing so. This is misleading because these two assumptions conflate two notions of a profoundly different kind: that decision-makers *ought* to make rational decisions and that they *are likely* to do so.

The means by which decision makers or decision-making bodies exercise control or domination over people within organisations, and the contribution made by overall – rationally conceived – organisational objectives, is one way of thinking about strategies in organisations. The articulation of institutionalised values to which all else, including individual aspirations, is subordinated to a (supposedly) collective will, is a large part of managerial strategic activity. However, in this chapter, the focus is on the external relations of organisations in the public sector. Here, it is the articulation of social values which dominate the organisational strategies of both public and private sectors.

Another assumption often made in promoting the rational model, which sometimes finds its way into specific policy proposals (DHSS, 1983), is that the model can be readily transferred to public sector service organisations and should be. The ability of public sector service organisations to make decisions and to devise strategies is expected by many to be judged in the same way and according to similar criteria as organisations which compete in the market. To stay with our example a little longer, Bob Johnston's chapter begins with an introduction which outlines the importance of the service sector to Britain's economy. His definition of the service sector includes 'social components such as; health, education, welfare and public administration'. Bob Johnston's message is that – to be successful – organisations must integrate and that this integration must incorporate their customers and competitors as well as the services being delivered. To do this, objectives must be set. Organisations must adhere to their objectives, and ultimately must measure performance in relation to them. All this so that they can compete effectively. The reason for pointing to criticism of this model is that such models continue to be presented as an ideal to which the public sector might aspire. (Recent examples which are explicitly related to the public sector will be discussed further on into this chapter). The usual explanation offered for the persistence with which so-called rational models continue to be presented relate to ideologies and the political values which are said to dominate in our society. Perhaps this is true, but it would also be fair to say that there is a paucity of understanding about how public sector organisations operate. Of course, this lack of understanding may also result from the influence of these dominant values. While an exploration of these issues might be interesting and useful, what I want to establish here is that, for whatever reasons that might be proposed, there are fewer ideas about how public sector service organisations operate. Discussion has to begin with the rational model of organisational behaviour, however inappropriate, because there are few other models at hand. Organisations are defined in rational and functional terms.

Initially, such models might be considered inappropriate because of an assumption that public sector service organisations do not compete in the market. But, this will not do because all organisations compete for a share of society's resources. However, there are a variety of other reasons why such models are of little help in understanding strategies in the public sector. There are differences between the public and private sectors which prevent the market analogy having any value in understanding public service organisations. This chapter is intended to demonstrate what those differences are.

So, this chapter will compare the meaning of strategy in public sector services with its meaning in other service sectors. It will look closely at the ability of public services to respond to demand and to act against popular demand. Then it will look at how strategic decisions are taken by public sector organisations and at how these processes are being influenced by commercial methods of decision making. Examples from a variety of public services will be used to illustrate strategic policies but particular attention will be paid to the UK's health service sector where these influences have been most strongly felt over recent years.

Strategy: public service and private service

It is tempting to regard all strategic planning matters in the public services as the preserve of central government. However, this is rarely the case because local government organisations and local health authorities command significant resources. Even a small district health authority will have an annual revenue in excess of £35 million. In order to plan for a new hospital or a new way of delivering its services, it will have to engage in strategic planning over very many years. Central government finds it necessary and convenient to delegate this kind of strategising to local authorities and to allow them considerable autonomy. Arguments over the extent of local authority autonomy have persisted and show no sign of lessening. It is a contentious topic and the reasons for this should be apparent in reading this chapter.

Government also finds it convenient – or necessary – to delegate major strategic decisions to professions. An extreme example of this being the powers of medical professionals who collectively are able to determine whether some forms of treatment should be available in the private or the public sector. The ethics of professional practice are often controlled by professional bodies, not government. This is an area which extends into what sorts of treatment/service should be offered. So, the influence of the state on services may appear to come from many directions. Government has to make arrangements for provision which are possibly very cumbersome. Public sector services are rarely the responsibility of just one arm of government: often several ministries or departments are involved, as are local government and other agencies. These divisions of responsibility result in the necessity for joint strategies to be devised.

The complexity of arrangements, responsibilities and powers means that strategies in the public service sector inevitably involve more than any single organisation. To take an example, the most significant strategic changes occurring now in the public sector relate to the policy of promoting 'community care'. It is difficult to be sure where the impetus for this idea originated and it is equally difficult to be sure exactly what it means. The fact is that it has come to mean different things to all those involved. Perhaps because people in general have changed their attitudes towards the mentally ill and the mentally handicapped, or perhaps because doctors found they could 'cure' their symptoms or control their behaviours, or perhaps because central government realised it could not afford to replace the asylums erected during Victorian times; the current policy is to close the institutions, de-institutionalise the patients (and staff), and to treat these people as much like normal people as possible. In no way can this be judged as a response to the demands of mentally ill and handicapped people, or their relatives, or the communities into which they are to be decanted. Nonetheless, these people have to be convinced, as do the staff presently responsible, that community care is in their own best interests. De-institutionalisation plans may originate from staff employed by the health service but must involve community health services, social services, housing departments and voluntary organisations. In the community health services, GPs are independent contractors. Social services are organised by county councils, housing services are organised by both county and district councils, and voluntary organisations are sporadic. The areas served by voluntary organisations, for instance, rarely match the county or district administrative boundaries. The scope, then, for strategic changes in the public services to run up against organisational inertia or for original intentions to be misunderstood and wrongly implemented is enormous.

One final point to make here is that the term 'services' must be understood differently when used of the public sector from when it is used to describe the activities of service sector industries. The provision of services and the allocation of resources towards public services is a comparatively recent development of government's activities. Until the mid-nineteenth century, government activities were restricted to defending the state and policing its inhabitants. The armed forces, police, prisons, and the administration of individual justice pre-date more recent public sector organisations. Many of the more recent developments, commonly associated with the welfare state, are extensions of the state's earlier 'policing' and 'justice' functions. Social services, for instance, have a major legal responsibility for preventing violence to children in the home. Again, the social security system plays a role in providing incentives to work. While the term 'services' is often applied to public sector organisations, such organisations have a role in regulating individuals (Foucault, 1965, or 1978). Marxists take this further and argue that the welfare state and its services function to regulate social classes (Gough, 1979).

Demand and allocation

Every society has to make arrangements for the distribution and redistribution of its resources and in Britain, like most Western states, the market is the chief means by which this is accomplished. But it is not the only one. The re-allocation of incomes, for instance, is accomplished by a mixture of state services (pensions and supplementary benefits) and private provision (charities and private pension schemes). Evidence suggests that even in Britain's so-called welfare state, the private provision of welfare is larger than the public sector (Titmus, 1963; Townsend, 1984; Sinfield, 1978). Incidentally, the national accounts may show that nearly half of Britain's economy is conducted in the public sector but a large part of these figures are transfer payments. Also, organisations like the NHS or the defence ministries spend large proportions of their budgets in the private sector.

As was stated earlier, it may initially appear that government has the major strategic role in deciding the mix of private and public provision in society. While the evidence of the Conservatives' privatisation policies supports this view, other parts of society are influential – the professional providers of services (doctors, teachers, lawyers, and town planners) for instance. In examining the government's role it is, in any case, important to remind ourselves that such policies could not have been pursued if people did not persist in the belief that government should not be involved outside of its more traditional spheres of activity and that private or individual forms of service were intrinsically better. These beliefs and attitudes need to be examined because they have effects on the way we think of the public sector which in turn has effects on public sector activities and policies. Such thinking is based on fundamental assumptions about people's ability to make rational choices. It is assumed that this ability affects their behaviour and can be used to make predictions. It is a mode of thought which stems from the dominance of economics as a means of understanding society (Hindess, 1984). Perhaps, it is this dominance which has resulted in the activities of the (welfare) state being conceived of as services rather than as regulatory. The point is, however, that with an absence of any appreciation of how public sector organisations are managed, similarities have been sought between them and private sector organisations. Any differences which are acknowledged in these attempts are generally the wrong ones.

In many areas of public service provision (education, housing, welfare benefits and income maintenance), there are unresolved conflicts over what the objectives ultimately are. The problem is not restricted, as is implied by those who wish it were so, to that of how the objectives can be reached. Certainly, as far as the state provision of health services through the NHS is concerned, the objectives have never been agreed or determined. There is no consensus and this may result from the difficulties people encounter in defining what health and sickness are. The purposes of medical intervention and health care services differ within the different branches of the medical profession. Governments assume a responsibility for making strategic decisions about health care which others find difficult to accept and, in any case, the ultimate health service objectives of government alters at least as often as governments change. As for the individual making a choice, the priority tends to be placed on the immediate personal need and not to be concerned with the future possibility of ill-health, severe accident, or chronic sickness. For obvious reasons, individual choice is not at all consistent: as taxpayers, individuals want to pay less and want more efficient public services, as patients and as clients, they want more effective services.

Lessons from commerce?

The most obvious distinction between public and private sectors is often said to be the existence of the profit motive in the private sector. It is assumed that privately owned companies measure their performance, and set their objectives, by their ability to make a profit. It is also assumed that public sector services do not use the same criteria: they do not need to make profits. While this is true and while it also has important consequences, too much can be made of this distinction, even where it still holds good. The argument often runs on from here to say that the profit motive in the private sector ensures competition which in turn ensures efficiency (and increased customer satisfaction). So, without the requirement to make a profit, organisations in the public sector can ignore the demands of the people receiving their services and ignore any necessity to become more efficient.

There are two major objections to this argument. First, no matter how much money is made available to public sector organisations, the demands made on services will always increase. This makes efficiency a constant objective. This can be seen in any historical account of the NHS, for example, where the search for efficiency predates Mrs Thatcher's Conservative government (Butler and Vaile, 1984, p. 140). Second, competition between companies is, in any case, not always guaranteed by the market. Collusion over market sectors is quite normal. It does not follow, therefore, that companies will become more efficient and provide the services that people want. For example, privately owned transport services were unable to make sufficient profits when in competition with each other. The duplication of transport networks was not the best means of allocating society's scarce resources. As a result, they were merged under nationalisation or municipalisation schemes. Once in the public sector, however, they were starved of sufficient investment, and over time the inadequacies of public transport services have led people to an increased dependence on privately owned cars operating on publicly owned roads. Resistance to public support has meant that a system has been adopted which is probably more convenient for those with access to cars – less so for those without, and certainly less safe. In cities in some other countries, where this resistance has been absent, public transport competes on convenience as well as price. So we cannot be wholly certain that private solutions result in a better allocation of society's scarce resources. Nonetheless, this was the argument used by government for their recent reprivatisation. Perhaps there was an unspoken objection that the existence of public transport prevented the remaining private transport companies from increasing their prices to more profitable levels. It is here that the articulation of such notions as consumer sovereignty and individual choice is revealed as a political mechanism because people are prepared to believe that they have sovereignty as consumers and not as clients and that they are capable of making rational, informed choices.

Despite these objections, the claim that public sector organisations are necessarily less efficient is supported by the fact that governments have, from time to time, pumped money into the public sector in order to stimulate the economy and that, whenever this has happened, a temporary decrease in the value obtained for the money invested was the result. Nonetheless, governments have equally pumped money into the economy via the private sector, usually through tax concessions. Criticisms of private firms or private individuals for then spending their money in ways which others might consider unwise or foolhardy remains muted. This observation reminds us that we and our governments adopt entirely different attitudes towards spending by private individuals or firms from the attitudes we adopt towards spending by public sector organisations. Private money can be spent in any way its owner may choose. Public organisations, in contrast, are accountable for every penny spent. Yet, private provision is defended on the grounds that it ultimately results in the most efficient distribution of society's resources, so there is a recognition that, ultimately, the resources used are everyone's. This inconsistency is supported by the assumption that private individuals or companies will use their resources to maximise their investment.

The results of this inconsistency can be seen in recent government policy making. Governments have claimed that the public sector spends the nation's wealth, while the private sector creates it. However, nobody needs police services, social services, or health services in the same way that they need consumer durables. Private companies which successfully make profits by manufacturing or selling such goods as beer, tobacco, dairy produce or automobiles, are said to be 'wealth-creating'. Doctors, clinics and hospitals treating people suffering with the consequences – cancer, heart disease or road accident injuries – have been told they are a drain on the wealth-creating sector. This leads us back to the distinctions which were remarked upon earlier. There may be some fundamental rationality to which organisations must direct themselves, but there is no one person, or authority, who is able to persuade everyone else what it is. Organisational analysts who adhere to the rational model cannot actually extend their ideas to private companies because these do not work well when run as fiefdoms. The extension of their ideas into a democratic and pluralist society and the institutions and public services it collectively owns is even less likely to work. Nonetheless, when capitalist enterprises are run by people who associate individual enterprise, private ownership of companies, and the free market with democracy, it is only to be expected that an attempt will be made. Some democratically elected governments, such as Mrs Thatcher's and Ronald Reagan's, have been influenced by the thinkers of the 'new right' and have clearly been willing to make this association. In Britain this has resulted in determined efforts being made to make public sector organisations behave like private sector organisations. One example of this is seen in the moves made to measure outputs. In a private company, such outputs might well lead to alterations in strategy. In the public sector this may not happen. As public sector organisations are supposed to respond to the democratic will, it is also arguable that it should not.

Measurement of success towards reaching objectives

The primary distinction between private and public sector organisations concerns the measurement of success. Private sector companies are successful if they are able to attract investment by demonstrating their potential for earning a sufficient return on investment. Past performance is one indicator, ownership of assets is another. Both these indicators correspond to financial values and so companies can be compared in quantitative terms. It is axiomatic that success measured in these terms will be supported by further investment and that failure will not. In public services, almost the reverse is true. If a public service fails to provide an adequate service, then more resources may be allocated to it. Perception of success, on the other hand, will not create the demand for more investment. Hospital waiting lists have long been used to win extra resources. Police services argue for more resources when they are faced with rising crime rates, not with demonstrations of their ability to clear them up. Success for public services is rarely measured in quantifiable terms. Recent attempts to do so have been made, but generally have given a false impression. Increases in the numbers of pupils gaining 'A' levels do not, for instance, correspond neatly with what is meant by improved education; an increase in the numbers of people receiving supplementary benefit is not necessarily a good thing, nor is it necessarily a bad thing. Even allowing for the difficulties in accounting for community care services, increased throughput in hospitals is not necessarily an indication that people's health is better. Indeed, until very recently, hospital discharge statistics included those who were discharged via the mortuary.

However uncomfortable it may be for those who wish to impose accountability and management by objectives, the measurement of success in achieving objectives in the public sector is made additionally complicated because the objectives remain obstinately vague. Medical intervention, for instance, may not save a person's life. The patient may well be discharged via the mortuary despite receiving the very best of care. This does not mean that medical intervention was a failure or that it is pointless for those who are going to die anyway. Even those whose life chances were small (and generally the chances remain unknown) have a right to be given the same standards of care as anyone else – perhaps more. Rights of this kind are often acknowledged in the public sector, even if they are never adequately respected.

The private sector is rarely faced with such difficulties. Its strategies are defined from the outset because people get what they pay for (if they can afford it in the first place!) and nothing else. They are entitled to their money back if services are not delivered after they have paid. If someone does not have the money to pay, then they cannot demand service. Private sector service managers make their strategic decisions in this context. For this reason, the goods and services on offer are rarely so vital. The public sector, on the other hand, exists to provide services according to proven need – regardless of the individual's ability to pay but with regard for another important distinction – that needs cannot always be self-diagnosed.

This leads onto a second major distinction between private and public services.

In the private sector, consumers are able to express their preferences – however inadequately – through their ability to pay. Leaving aside the ways in which these preferences can be manipulated and the problems of those unable to pay, they are 'free to choose' (Friedman and Friedman, 1980). In the public sector, the individual's choice is sometimes limited and sometimes absent altogether. Instead, the service is provided because it has been made obligatory. Education from five years to sixteen is compulsory. Mothers bearing children must avail themselves of a midwife and increasingly must have the child born in hospital. Taking a child into care – or allowing a child to be cared for by its parents or foster parents – is a process subject to legal requirements. The same degree of legal process applies to other groups of people such as the mentally ill or the mentally handicapped. Where the law does not make it compulsory, there are often irresistible social expectations: someone absent from work through ill-health is required to seek medical advice and to take it (Levine and Kozloff, 1978). In this sense, public services are quite distinct from those provided by the private sector. The consequence is that the judgement over whether good value for money is being obtained is not made by the receiver of the service. Instead, these judgements are made by the government and its agents or, where rates contribute, by local government. Public sector services are often, quite rightly, accused of denying choice to the public, but to talk of them offering services to customers is highly inappropriate. Despite this, attempts have been made in recent years to apply the model of consumer choice to public services. That these moves should come from government is particularly telling, but there are many people – of varying political persuasions – who want to see public services far more responsive to people's expressed needs.

Public demand for services

Some services are, of course, provided in response to demand. Unfortunately, demands generally outstrip the abilities of the service to meet them. To some extent this must be because the service is provided free of direct financial charges, although there are always other costs to be borne by the user. The consequence is that services have to be rationed by some means other than the price mechanism. So, queues, waiting lists, geographic inequalities, and refusal of rights have become abiding features of public services.

Faced with demands which cannot all be met, society is faced with a number of questions and has not always been too sure what the answers are. Given that all needs cannot be met, how are decisions to meet some needs but not others to be reached? Then, if decisions are reached, what justifications can there be for not meeting identified needs when the result may be tragic for the individual concerned? How can the strategy of spending millions of pounds to help the relatively small numbers of AIDS victims be justified to the many elderly people waiting for the NHS to provide them with hip replacement operations? In the private sector, nobody has to justify inadequacies in provision. The inability of a firm to make a sufficient return on its investment is justification alone. Private provision of an activity such as health care means that no justification has to be offered when people are unable to afford the health care they desire. Private provision is only open to criticism when it fails to deliver the goods which have been paid for directly. In the public sector, strategies have to be adopted which entail denial as well as provision and there are no simple answers. It is, therefore, no surprise that these decisions are often difficult to reach. Equally, it is no surprise that responsibility for decisions is often difficult to track down. In the private sector, the dissatisfied customer can take his or her custom elsewhere. Providers have, therefore, a vital interest in their customer's opinion. They take steps to find these out and to analyse their customer's behaviour. In the public sector, because there are often legal responsibilities associated with the provision of services, complaints are often extremely difficult to make. There is no financial loss to the public sector provider if the dissatisfied user goes elsewhere, and so dissatisfaction is almost as effective as non-provision as a means of rationing resources. Non-provision can be an effective means for governments to free resources to meet other demands.

Conclusion: decision-making processes in the public sector

The problems involved in deciding whether people are to be denied or provided with some public service are sufficient to ensure that such decisions cannot be considered as ethical decisions only. They are conducted in the political arena. However, politicians find such decisions no more comfortable to make than anyone else. The result is that decisions are often delayed and never made completely clear. Often too, the process is delegated down to professionals and their professional organisations who have claimed a special authority or a special expertise. Here, too, decisions can be blurred. Moreover, until very recently, the decision-making processes tended to involve many individuals with different responsibilities. In recent years, efforts have been made by governments to apply commercial management techniques to public sector service organisations. Such decision-making processes have been anathema. The health service is an interesting example because it was the most resistant to these changes. Proposals to introduce chief executives were made periodically (for example, in the Royal Commission on the NHS, 1979) but the idea was rejected on the grounds that it would infringe the legitimate interests of professionals to be represented in decision making. Only since the Griffiths' report (DHSS, 1983), has the government been able to introduce the idea. General managers have been recruited, occasionally from private firms or the armed forces, but generally from within the NHS. The difference is one of principle: general managers (or chief executives and managers in local authorities) have an individual responsibility. It is this principle which replaces the earlier one of collective responsibility which was reliant on achieving consensus between doctors, nurses, accountants, and administrators.

The suggestion here, though, is that the old methods were not as faulty as the government had claimed. There is no doubt that in some circumstances the government's diagnosis was very accurate. Decisions to cutback on provision were proving difficult to make and sometimes impossible. Decision making in the NHS was also accused of being dominated by the medical professions and that this had allowed the development of some aspects of provision and a corresponding lack of development in areas where medicine was not the major requirement – the care of the mentally ill, for instance. However, while delay and indecision were possible where everyone on the decision-making team retained a veto, most health authority management teams adopted an informal arrangement and distributed responsibilities among individuals (Rea, forthcoming). So, for instance, nursing matters were the responsibility of the Chief Nursing Officer (a post which is now defunct but which used to be mandatory). Organisational matters were acknowledged to be the responsibility of the Administrator, financial matters the responsibility of the Treasurer, and medical matters were distributed among elected representatives of the medical profession. In future, the responsibility for reaching decisions will nominally rest with one person, but all the evidence suggests that general managers have resorted to the same type of informal arrangement as previous management teams found necessary. Where they have not, then they have found themselves under attack for making the wrong decision and making it too soon. Unfortunately there are decisions which cannot be reached on criteria which can honestly be described as objective or rational. If one set of criteria are agreed by some, others will oppose them as inhuman or inequitable. It may sound banal but to some questions there are no ready answers. Delay sometimes is the only reasonable course.

The fact is that, with finite resources, there can be no *right* decision. An increased allocation of resources for one activity, say care of the mentally ill, will result in decreased resources being available for other activities. If public sector services have proved slow and have been judged incorrect when making strategic decisions, then surely it is because they have been asked to make decisions which governments and politicians have also realised were difficult. Public sector services have proved difficult areas in which to make strategy, and government's regret that they do not behave like private companies is genuine. There are real dilemmas to be resolved and their existence is as real when decisions have to be made over whether to resource other public sector services. As more is spent on education, say, less can be spent elsewhere. Services cannot be devised in response to market pressures – not because those pressures do not exist but because decisions have to be reached over whose demands are most pressing.

To return to the starting point of the argument presented in this chapter – the so-called 'rational' models. With government's acceptance of the Griffiths report and its proposals for general management, there has been a renewed impetus for people to persist in putting them forward. Chambers (1987) and Rathwell (1986) are recent examples from the *Hospital and Health Services Review*. The best of these acknowledge the limits of their proposals. Rathwell, for instance, notes of strategic planning 'that choice must be made between the range of demands to be satisfied' and that the 'feasibility of the alternative means must be judged and evaluated according to political, social, economic and technical criteria which can only be determined in the light of local circumstances' (p. 55). He also notes that 'generating commitment is a *sine qua non* for strategic change.' (p. 56). Rathwell is quite right, of course. His omission, and it is an omission from the 'rational' model of organisational or economic behaviour as much as his own particular proposals, is a failure to address how these significant snags can be overcome in a public service. It is perverse to limit rationality to those human activities which are defined as economic. To do this under the flag of rationality is peculiarly ironic.

The persistence with which the 'rational' model is presented is enhanced by the activities, statements, and policies of governments. For governments are comprised of politicians who are responsible for services which they know to be imperfectly responsive to public demand which is often contradictory when not absent altogether. They are equally aware that they are governing by virtue of imperfect political mechanisms in which the electorate's views are similarly often contradictory if not altogether absent. Governments and politicians have good reasons for preferring difficult choices and decisions to be presented as being open to technical or economic solutions once the correct structural machinery is in place to ensure that choices are made on a purely *rational* basis.

References

Butler, J. R. and Vaile, M. S. B. (1984) *Health and Health Services: an Introduction to Health Care in Britain*, Routledge and Kegan Paul.

Chambers, N. (1987) 'Developing a consumer strategy in the NHS or getting things right', in: *Hospital and Health Services Review*, January, pp. 12–14.

DHSS (1983) *NHS Management Inquiry*, (Griffiths report). HMSO, London.

Foucault, M. (1965) *Madness and Civilization: a History of Insanity in the Age of Reason*, Random House, New York.

Foucault, M. (1978) *History of Sexuality, Volume I: An Introduction*, Random House, New York.

Friedman, M. and Friedman, R. (1980) *Free to Choose*, Secker and Warburg.

Gough, I. (1979) *The Political Economy of the Welfare State*, Macmillan.

Hindess, B. (1984) 'Rational choice theory and the analysis of political action', *Economics and Society*, Vol. 13, No. 3, pp. 255–77.

Levine, S. and Kozloff, M. A. (1978) 'The sick role: assessment and overview', *The Annual Review of Sociology*, 4: 317–43.

Lindblom, C. E. (1959) 'The science of muddling through', *Public Administration Review*, Vol. 19, Spring, pp. 79–88.

Rathwell, T. (1986) 'Strategic management – a change agent for the NHS', in: *Hospital and Health Services Review*, March, pp. 54–6.

Rea, D. M. (forthcoming), *Power in Health Services*.

Reed, M. (1985) *Redirections in Organizational Analysis*, Tavistock.

Royal Commission on the National Health Service: *Report* (1979), (Chairperson: Sir Alec Merrison), HMSO, Cmnd 7615.

Simon, H. A. (1957) *Administrative Behavior: a Study of the Decision-making Process and Administration Organization*, Second edition, Free Press, Collier-Macmillan, New York.

Sinfield, A. (1978) 'Analysis in the social division of welfare', *Journal of Social Policy*, Vol. 7, No. 2, pp. 129–56.

Titmus, R. M. (1963) 'The social division of welfare' in: *Essays on 'The Welfare State'*. Second edition, Allen & Unwin, London.

Townsend, P. (1984) *'Why are the Many Poor?'*, Fabian Tract 500, Fabian Society.

10 Service organisations – structure and performance

PETER JONES AND SUE RICKS

Introduction

The basic premise of this text is that service industries are in some ways different from manufacturing industries. It follows, therefore, that it is likely that the structure and nature of firms and organisations in these industries will be different too. This chapter examines the extent to which this hypothesis is valid. It begins by briefly reviewing the range of organisational forms that exist. It considers the range of factors that affect organisational design and relates these to service operations. From this it is possible to evaluate whether or not there is a theoretical basis for assuming service organisations will have a distinctive structure or form. Some consideration is then given to empirical evidence that may support this view, although such evidence is partial and limited. Finally, the impact of organisational structure and design on service firm effectiveness is discussed.

The debate about the nature of services and their distinctive characteristics in comparison with products is long standing. It has been suggested that most 'goods' are bundles of both a physical product and an intangible service (Sasser et al, 1976; Shostack, 1977). A significant trend in the 1980s has been the recognition by so-called manufacturing firms of the significance of this service element. Many firms, for instance IBM, now actively promote internally and externally the idea of themselves as service organisations. As Levitt (1981) has said: 'Everyone sells intangibles in the market place no matter what is produced in the factory'.

But it is not just the specific characteristics of the firm's output that has implications for the organisation. It is increasingly rare for firms to have a single output. Many large organisations will be supplying customers with goods that are predominantly products, or predominantly service, or any 'bundle' in between. Within the organisations the processes that enable the firm to supply the customers will involve some employees in product-related activities and others in service-related activities.

Another feature of modern business is the idea of 'internal' markets and customers that encourage parts of the organisation to view other parts of the organisation as if they were 'real' customers. An alternative approach has been the contracting out of some activities, particularly those not related to the firm's mainstream business. One of the reasons for the growth of services in the UK has been this trend to contract out service functions, such as data processing, catering, marketing and so on. In summary, therefore, it is extremely difficult to differentiate between service organisations and non-service organisations.

Organisational forms

Hunt (1987) provides a taxonomy of organisational forms. These are based primarily on the nature of structural form, in particular the type of hierarchy. These can be related to the level of environmental uncertainty and complexity, as illustrated in Figure 10.1.

No clear empirical evidence appears to identify whether or not one or more of these alternative structures exists predominantly in service industries. It could be argued that the bureaucratic organisation is stereotypically associated with public services, but even this may be less true now than in the past.

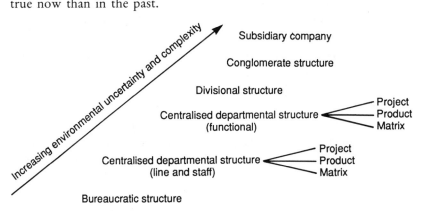

Figure 10.1   A continuum of hierarchical types
(*Source*: Hunt, J. (1987) *Managing People at Work*, McGraw-Hill Book Company (UK) Ltd.)

Factors affecting organisation design

One implication of the suggestion that organisations evolve over time through a sort of hierarchy of types is that organisational design is a rational process. It also implies that the structure of an organisation will closely reflect the length of time that organisation has been in existence, so that the older an organisation the larger and more complex it is. This suggestion is of course fallacious. First, the size of an organisation is based not on how long it has been around but on how successful it is. Second, complexity, and size too for that matter, tend to be related to the 'technology' of the industry sector in which the organisation operates. And finally, the environment of the organisation, and especially its relative stability or uncertainty, will greatly influence the form the organisation takes. Chandler's pioneering work (1962) concerning strategy and structure identified the extent to which there is internal resistance to change within organisations. Often the trigger for successfully introducing change is the decline in performance that results from a lack of fit between the organisation's environment, strategy and structure. Therefore, the values and ideologies of the senior managers of organisations are also key factors in organisational design. Research in this area has been well documented by Miles and Snow (1978).

In terms of *age and size*, it has been found (Mintzberg, 1979) that older organisations tend to have more formal structures, with an emphasis on close control and hierarchical form. As we shall see, this 'traditional' organisation is in decline as more and more companies recognise the dilemma of growth and large size, and the accelerating pace of change. Large firms tend to have to create structural differentiation that creates the need for co-ordination by a central administration and lateral communication links between sub-divisions. At the same time, one of the driving forces of growth is to achieve economies of scale, particularly in terms of these central functions and organisational administration.

The impact of *technology* on the structural characteristics has been well established (Perrow, 1967). An organisational technology focusses on the means of production, that is the way resources (inputs) are transformed into goods and services (outputs). The key aspect of the technology is the degree of routinisation and this is directly related to the organisation's structural characteristics. A routine technology exists when there are few exceptions and problems are easily analysable. Retail banking and fast-food operations are service sector examples of this type of technology. Non-routine technologies reflect work involving many exceptions and problems difficult to analyse. Management consultancy and other professional services exemplify this type of technology. This dichotomy is further developed when we consider aspects of service firm organisation.

The *environment* and the degree of uncertainty has been recognised as a factor affecting the structure and actions of complex organisations (Thompson, 1967). Organisations that operate in relatively stable environments tend to be more mechanistic in nature, making greater use of prescriptive procedures, standard methods and stated rules to control operations, whereas organisations operating in dynamic environments tend to be organic and very much more flexible.

However, there are two problems with relating age and size, technology and the environment to *service* organisations. First, the research and evidence to support the broad conclusions identified above are now almost twenty years old. More recent research (Peters and Waterman, 1983) suggests that other factors may have more impact or be of greater import- ance. These authors stress the role that corporate management can play in structuring, designing and influencing the organisation according to what- ever criteria they regard as being most likely to result in improved performance. The second problem with the analysis is that much of this early research was carried out in manufacturing sectors at a time when these were a much larger part of the economy.

Should service organisations be different?

If the research evidence is scarce, what conclusions can be drawn about the nature of organisations in the service sector? One major distinction proposed (Sasser et al, 1978) is between those service firms serving mass- market consumers, such as retailing, banking and catering, and what they called 'professional service organisations', such as lawyers, consultants and doctors. They use this dichotomy to illustrate key features of structure and systems. These are summarised in Table 10.1.

Are service organisations different?

Channon (1973, 1978) studied structural change in UK manufacturing and service industries in the 1960s and 1970s. Overall, he found there was a move away from functional and holding company structures towards diversification. The trend was associated with increasing diversity, although in service sectors it happened somewhat later. Up to 1965, 62 per cent of the service industries Channon studied were dependent on a single 'product' base. From 1965 to 1970 the figure was 42 per cent. But much has changed since this early research, as Heskett (1986) identifies there is now a 'service economy'.

Peters in his most recent work (1988) now emphasises the importance of a 'lean' structure, irrespective of whether a company is in manufacturing or services. He advocates no more than five management layers, just as Drucker thirty years earlier suggested no more than seven (1955). Peters

Table 10.1 A comparison of professional and consumer service organisations

	Professional Service Organisation (PSO)	Consumer Service Organisation (CSO)
Type of Product	Nonstandard with high knowledge and/or manual skill content	Standardised with low knowledge and/or skill content
Type of customer contacts	Medium to long-term contact with professional individuals	Short-term contact with a variety of service employees
Geographical dispersion	Single centralised office or few major offices serving local regional or national markets	Multisite operations each serving local markets
Transaction volume per time period	Low	High
Value of individual transaction	Large	Small
Locus of profit control	Individual contract	Operating unit
Initial sale	Personal selling by professionals or marketing team	By advertising and promotion
Repeat sales	By professionals delivering service	By service employees delivering service
Customer loyalty	To service provider	To concept
Type of organisational structure	Flat unstructured hierarchy with loose subordinate-superior relationships with broad discretion at all levels	Rigid pyramidal hierarchy with standard operating procedures and close top-down control
Centralised functions	Planning and state of the art knowledge	Planning Procurement Advertising Budgeting Cost control Facilities design Product design Pricing
Type of middle management	Professionally trained, self-motivated individuals who also participate in delivering the service	Operating skills geared to managing people and meeting predetermined goals
Type of operating personnel	Professionally trained, self-motivated individuals	Low and unskilled operators
Orientation of facilities	Non-standard, pleasant, unstructured environment for employees	Multiple standardised facilities and structured environment for employees with atmosphere geared to customer requirements
Quality control	Peer and client evaluation	Built-in training programs and random inspections

Source: Sasser, W. E., Olsen, R. and Wyckoff, D. D. (1978) *The Management of Service Operations*, Allyn & Bacon Inc., Newton, MA.

also advocates that the organisation chart be turned upside down and the role of middle management be reconceived – repeatedly advocating horizontal communication and responsibility. Winning companies are 'constantly adapting'.

Morris and Johnston (1987) also conclude that the evidence for a difference in organisational forms between services and manufacturing is weak, resting largely on the belief that common sense suggests this is so. In most service organisations the single most important reason for behaving differently from manufacturing firms is the interrelationship between production and consumption. In some cases, customers actually participate in the production of the service itself, and in many others they are present in person. Although in operational management terms the service customer may be processed in a similar way to information or materials, this is likely to be carried out in a more dispersed way than in manufacturing, as illustrated in Table 10.1.

But this necessity for dispersed operations does not necessarily imply the dispersal of other functional management parts of the organisation. Quinn and Gagnon (1986) conclude that services and products are becoming so widely substitutable that distinctions between the sectors seem more arbitrary than helpful. They refer in particular to increasingly sophisticated technology which creates economies of scale and scope. It breaks down boundaries, permitting the management of new levels of complexity. For instance, a manufacturer/retailer such as General Motors has used its strength in consumer credit to compete with financial services firms. Such actions erode the distinction between financial services and product marketing to the point where the two are inseparable. The implications of information service technology for competitive strategy in product-oriented companies is evident – profits depend on the development of knowledge about market sensitivities, supplier costs, exchange rates and so on. It can be argued that more money is made in the product-oriented sectors through information and services than through production activities.

Summary

In conclusion it seems that in order to facilitate organisational effectiveness, the key issues are similar whatever the industry orientation. What is needed is a responsive, flexible business providing added value where customers genuinely request it.

References

Chandler, A. D. (1962) *Strategy and Structure, Chapters in the history of the American Industrial Enterprise*, MIT Press, Cambridge, MA.

Channon, D. J. (1973) *The Strategy and Structure of British Enterprise*, Macmillan, London.

Channon, D. J. (1978) *The Service Industries – Strategy, Structure and Financial Performance*, Macmillan, London.

Drucker, P. (1955) *The Practice of Management*, Heinemann, Oxford.

Heskett, J. L. (1986) *Managing in the Service Economy*, Harvard Business School Press, Boston, MA.

Hunt, J. (1987) *Managing People at Work*, McGraw-Hill, Maidenhead, Berks.

Levitt, T. (1976) 'The industrialisation of service', *Harvard Business Review*, September–October.

Levitt, T. (1981) 'Marketing intangible products and product intangibles', *Harvard Business Review*, May–June.

Miles, R. E. and Snow, C. C. (1978) *Organisational Strategy, Structure and Process*, McGraw-Hill, Maidenhead, Berks.

Mintzberg, H. (1979) *The Structuring of Organisations*, Prentice-Hall, Englewood Cliffs, NJ.

Morris, B. and Johnston, R. (1987) 'Dealing with inherent variability: the difference between manufacturing and service?' *International Journal of Operations & Production Management*, Vol. 7, No. 4.

Perrow, C. (1967) 'A framework for the comparative analysis of organisations', *American Sociological Review*, 32.

Peters, T. (1988) *Thriving on Chaos*, Macmillan, London.

Peters, T. J. and Waterman, R. H. (1983) *In Search of Excellence: Lessons from America's Best Run Companies*, Harper & Row, New York.

Quinn, J. B. and Gagnon, C. E. (1986) 'Will service follow manufacturing into decline?' *Harvard Business Review*, November–December.

Sasser, W. Earl, Wyckoff, D. D. and Olsen, R. P. (1978) *The Management of Service Operations*, Allyn & Bacon Inc., Newton, MA.

Shostack, G. L. (1977) 'Breaking free from product marketing', *Journal of Marketing*, April.

Thompson, J. D. (1967) *Organizations in Action*, McGraw-Hill, New York.

11 Management contracts
DR MICHAEL Z. BROOKE

Introduction

An intercontinental journey can involve:

- travelling by an airline which is a flag carrier for its third-world country, but is managed under contract by another airline;
- staying in a hotel with a world-famous name, owned but not managed by a local entrepreneur;
- drawing cash on a bank that is locally owned but managed from abroad.

These are examples of contractual arrangements under which one party manages an enterprise on behalf of the owner. A management contract differs from franchising in which the local owner is also the manager; it also differs from direct investment when a foreign owner runs the business. Many companies use all three arrangements according to the circumstances. Direct investment is employed where the costs and benefits of managing the operation internally offer more satisfactory results than contracting out. Franchising is employed where the risks are reduced by subletting the commercial formula, and management contracts where franchising might be preferred but no satisfactory expertise is locally available.

The last paragraph over-simplifies a subtle choice of strategy which will be examined in more detail. In fact there are two different uses of the phrase 'management contracts' employed in the service industries. One is specific to the construction sector, the management of subcontractors by a main contractor. The other use, the one employed in this chapter, is the management of one company by another; frequently, but by no means always, the two are in different countries. The words may differ – a joint venture, associate company, technical cooperation agreement and other similar terms are used interchangeably – but the fact remains that of one company managing another with either no or minimal equity. Figure 11.1 illustrates the concept.

In a pure franchising arrangement, the client pays a fee for the business system which the franchisor has devised. The agreement is likely to include

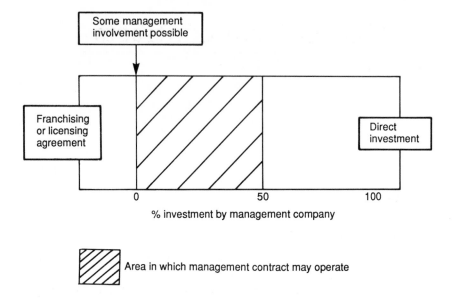

Figure 11.1   The management contract for service industry organisations

conditions about the use of the system and the management methods to be employed. Financial controls and marketing techniques will be stipulated, while the client may have to use the franchisor's training courses; but, on principle, the franchised business is independently owned and managed. The arrangement becomes a management contract when the franchisor sets up a direct management system with planning and control administered from its head office.

A management contract, like a typical franchising agreement, frequently includes zero equity on the part of the contractor. There may, however, be some participation for a number of reasons discussed later; at the same time, a contract may be designed to support a joint venture in which case the contractor holds up to 49 per cent of the shares.

Motives for contractors

The main advantage for the contractor is the opportunity to generate more revenue out of expensively acquired knowledge; this is frequently accompanied by the ability to sell related goods or services. For the client, there is the ability to acquire expertise or simply to put funds to work profitably. The following is a list of all the motives mentioned in a series of surveys.[1]

A contractor is likely to enter into a management contract when:

- its expertise proves saleable;
- it has spare resources in management, knowhow or equipment;
- new business can be generated by a means which offers low risk market entry;
- an established business is to be disinvested – to reduce risk or use resources elsewhere – but management control remains feasible;
- the contract will produce or secure additional business in the sale of other goods or services;
- a source of supply can be safeguarded this way;
- a valued customer (or third-world government) invites the contractor to supply management services;
- a management contract provides a competitive advantage for a company negotiating for new business (for example, an offer to operate a facility like a hospital, a prison or a steelworks after construction is completed);
- an existing business is under threat and a management contract appears to be the most cost effective alternative.

This can arise in a number of ways, for example:

- an investment is threatened by nationalisation (or indigenisation, local but not necessarily government ownership), but the former owner is invited to continue as manager;
- a minority holding is undertaken when the majority shareholder is incapable or unwilling to undertake management control;
- a franchisee or other collaborator is lacking in management expertise and the contractor has to accept more responsibilities than in a normal franchising arrangement;
- an export market is likely to close and a management contract is a viable means of continuing to gain revenue from the market.

Most of these motives are of a defensive nature, it will be noted. A company is entering a management contract to defend an existing business and this is one of the options available for the defence. In the case of a loss of an export market – due to import controls, tariffs or local competition – direct investment is frequently preferred. A management contract is probable instead when:

- a company does not have the resources for direct investment or is committed to using them for other purposes;
- direct investment is not permitted;
- a suitable collaborator is available.

Under these circumstances, a management contract fulfils the same objectives as direct investment. The one is a substitute for the other – mainly, but not exclusively, in international operations. In franchising, the substitution of a management contract applies equally to domestic operations. In this case a company may find that the franchisee is not capable of managing the project successfully or that a suitable franchisee cannot be found.

The aggressive approach is to consider management as a saleable commodity in its own right or in close connection with other expertise. As a result the contract becomes a means of expanding into other markets. Many firms have learnt the technique of promoting management contracts from necessity. Assets have been nationalised. As a result of this learning process, it has become possible to use contracts as an option when considering new developments. This has occurred frequently in tropical agriculture, where plantations were taken over and the previous owners invited to stay as managers, but less often in the service industries. A similar principle applies when indigenisation forces a company to sell off more than half its holding; the lessons learnt during the exercise can be applied elsewhere.

A market extension use of management contracts occurs when an entrepreneur approaches a company and proposes a contract venture. This is found most commonly in the hotel industry; banks also provide examples. Equally, third-world governments may look to experienced companies in construction, tourism and other sectors to help establish new industries. In this case, the contracts will have a limited life. Another motive arises when a company is into the transfer of technology. The sale of technical expertise is often accompanied by management techniques, and consultants in advanced technologies – like deep sea mining – have set up management contracts to oversee the transfer of the skills required.

Motives for clients

A client is likely to seek a management contract with a view to attaining a number of objectives.

1 The development of a viable business where capital is available but the necessary technical and managerial skills are not.

2 The profitable exploitation of a market in a partnership which avoids unwanted conditions.

3 The acquiring of new business skills including training.

4 When a management contract with an established operator provides extra credibility for seeking finance. Internationally this applies to devel-

opment loans, nationally to business start-up schemes and to bank loans and debentures in both cases.

Theory and practice

Precise arrangements vary from venture to venture with an initial agreement which stipulates the contribution of the parties. Typically, a management contract is a three-cornered arrangement in which one company (the contractor) agrees with another (the client) to set up a third (the contract venture) to bring together the contractor's expertise and the client's capital. But it is not as simple as that. The client company is not just a sleeping partner. It plays a more active part in the project than that of an ordinary shareholder. This method of conducting business carries one stage further the long-developing relationship between ownership and management. Companies start with owner-managers; they move into a regime of professional management under which the owners are shareholders will little involvement in management. There are many variations of those two common situations; the further stage described in this chapter includes the emergence of the professional owner who is not prepared to delegate all the decision-making to the manager, but is forging a new relationship whether realising the fact or not. Various outcomes of this relationship are possible, but some patterns are emerging. The following are among the decisions on which the owner is likely to intervene more directly and more consistently than a shareholder in a normal business.

1   The balance between dividends and retained earnings. This is a cause of disagreement if the two parties are working to different time scales. The manager may, for instance, be looking for income in the short term, while the manager wants to plough all the profits back to enhance his performance over the lifetime of the contract – especially if a performance clause is attached to renewal clause. On the other hand, a contractor with some equity may seek a high dividend as part of the remuneration while the client is taking a long-term view.

2   Entering new products or markets. The two parties are likely to reach agreement on this, if it arises, readily enough; but, again, there is scope for disagreement. The contractor will be looking for business opportunities that match his plans and these may not fit with those of the client.

3   Seeking new methods of loan financing. The contractor is likely to possess expertise about the most suitable financing package for the particular business as well as contacts with sources of finance; the owner is likely to regard this expertise as advisory rather than mandatory.

4 Making senior appointments. The contractor will wish to place experienced executives into key posts, whereas the client may have other criteria for appointments, including rewards for services in other connections.

5 Organising a staff training programme. This is an issue on which there is general agreement, except that formal training frequently has higher priority for the client than the contractor. Complaints are frequently heard that inadequate or inappropriate training is being offered.

On all these issues, there is scope for disagreement, but the impression should not be given that the relationship is necessarily antagonistic; on the contrary many profitable partnerships have emerged from management contracts. It remains that methods for the settlement of disputes are always required even if they are not used.

There is always potential for conflict when an owner plays part of a role which a manager expects to monopolise. In fact, most of the disputes that have come up for arbitration have hinged on this issue; those that have come before the court established in Paris by the International Chamber of Commerce have mainly been in the hotel industry. This sector provides special opportunities for management contracts and with them special scope for conflict. The owner sees himself as a leading citizen in his locality, deeply rooted in the local culture. He reaches agreement with a contractor in the form of an international chain of hotels which can provide both management techniques and marketing muscle. The conflict usually begins as a clash between the international culture of the chain and the opinions of the locals voiced by the owner. It may start over simple issues like the decoration of a lounge, the furnishing of the bedrooms or even the national bias of the menu, it ends with both parties claiming that the other has exceeded its rights in the agreement.

One of the problems of adjudicating disputes is that managers are often more skilful at presenting their case than owners. Even so, most disputes are settled in the local courts in spite of the conventional wisdom that advises contractors to organise redress according to the laws of their own or a neutral country. This may well be the route to a pyrrhic victory in which the contractor cannot enforce the court's decision. In one example of the reverse, a Nigerian court found in favour of a foreign contractor. Had the case not come before the courts of that country, the compensation might well have been blocked. As an alternative, an international body is sometimes used, but infrequently. In addition to the International Chamber of Commerce, there is the International Court for the Settlement of Investment Disputes established by the World Bank.

The national advantages

Management contracts are used domestically and internationally. In both cases, they provide advantages to a country in the dissemination of management expertise. In other respects, international management contracts provide a number of advantages.

For the contractor country, there are several benefits. The most important is the acquiring of foreign expertise on acceptable terms. The exact terms vary from country to country, but there is usually a wariness about making a national economy too dependent on foreign domination even in countries which encourage foreign investment. Some equity on the part of the contractor-company may be favoured in order to increase its commitment, but the management contract stimulates local business without overall or permanent control. The stimulation is all the greater in a developing economy where a contract in one business provides effective competition to force others to improve.

Some examples

The hotel industry provides a number of examples, both domestic and international. Holiday Inns, for instance, announced in 1984 an expansion in Europe by means of a minority investment and contracts which would allow control of the properties taken over. In 1980, a United Nations report[2] showed that management contracts were the largest single method of conducting business used by hotel groups – 31.4 per cent of the rooms in foreign-owned hotels were in establishments operating under management contracts. Naturally the percentage was higher in the third world, but even in the industrialised countries it came to 23 per cent. There is evidence that the proportion has increased since that report was issued.

Health care is another sector in which contracts are common. Both private and public sector hospitals in many countries are managed by specialist health care companies. An intriguing example in Britain was reported recently (14 February 1988). In this case, one private hospital company was managing a hospital for another. The context of a press report about this was that the client company had finance from a government-backed scheme for new business.[3]

Transport and tourism provide numerous examples of contracts. Canadian National, for instance, has operated railway contracts in several African countries, as has the Indian railway administration. The latter is one of many examples of management contracts where both the contractor and the client are from developing countries. Airlines, bus operators and tourism facilities are also frequently managed under contract. Some of these contracts are in the hands of consultancy companies.

The construction industry uses management contracts both for main and for subcontractors where it is more suitable to sell the expertise rather than to provide the service directly. Sometimes the contract may be an extension of a conventional turnkey arrangement – where the new facility is handed over in working order – to a contract under which the construction company undertakes to provide management for a fixed number of years. One company reported the loss of a deal where it had only proposed a turnkey arrangement, while the successful competitor had offered a management contract.

Finally management contracts can enable a company to sell its skills in unlikely places where other business methods would be unacceptable. One example is the management of a military maintenance depot.

In conclusion

Wherever there is specialised expertise, there is scope for the sale of management services. Examples include the intricate and testing requirements for managing a hospital, the scheduling and arranging of public transport, the setting up of construction projects and other operations, domestic and international. In particular, it has been noted that the contract form of business is part of two significant trends:

- a redefinition of the relationship between owners and managers,
- a trend to the service industries in the internal economies and the external trade of the industrialised nations.

In this latter connection, the trade in knowledge for the primary and manufacturing sectors is itself a service industry. A significant growth area is that of consultancy offshoots of manufacturing companies which offer management contracts as one of their products. From sugar to steel, a large number of such undertakings are providing this service.

The other issue which distinguishes management contracts is that they provide a route to business innovation which avoids the disadvantages inherent in investment. For the contractor there is a low risk opportunity which makes limited demands on capital resources; for the client there is a partnership with limited restrictions and the opportunity to go independent later if required. In the last ten years, knowledge about management contracts has increased rapidly. In the 1970s they were seldom on the agenda of companies to whom they might be useful. Now they are on the list of options; in the 1990s their use is likely to increase rapidly.

Notes and references

1 The surveys were conducted under the supervision of the author between 1979 and 1984; the earlier surveys were financed by the Leverhulme Trust whose assistance is gratefully acknowledged. Many of the generalisations contained in this chapter come from this research, although more recent evidence is incorporated. The results of the research were published in *Selling Management Services Contracts in International Business*, by Michael Z. Brooke, Holt, Rinehart and Winston, 1985.

2 See United Nations (1980) *Transnational Corporations in Transnational Tourism*, United Nations Centre for Transnational Corporations, New York.

3 See the *Guardian* (London) 14 February 1988.

Bibliography

Brooke, Michael Z. (1985) *Selling Management Services Contracts in International Business*, Holt, Rinehart and Winston, Eastbourne.

Ghai, Y. (1984) 'Management contracts in Africa', *The Africa Guide*, World of Information.

Sharma, D. D. (1983) *Swedish Firms and Management Contracts*, Uppsala University. United Nations. *Management Contracts in Developing Countries: An Analysis of their Substantive Provisions*, United Nations Centre on Transnational Corporations.

World Tourism Organization (1980) 'Accommodation management methods: the management contract', Paper presented at a workshop on regulating and negotiating with transnational corporations for Pacific Island countries, Tonga.

12 Franchising services

PROFESSOR M J K STANWORTH

Introduction

Historically, businesses in Britain have tended towards a policy of achieving control over their environment by directly owning and managing as much of it as possible. In more recent times, however, we have witnessed a movement towards more 'arms-length' forms of business relationship such as subcontracting and franchising as methods of allowing the large organisation to concentrate its resources to greatest effect.

Franchising, at its most effective, combines the strengths of both small and large scale. The franchisee, being usually small, can offer clients a personal service, has a thorough knowledge of local market conditions and can make decisions quickly so as to ensure a rapid response to problems and opportunities. The franchisor, on the other hand, has the contrasting advantages of size – bulk buying power, national marketing and advertising and on-going product or service development. Furthermore, the franchise can exploit opportunities in small localised and geographically dispersed markets which would not bear conventional head-office overhead costs. Obviously, the rapidly growing service industries are just such a case in point.

A franchise can take various forms. Typically, however, it involves satellite enterprises (run by franchisees) operating under the trade name and business format of a larger organisation (the franchisor) in exchange for a continuing fee. The franchisee sets up his/her own business, operating along lines specified by the franchisor and trading in the product or service previously market tested by the franchisor.

The main advantage of franchising to the franchisor is that it facilitates national coverage for a product or service more quickly than could be achieved otherwise. Most of the necessary capital is put up by franchisees and the latter, being self-employed, are usually motivated to work hard in building up their businesses which, at the same time, ensures success for the franchisor (sometimes the franchisee will be a large company looking for diversification but, more commonly, we are looking at an individual or small business).

The franchisee, on the other hand, gets the chance to run his/her own business, use of an established trade name, prime rights to a particular geographical territory where appropriate, head office advice and administrative back-up, plus the benefits of continuous market research and product or service development.

History and development

Franchising is frequently seen as a relatively recent phenomenon imported from the United States, but the real pioneers of modern franchising were almost certainly the British brewers of the 18th century who created a system of 'tied' house agreements with publicans which remains widespread to this day. It is true, on the other hand, that franchising is today economically more important in America. Franchise activities in the United States now account for around 34 per cent of all retail sales and 10 per cent of gross national product. It is estimated that, in America, there are approaching 500,000 franchise outlets (including around 90,000 franchisor operated) with a combined turnover of around $600 billion (US Department of Commerce, 1986).

As yet in Britain, there exists no centralised statistical intelligence gathering machinery to match that operated via the US Department of Commerce. However, non-government estimates indicate that, taking into account the fact that Britain has a substantially smaller population than the United States, the imbalance in the extent of franchising in Britain may not be as great as is sometimes supposed. For instance, one estimate (Stanworth, 1984) has suggested that the number of franchised outlets in the UK is around 80,000.

This includes retail petrol outlets franchised to independent owners, franchised car distribution outlets, tenanted public houses and voluntary group wholesale-retail franchises operating in areas such as food retailing and photography. In short, it includes most areas of activity likely to be encompassed in US official estimates of franchise industry size even if some of the areas, such as petroleum and automobile distribution, are frequently excluded from franchise industry figures in Britain.

A more recent estimate of franchise industry size in Britain, funded by the National Westminster Bank and restricting itself largely to the growth area of 'business format franchises' (thus excluding most of the businesses mentioned in the above paragraph), estimates that there are around 250 franchises with 15,000 outlets, employing 145,000 people and turning over something in the region of £3.1 billion (Power, 1987). The same author, in an earlier report, estimated that probably only around 50 of these franchises were in operation at the beginning of the 1980s and that now 'franchising is becoming increasingly polarised between the established systems and other less predictable new arrivals in the industry'.

Since franchises often differ so greatly from one another, it may be useful to form them into sub-groupings after the fashion suggested by a leading American expert, Charles Vaughn (1979):

1 The manufacturer–retailer franchise

Here the manufacturer is the franchisor and the franchisee sells direct to the public. The franchisee may operate the franchise as his/her sole business concern or, alternatively, as an activity within an existing business. Car/truck dealerships and petrol service stations are examples and these cover a large proportion of franchise activities overall (they accounted for 36 per cent of all outlets and 72 per cent of franchise sales in the US in 1986).

2 The manufacturer–wholesaler franchise

The outstanding example of this type of franchising is the soft drinks industry dominated by Coca-Cola, Pepsi-Cola and Seven-Up who franchise to independent bottlers which, in turn, serve retail outlets.

3 The wholesaler–retailer franchise

The best-known examples here are the 'voluntary' groups in grocery retailing where the wholesaler (the franchisor) supplies products to the retailer (the franchisee) who is signed up on a voluntary franchise basis. Examples are Spar, Mace, VG, Londis, etc., and similar operations in other areas of retailing such as photography.

4 The trademark, trade-name, licensor–retailer franchise

This is the franchise sub-group that has grown so remarkably quickly over the last three to four decades (especially in the US) and is still developing on an international basis. The franchisor, who may not be a manufacturer, has a product or service to be marketed under a common trade-name by, usually, standardised outlets. This sub-group approximates to what are often now known as 'business format' franchises which have a high service element, e.g., fast food, fast print services, cleaning and related hygiene services, car-hire, car tuning, etc.

It is clear from the above that much franchising activity is based in the

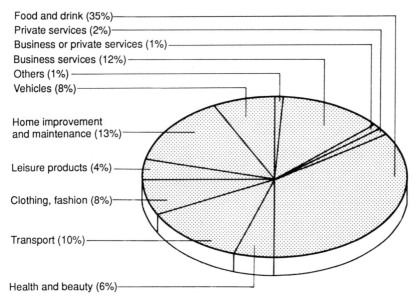

Food and drink (35%)
Private services (2%)
Business or private services (1%)
Business services (12%)
Others (1%)
Vehicles (8%)

Home improvement
and maintenance (13%)

Leisure products (4%)

Clothing, fashion (8%)

Transport (10%)

Health and beauty (6%)

Figure 12.1   Analysis of units based on turnover
(*Source*: Power Research Associates)

service sector. This is not surprising as one of the fundamentals of the concept is the geographic coverage of a market with a 'product' through independently owned operating units. Thus franchising is particularly important in the retailing, hospitality and personal services sectors of the economy. In terms of the percentage of units based on turnover, 35 per cent of franchises are related to food and drink, and a further 31 per cent to the retailing of goods such as vehicles, clothing, DIY products and leisure products. This is detailed in Figure 12.1. Thus, strategic management, i.e. franchisors, and operational management, i.e. franchisees direct their businesses not only in the context of issues and trends relating to franchising, but also the issues and trends relating to their specific industry sector, as discussed in Part I.

Getting started as a franchisor

Given the current rate of growth in franchising and the long-term trend towards growth in the service industries, it would be surprising if franchising did not assume an increasingly important role in our economy into the foreseeable future. Any individual or organisation wishing to set up a franchise network needs to exercise not only the degree of planning and attention to detail that any new business venture requires, but an additional element since, in essence, two business ideas not one may be on trial. After all, the budding franchisor may be testing a new business idea in the marketplace and also establishing and perfecting a format for, in effect, cloning that business.

There are three principal sources of new franchises. First, overseas imports bring in many new ideas ranging from the American fast-food franchises to the recently arrived Australian Jenny Craig Weight Loss franchise. These are already established elsewhere and usually come here well funded and staffed by people who know what they are doing. Second, there are the big company divestments. More and more, large companies are subcontracting their activities and franchising is one method of doing this. Examples here are Holland and Barrett, Sperrings, Sketchley and the Co-operative Wholesale Society's Late Late Supershops. The Abbey National Building Society has plans to franchise its Cornerstone estate agency chain in the near future. There can be problems here since the people concerned are used to thinking 'big' and may have difficulty in seeing the world through the eyes of potential franchisees or local consumers. However, they usually have good financial stability and money buys time whilst these firms are learning the ropes.

Perhaps the most interesting and challenging source of new franchises is what might be called the entrepreneurial franchise where an individual is setting up from scratch. Sometimes these ventures fail and it might not be because the idea was not a good one – rather it can be simply because some key steps in the process were missed out.

Obviously, step one is to get the product or service tested, marketed, priced, and staffed with all the ancillary business services needed – lines of supply and delivery established, administrative and financial control procedures set up, etc. This is the *pilot stage* and key decisions have to be made here. For instance, does the business require sites with high street visibility with all the associated costs, or can it flourish in a secondary site? Who or what is the target market and what kind of marketing strategies and budgets are required to reach it? What kind of prices will the market bear and what is the competition?

Entrepreneurs are renowned for carrying a great deal of information around in their heads rather than putting it down on paper. In the case of a franchise, it is essential to build up comprehensive paperwork systems since this will form part of the business format to be subsequently offered to potential franchisees – the 'painting by numbers' analogy is one that budding franchisors might be well advised to keep in mind here.

Once the first outlet is up and running, the founder has a business with franchise potential. The next step is to develop that potential. Given that the basis of franchising rests on the ability of the franchisor to establish businesses for other people, he should next begin the process of replication. That is, he should set up a second outlet in a new geographical location. This, obviously, will involve recruiting and training new staff, dealing with a new landlord, expanding lines of supply, etc.

At this stage, it is important not only to develop staff who can deal with certain specific tasks themselves but who can train and assist others later. Also, they can have a role in developing training and reference manuals for later use by franchisees. Even at this early stage in the life of a budding franchise, advice can be sought from the British Franchise Association and certain categories of membership are open. Membership can be a useful source of contacts and connections within the industry and may also assist the franchise's credibility when it comes to recruiting franchisees.

Before franchising, a company should design a logo and settle on a name which is distinctive, original and, usually, one which describes the business they are in. Few franchise businesses have titles of the 'R. Jones & Son' type since marketing is a key aspect of a business format franchise and such a name does not enhance the public awareness of the business.

Finally, a scale of fees needs to be arrived at. This usually includes a once-and-for-all license fee for use of the trade name and then a royalty or service fee which is on-going and related directly to the level of sales turnover. Also, the cost of business premises, shop fittings, equipment, vehicles, working capital, etc. all need to be calculated in order that potential franchisees know the full financial requirements of buying into the franchise.

Managerial control

Commenting on the disadvantages of franchising from their viewpoint, franchisors concede that franchising inevitably means a certain loss of control compared to the conventionally managed outlet. It requires a more persuasive style of management since franchisors are well aware that attempts to control franchisees too closely are likely to be counter-productive. This, however, does not stop them from exerting very close control over particular franchisees from time to time, even to the point of terminating the contract if necessary, but this is relatively rare and, obviously, not desirable on a wide scale.

It might be thought that the franchisor–franchisee relationship is inherently fragile. The franchisor has an overriding interest in ensuring that business conducted in the name of his franchise conforms to certain laid-down practices and procedures. The franchisee, on the other hand, is running his or her own business which is not only self-funded but is a legally separate entity.

It is sometimes questioned whether the franchisee is, in reality, anything more than a manager firmly controlled by the franchisor and whether talk of self-employment represents little more than a pipedream. However, research indicates that most franchisees feel their needs for independence and autonomy to be largely met. These may be somewhat less than would be the case with a conventional small business but, in reality, franchisees exchange a degree of independence for security and know-how. Also, it should not be forgotten that conventional small business owners, in practice, tend to find their independence whittled away by various external constraints to a fraction of what it might be nominally.

Research (Stanworth, 1984) shows that, in order to understand the franchisor–franchisee relationship properly, it is necessary to go beyond an examination of the formal contract, which is the document binding the parties legally. Franchise contracts are frequently long and detailed and often appear to specify in detail how almost every facet of the operation should be conducted.

However, if we shift the analysis to the operational day-to-day level, an altogether different picture emerges. The contract, though central in the legal sense to franchisor–franchisee relations, does not occupy a similarly prominent position in day-to-day reality. In short, the franchisee's scope for independent decision making is much greater than an examination of the formal contract would imply.

In certain areas of operational day-to-day decision making, both parties are usually agreed that decision making is largely at the discretion of the franchisee. This is true when considering, for instance, hours of operation, employment of staff, wage levels and bookkeeping procedures. In other areas, such as product/service mix and pricing levels, the responsibility rests largely with the franchisor.

There are other areas, however, where both parties may claim responsibility, such as local advertising and standards of customer service. But these differences seem to result not so much from confusion or disagreement as from genuine differences in views. For instance, franchisors usually claim that customer service standards are fully prescribed in the contract and monitored by field supervisors, the use of 'dummy' customers and/or invitations on promotional literature or invoices to contact the franchisor direct.

Franchisees, on the other hand, often tend to feel that these arms-length quality control methods are only likely to identify customer dissatisfaction when it has reached crisis proportions. For maintaining good customer relations day-to-day, franchisees usually feel they are the prime initiators.

On local advertising, the franchisor may feel he has responsibility since he may give guidance on content and have final powers of veto over what is published. Franchisees, on the other hand, usually pay for the advertisements, decide the media and, indeed, often decide on the sheer volume of local advertising.

Perhaps a very good indicator of the nature of the relationship between franchisor and franchisee is the frequency and nature of contact between them. Research (Stanworth, 1984) shows that around one-third of franchisees report contact with the franchisor as occurring at least once a week. The remainder report contact occurring about once a month.

But most of these contacts are initiated by franchisees treating their franchisors as a resource for solving operational problems. Franchisors typically visit franchisees every 1–2 months though there are wide variations. New franchisees expect to be visited much more frequently to help them get fully established, whilst some established franchisees claim to be very rarely visited.

Only 5 per cent of franchisees in the above research felt themselves to be 'over-supervised', whilst 12 per cent would have liked more supervision. The great majority – around 80 per cent – felt the existing level of supervision to be about right.

Methods of on-going franchisor–franchisee communication include joint consultative committees, annual conferences, newsletters, bulletins, competitions and special award schemes. Joint consultative committees, as in other sectors of the economy, tend to serve as tension-management devices. Franchisees feel that they (or their representatives) have the ear of the franchisor whilst the franchisor has the ear of franchise opinion-leaders.

At times, such a platform for consultations can fail to satisfy franchisees who may then form an independent franchisee association. This can have something of a trade union character about it. The formation of such associations often coincides with the franchisor seeking to impose far-reaching changes upon franchisees.

Franchising, as a business format, offers a viable alternative to conventionally operated businesses in many increasingly important areas of economic activity. At the same time, it produces its own distinct patterns of personal relations calling for particular skills on the part of the franchisor.

Franchise funding

Almost without doubt, the biggest single boost to the prospects for franchising in Britain has come from the recognition and support extended by the clearing banks following the lead of National Westminster in 1981 (Stanworth and Stern, 1988). Interestingly too, the banks have recognised franchising very much as an avenue into small business rather than viewing it as a large business activity. In fact, the NatWest bank, in taking a lead here, was quite explicit in its early promotional literature, going into print with a statement such as:

> 'The bank has recognised the part that franchising can play in the creation of new small businesses and has appointed . . . Franchise Managers with specific responsibility to assist the development of new businesses through franchising'
> (*NatWest Franchising Services pamphlet, 1981*)

Before agreeing either to fund a franchisor or establish a franchisee finance scheme, each franchise is subject to a thorough evaluation. This includes an examination of the pilot operation, financial stability, management structure, marketing ability, product/service quality and brand awareness of the franchisor. It is also examined from the viewpoint of the kind of information provided to, and the selection of, prospective franchisees as well as the nature and quality of services provided for franchisees.

Of particular interest to the banks is the quality of the franchisor's field support services since the franchisee's ability to meet his obligations to the bank can be highly dependent on his ability to deal with problems before they become serious. The franchise agreement is scrutinised with attention focusing on the rights and obligations of both parties, any onerous clauses which could affect the bank, bases for contract termination or non-renewal, transferability and the conditions attached to sale.

The bank is particularly concerned that the franchisor should have the ability to maintain the franchise chain as a whole. It is to this end that the prospective franchisee who wishes to be funded by one of these schemes is required to sign a mandate which allows the bank to inform his franchisor should he get into difficulties. Additionally, the franchisor is expected to consult with the bank should he suspect that the franchisee is encountering difficulties, e.g., failing to make service fee payments, and certainly before termination.

One of the advantages of this form of funding over more traditional forms is its integrated nature. This may include a higher level of loan funding than the bank would normally consider and at a lower rate of interest. Whilst a conventional small businessman could usually expect to receive bank support on no more than a 1 : 1 own funds/loan finance basis, a franchisee using a bank package can expect this ratio to improve to 2 : 1. Up to two-thirds of the total start-up capital, including working capital, may be provided.

As far as security for two-thirds finance is concerned, the bank usually expect at least 60 per cent of the facility to be secured more often than not by personal assets with the balance unsecured. In a situation where there is only, say, 20 per cent security available, the bank can utilise the Government backed Loan Guarantee Scheme which is designed to assist small businesses seen as worth supporting but deficient in security even after the applicant has pledged his/her personal assets.

The bank takes no security from the franchisor when assisting a franchisee since the two are seen as separate business entities. The reason for the higher than conventional gearing ratios and lower interest charges is that, whilst the prospective franchisee may have no previous business experience or record himself, the franchisor does. Loans may be on fixed or variable interest rates, and can include a capital repayment holiday.

On the information and evidence available so far regarding relationships between the clearing banks and the franchising industry, it would appear possible to conclude two points. First, that many franchisees are in an advantageous position with regard to access to initial funding because they have taken a franchise as compared to a totally independent business. The main advantage here lies in the transference of the record of previous franchisees to their business. The franchisor is therefore able not only to provide introductions to prospective sources of funding but, especially if well established, to have funds made available at lower cost.

Second, it appears clear that the banks have recognised the reputable business format franchise as a relatively secure outlet for a proportion of their small business advances. The development of franchisee finance schemes provides an important marketing tool with which to attract an increased share of franchise borrowing, while facilitating increased administrative efficiency at branch level as a result of centralised vetting and information dissemination services.

It appears then that the proportion of franchisees obtaining a significant slice of their start up funds from the banks will increase significantly over time. With this may also come some subtle changes in the franchise relationship as both franchisors and franchisees become more accountable to a third party – the banks.

The record of the clearing banks indicates that franchise lending, subject to the checks and forms of scrutiny outlined above, represents a relatively safe form of bank investment compared to conventional small business start-ups. The precise level of failure amongst franchise outlets is not easy to estimate and has been the subject of much previous discussion (Stanworth, 1985 and 1986/7). However, a picture is gradually emerging. The overall failure rate appears at least lower than for small businesses generally (particularly considering the sectors in which they operate).

Power estimated in 1986 that, in the space of a year, up to 10 per cent of franchise outlets either cease operation altogether or change hands – the latter is often seen as a form of disguised failure (Ozanne and Hunt, 1971). However, it appears that most failures occur in what Power has termed the 'less predictable new arrivals in the industry'. Thus there appears to be a continuum of risk probabilities within the industry ranging from low amongst what Power terms the franchising 'establishment' to a somewhat higher level around the periphery of the industry.

Future trends

The current rapid rate of growth of franchising in Britain (Power, 1986, 1987) and, indeed internationally, appears set to continue. A number of factors appear to be at play here. First is the general worldwide decline of traditional manufacturing industry and its replacement by service sector activities. Franchising is especially well suited to service and people-intensive economic activities, particularly where these require a large number of geographically dispersed outlets serving local markets.

A further factor here is the growth in popularity of self-employment. Most governments in the Western world are looking towards self-employment and small business as an important source of future jobs and, in Britain, over the last decade, the proportion of the labour force in the self-employed sector has increased from around 7 per cent to around 12 per cent (Meager, 1987). As franchising becomes increasingly well known and understood, the chances are that it will appeal to a growing number of people. Alongside this trend, we may expect to see an increase in the number of franchise opportunities. This process will be assisted, not least, by large companies following the current trend towards divestment from centralised control of an increasing proportion of their business activities.

Substantial developments in the field of franchising between now and the end of this century are also likely in the areas of business education and commercial legislation. In both areas, there is also likely to be considerable emphasis on harmonisation across regional and national borders.

On the first point – training – it has to be said that, despite the growth of franchising and despite the rapid increase in the number of business schools and management centres running undergraduate and graduate courses on small business and entrepreneurship, the attention paid to franchising as a viable business option has generally been overlooked and is seldom mentioned. It is likely that the future will witness the development of a growing liaison between the worlds of franchising and management education with a view to integrating the topic of franchising fully into teaching programmes in the universities and polytechnics of Britain and their counterparts abroad. Given the flexibility of the franchise concept for movement across national boundaries, it is important that this initiative be based on an international perspective.

Last but not least, we come to the legislative aspect of franchising and here current trends are hopeful. On a number of occasions recently, in locations as far as America, Australia and the EEC, the issue of the legal framework surrounding franchise operations has come into question. What has tended to happen here is that the early fears of franchisors – that over-zealous legislators, with only an imperfect understanding of franchising, would force through inappropriate legislation – have not been realised.

In the US, legislation has tended to be patchy and sometimes erratic, varying on a State-by-State basis. In Australia, representations made to Government by franchisors appear to be bearing fruit and likewise in Europe. For instance, the EEC has recently published the first draft of a block exemption regulation designed to allow franchising exemption from competition laws framed for different kinds of business but which have, on occasions, threatened to encompass franchises as a result of separate legal entities within a given franchise operation co-operating (or, appearing to act in restraint of trade). The most recent EEC initiative will allow franchisors to grant franchisees territorial immunity which appears quite logical given the original intentions of the relevant legislation – the Restrictive Trade Practices Act (Stanworth, 1984: 120–121). It is interesting that the International Institute for the Unification of Private Law, representing 51 member states from five continents, is currently addressing itself to the topic of franchising and its legal framework.

References

Meager, N. (1987) 'Self-employment: serious trend or statistical hiccup?, *Manpower Policy and Practice*, Summer, pp. 40–41.

Ozanne, U. B. and Hunt, S. D. (1971) *The Economic Effects of Franchising*, Washington D.C., US Government Printing Office.

Power, M. C. (1986) *Franchising – The Industry and the Market: Changes in Scale, Structure and Character 1984–66*, (Follow-up study, 1987.)

Stanworth, J. (1984) *A Study of Power Relationships and their Consequences in Franchise Organisations*, SSRC Report.

Stanworth, J. (1985) 'Predictions', *Franchise World*, April–July, p. 16.

Stanworth, J. (1986/7) *International Small Business Journal*, Winter, Vol. 5, No. 2, pp. 68–70.

Stanworth, J. and Stern, P. (1988) The Development in Franchising in Britain over the Last Decade with Particular Reference to the Role of the Clearing Bank, *National Westminster Bank Review*, May 1988.

US Department of Commerce (1986) *Franchising in the Economy 1984–86*.

Vaughn, C. L. (1979) *Franchising*, Lexington Books, 2nd Edition.

Part III

Management issues in service industries

Whatever the strategy and structure of the service organisation, it is almost certainly the case that there will be managers with responsibility for four main functions – operations, finance, marketing and personnel. Since this book is concerned with the issue of management, in Part III we consider how these four different types of manager should and do behave. In particular, the authors of these four chapters focus on how these managers in service firms may each have different issues to face and different responses to their counterparts in manufacturing industry.

For Robert Johnston, in Chapter 13, the major factor affecting service operations is the customer. Both managers and employees of service firms come into direct contact with the consumer in order to deliver the service. This introduces the strong likelihood of inherent fluctuations in demand and problems of matching individual customer needs with the ability to deliver the service. Johnston discusses how operations managers respond to these two major factors.

In view of the relatively high level of contact between customers and employees, human resource management in service organisations also has some specific characteristics. These are discussed by Paul Willman in Chapter 14. He identifies five alternative ways of managing this point of contact and focusses on task complexity and customer uncertainty as key factors in affecting human resource management in this context.

Brian Adams and Paul Colebourne, in Chapter 15, examine the role of financial management in service organisations. They highlight another common theme that runs through many of the contributions to this book, that of the appropriate 'service culture'. In their review they consider strategy, quality, and human resource implications.

Finally, in Chapter 16, Francis Buttle evaluates the nature of marketing in service industries. He draws attention to four key characteristics of services that have been implicit in much of the discussion in other chapters, namely intangibility, simultaneity, heterogeneity, and perishability. He goes on to identify the marketing manager's response to each of these problems.

Much of the debate over whether services are different from manufacturing has been fought over the battleground covered by these four chapters. Part III reviews this debate and, it is to be hoped, provides additional insights as to the relevance or otherwise of thinking in these terms.

13 Operations management issues

ROBERT JOHNSTON

Introduction

The service sector is a diverse sector. Within this sector there are three main types of industries. First, there are those industries concerned with the meeting of personal needs, for example, tourism and leisure, hotel and catering, retail and personal service activities. Second there are industries that are concerned with providing the technical components of the country's service infrastructure, such as financial services, transportation, communications and business services in order to meet industrial needs. Third, there are industries that provide the social components, such as health, education, welfare and public administration to meet broader social needs (Johnston, 1988). Despite this diversity, service sector operations have similar elements and similar management issues and tasks.

This chapter identifies some of the issues involved in managing service operations. It is divided into four parts. The first section describes the service operation. The second and third sections consider the two main tasks of the operations manager, the provision of customer service and managing operational resources. The final section considers the link between these two and the challenge currently facing service operations managers.

The service operation

The service operation is the part of the organisation that is concerned with creating and delivering the services and goods to the customer. In many personal and social services it involves dealing directly with the customer, as in leisure and health services. In other organisations, the operation may be concerned with the provision of facilities for the customer, as in tele-communications and travel, or the provision of goods for the customer, as in retail and distribution activities.

The inputs into the operation include human resources, buildings, equipment and material, and in many service operations the customer is also an input into the operation. There are two outputs from the service operation, goods and services. The goods are the tangible physical objects or products used within the service operation or removed from it by the customer (Sasser, 1982). A service may be defined as 'a change in condition of a person, or of a good belonging to some economic unit, which is brought about as the result of an activity of some other economic unit' (Riddle, 1986). Services are the processes of bringing about change in the operation's customers or in the goods they possess. Figure 13.1 is a simple representation of a service operation.

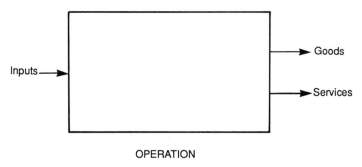

OPERATION

Figure 13.1　The service operation

Back office and front office

Within most service operations there are two distinct types of operations, namely back office and front office operations. The back office is the part of the service operation which the customer does not usually see, nor has access to. This is often referred to as the 'manufacturing' part of the service operation, for example the kitchen in a restaurant. The front office is the part of the operation that provides the service to the customer, usually involving some contact with the customer. This contact may be personal and direct, for example face to face with a bank clerk, or personal but indirect, for example discussing an overdraft with the bank manager over a telephone, or non-personal and involve customers interacting with equipment, a cash machine for example. The provision of service is usually a 'real time' activity, involving contact and interaction with customers (Chase, 1978). As a result, the operation is faced with a degree of uncertainty and unpredictability that has to be dealt with, in many cases, immediately.

The customer process

The customer process is the front office operation that delivers the service package (defined later) to the customer and interacts with the customer. The customer process will be different for each operation but there are usually some common elements. These are the point of entry, the response time, the point of impact, the delivery, and the point of departure (Johnston, 1987).

The point of entry is the place where the customer first makes contact with the service operation. Examples of points of entry are an entrance door or the start of a telephone call. Having entered the operation, the customer usually has to wait for someone to respond to his/her presence. This time is the response time and is usually spent in a queue. Queues may be of several forms; a physical visible line of people waiting for service, an invisible queue of incoming telephone calls, or a remote queue of customers in several locations waiting for a service to arrive. The point of impact is the moment when a service contact worker first acknowledges and responds to the customer. The point of impact is the start of the delivery of the service. The delivery is the activity during which the services and goods are provided and may involve many further points of personal contact. On completion of the service delivery, the customer leaves the service system. This is the point of departure.

Most service operations comprise several customer processes that may be in series or in parallel with each other. The size and number of processes and the interrelationships between them are indications of the scale and complexity of the operations management task.

The service package

The service package is the complex bundle that the customer purchases from the organisation (Voss, 1985). It comprises the services, the goods, and the environment in which the service takes place (Sasser, 1982). The environment includes the service location, its physical appearance, and the environmental conditions experienced by the customer during the service. In travelling by train for example, the package does not only include being transferred from A to B, but also the comfort of the seats, the food, the attitude of staff and the temperature and crowdedness of the train. This makes for a complexity in managing the operation as there is some difficulty in knowing what each customer is buying. Indeed, several customers using the same service may have different expectations and requirements. On a train journey, there may be customers who are on business and require a quiet and comfortable journey with space to work, there may be others who are on holiday and wish to enjoy and amuse themselves.

Field service operations

Many service operations create and provide the environment in which the services and goods are delivered. In these cases the customer has usually to travel to the operation, for example, banks, airports and restaurants. In the case of field service operations however, the services and goods are delivered at the customer's location and the environment may be beyond the control of the operations manager. Examples of field services are gas or electricity repairs, financial auditing and consultancy activities.

Goods and services

Most organisations, whether manufacturing or service, provide a combination of goods and services. Some organisations are more goods-orientated. The activities of a fish and chip shop are mainly concerned with cooking fish, chips and peas, for example. Interaction with the customer and treatment of the customer is limited. However, in the case of a restaurant, although the goods may be identical to those in the chip shop, though under the guise of cod meunière, french fries and petits pois, the customer requires, and is paying for, a substantial element of service. The customer expects a table and the appropriate utensils to be provided, to be greeted, assisted and cosseted through the meal.

Each service operation usually provides several services, and several types of goods. These can be classified as the core service, the main service that is provided; the supporting goods and services that enhance the core service but are peripheral to it; and facilitating goods and services that assist the organisation in the creation and delivery of the core service and the supporting goods and services (Sasser, 1982; Gronroos, 1987).

The core service is the fundamental service of the organisation, without which the remaining supporting and facilitating services would have little use. For example, the core service in an hotel is the provision of food, accommodation and sanitation. If this were not provided, however polite the staff, convenient the location or extensive the menu, the hotel could not function.

Supporting goods and services are the services and goods that enhance or complement the core service. Such goods and services might include, in the case of an hotel, the provision of a car rental service, a bus tour service, and the sale of maps, magazines or postcards. Over the last few years there has been a proliferation of the supporting goods and services in many service industries, as it has been felt that they enhance the perceived quality of the core service. Currently we are seeing a move away from this traditional proliferation to a more focussed approach that removes some, and in some instances all, of the non-core services.

Facilitating goods and services facilitate the organisation's provision of the core and supporting goods and services to the customer. In the case of the hotel, the restaurant facilitates the production and consumption of food, the computer facilitates the provision of bills and reservation services, and hotel cleaning services facilitate the provision of clean and tidy rooms.

Who is the customer

One important issue for service operations management is understanding who is the customer. In many service operations, for example, banks and restaurants, it is usually clear who the customer is. This is not always the case. Take, for example, an International Airport. The customers are not only the fare-paying passengers but are also the airlines for whom the airport assembles and prepares customers. The airport provides many services for the airlines, for example, cleaning and catering services, and landing and take-off facilities. Other airport customers include the 'meeters and greeters' for whom facilities have to be provided and also the 'spotters' for whom many airports also provide services. These are all examples of 'external' customers, where the customers are external to the organisation. There are also 'internal' customers who are a part of the same organisation, though possibly a different operation. For example, the accountancy department of an organisation, or the marketing department, provide services to the other parts of the organisation. In these cases the customers are people within the same organisation. Other examples include management services, computing services, distribution services, and research and development.

A second level of categorisation of customers, whether internal or external, is in terms of their involvement with the operation. There are three types of involvement; there are customers who pay for the service, customers who benefit from the service and customers who participate in the service. In the case of a restaurant for example, the person who pays, benefits and participates is usually the same person, and if anything goes wrong the customer can take steps to deal with it at the time.

In some cases the payer, beneficiary and participant are different individuals, or sections of society, and there may be conflicts between them that make the task of managing the operation particularly difficult. Take, for example, the prison service. The prisoners are the participants, the

payers are the taxpayers and society as a whole benefits from the removal
of the offender from society and maybe eventually from his/her reform.
In this example, there may be conflicts between the objectives of the
participating customers who may not wish to be there and the beneficiary,
society, who requires the offender to be there, thus making safety and
security a major task. This is further complicated by the conflicts between
the taxpayers and participants, one wanting to limit the amount spent on
the service but participants who have to endure cramped and primitive
conditions. A third conflict is between the taxpayers and society, the latter
wanting the offenders off the street for as long as it might take to reform
them, the former not wanting to pay for long sentences. This creates
difficult resource acquisition and allocation problems for the prison service
to add to the problem of managing inmates.

The role of operational staff

The service operations staff may be customer contact staff or back office,
non-contact staff or have a combination of roles. The nature of their role
in the front office will largely be determined by the degree and nature of
their contact with customers. Their impact upon the quality of the service
can be considerable as they have to respond to and deal with the customers
inside the system.

Operations management tasks

The operations manager is responsible for the design, planning and control
of the operation. He/she may be involved in the creation of the operating
system; the specification of the type of process, the degree and nature of
customer interaction, the goods and services to be provided and the type
of staff and environment required. Once the operation is established the
manager is concerned with the planning and control of the operation to
ensure that it is serving the market for which it has been created. This may
require a number of alterations to the design features as the market changes
or new opportunities are identified. Driving the decisions that the operations manager makes are the two basic objectives of operations
management, firstly to provide good customer service and secondly to
create and maintain an efficient and productive operation by the planning
and control of operational resources (Wild, 1977). The following sections
outline these two objectives and some of the issues for management in
achieving them. A final section considers the link between the two and the
need for service operations to develop a customer perspective.

Customer service

Good customer service results from providing the right service package; goods, services and environment, in order to fulfil a customer's needs and expectations. This will be the result of good process and product design, quality control of goods and services, supported by market research into the needs of the market, and appropriate organisational systems, policies and philosophies, for example, payment systems, recruitment policies, and management culture.

Many service industries seem to have difficulty in providing good customer service, indeed many service industries, particularly in the personal service sector, seem to be run with the object of causing the least inconvenience to their staff as possible rather than providing good service for customers. Most people can recount many instances of inadequate service, poor goods or an inappropriate environment. However, examples of excellent customer service seem to be few and far between. In the past, customer service has often been seen by some organisations as more of a nuisance than a requirement. However, many organisations are becoming concerned about their levels of customer service as it becomes increasingly apparent that adequate customer service is no longer enough to retain and attract customers in times of increasing customer awareness and increasing competition.

The issues for the operations manager are to design and control the quality of the total service package; the quality of the services, goods and the environment in which the service takes place in order to provide good customer service. Quality can be defined as the features and characteristics of a product or service that bear on its ability to satisfy a customer's need. The following parts of this section identify some of the quality issues in providing the service package. The final part of this section describes a strategy for implementing service quality.

Service quality

Service quality is the level of service that is delivered by the operation (Sasser, 1982). This is a vital component of customer service and one of the most difficult to design and control. The design of service quality requires that all the attributes of a service can be identified and service levels specified. Service quality control assumes that all the attributes are measurable and can be measured against specified targets. From a customer perspective, the measure of service quality is usually referred to as customer satisfaction. This section considers what is meant by customer satisfaction, and the issues of service quality specification and measurement.

Customer satisfaction

Customer satisfaction is the degree of fit between customer's expectations of the quality of the services to be provided and the actual quality of the service provided as perceived by the customer (Johnston, 1987; Gronroos, 1984). In most cases customer satisfaction will not be based on a single factor. Customer satisfaction will be the result of the combination of several factors that customers deem to be appropriate in the creation of satisfaction, though some factors may be more important than others.

Service quality specification

The greatest difficulty in the provision of customer satisfaction is that the factors that create satisfaction will vary from customer to customer, and the levels of service associated with each factor expected by each customer may also be different. Each customer's specification of service quality and levels of quality will be based upon that customer's expectations of the service to be provided. Such expectations may be created by market image, or information from other customers, friends and the media, some of which may be outside the control of the organisation. Furthermore, such expectations may not always be specified by the customer because they may not be consciously known. The issue for service quality design is to be aware of the determinants of customer satisfaction and the range of customer expectations for each factor for the market segment being served.

Service quality measurement

Many organisations tend not to measure the service aspects of quality because they are difficult to measure, and assume that non-service measures are adequate surrogates (Johnston and Morris, 1985). Often financial measures are used, but these tend to measure the symptoms rather than the causes. For some organisations, the main measure of service quality is the number of complaints. This is an inadequate measure as it only measures some of the dissatisfaction. For example, one general manager of a large hotel in Boston claimed that 96 per cent of his customers were satisfied. On questioning, this actually meant that 4 per cent of his customers complained. In his 1200 bedroom hotel with 800 guests per night, a 4 per cent complaint rate leads to about 1000 complaints per month. (He writes letters to all complainants. Assuming each letter takes 2 minutes, he must spend nearly a week every month just answering complaint letters.) No respectable manufacturing company would hand over responsibility for quality measurement to its customers alone.

The issue for service operations management is to be able to deliver the levels of service determined by the service specification and have procedures to deal with customers whose expectations either fall outside the specified service levels and/or who believe that they have received poor service. The final part of this section provides a description of a service quality strategy that deals with some of these issues.

Product quality

The operations manager is concerned with the design and control of the organisation's supporting and facilitating goods that are either used by the customer in the operation or removed from the operation. Product design issues include the specification of materials and suppliers, and the process of creating the products. Product quality control requires the identification of the variables and attributes of the products, the setting of targets, the measurement of the variables and attributes against those targets and the provision of corrective action if necessary (Voss, 1985). One issue of product quality in a service context that receives little attention is the presentation of the goods to the customer. This is of little importance in some operations; a chip shop simple style of wrapping is appropriate for its market and products, but would not be appropriate in the restaurant. To assist in the correct presentation of goods many restaurant chains, for example, besides specifying the nature of the product provide pictures of the finished dish indicating also how it is to be presented. Manuals are also used to specify not only with what, but how hotel bedrooms are to be cleaned and how the beds are to be made to ensure that consistent and acceptable standards are always applied. Inspection procedures may also be in place to ensure that the standards of presentation are met. These may be formal systems in the case of the hotel bedrooms where the housekeeper will inspect all or a proportion of the rooms before they are occupied. In the case of the presentation of the food, the restaurant manager may keep a watching brief over this and other aspects of product quality.

Environmental quality

The environment where the services and goods are delivered is important as it may have an impact upon the customer's perceived quality of the service package. The environment includes the location, its ease of access or physical appearance and the environmental conditions experienced by the customer in the process; the amount of heat, light and humidity for example, or the lack or abundance of other participants in the service operation. The operations manager has to identify the characteristics of the environment that are appropriate to and consistent with the other elements of the service package and, customer expectations. A second task is to ensure that all of these features are provided and maintained to create the complete service package.

Service quality strategy

A service quality strategy is a response to the issues of designing and controlling service quality. It is a set of plans and policies to provide a high level of customer satisfaction. It requires top management commitment, a clear understanding of the market, the implementation of control systems, backed up by staff development.

Top management commitment

The first requirement in the design and implementation of a successful customer service strategy is commitment by top management. They must not only provide 'support' but have corporate objectives that identify the need to provide and measure customer service.

Top management need to be exposed to, and aware of, the problems faced by the operation in providing good customer service, as it is they who are able to remove many of the obstacles. Some organisations require their senior managers to work in the operation for short periods. Hertz executives, for example, have to serve behind the counter for two weeks every year. George Davis, formerly chief executive of Next, reputedly periodically served on the shop floor.

Part of the role of top management is to create a culture that supports the improvement of customer service, whereby it is seen to be good practice to report problems or make suggestions.

Top management must also ensure that control systems, reward systems etc, support the provision of customer service and should seek out the obstacles that may prevent good service.

Understand the market

In order to be able to identify what is meant by customer service, it is necessary to identify and understand the market segment that is being catered for and the range of expectations of customers in that segment. It is also important to understand how those expectations are created before entry to the delivery system. This will facilitate the specification of service quality levels.

Design the operation

To provide the required level of service quality, operations management must design the operation so that it can provide the service within the required levels. It is important to understand how customer expectations and perceptions are managed during and after the provision of the service.

Create control systems

It is necessary to ensure that the required levels of quality are provided and maintained, so effective control systems are required. To do this it is necessary to define:

• What is to be measured
• What are the targets
• How is it to be measured and by whom

What is to be measured

The measurement of service quality must be from a customer perspective as it is they who are the market, the receivers of the service and the people with the expectations that the service is provided to fulfil. Complaints are inadequate, and a single measure is also inadequate unless it is used to establish the degree of conformance to overall expectations and follow up activities used to pinpoint the problem. A single measure would ask the questions; did the service meet your expectations, or was it worse or better than expected? A more comprehensive set of measures would be based on an analysis of the process in terms of the critical points and activities, identified in the first section of the chapter. This would assist in the identification of the main features in the process that create customer satisfaction. It is then necessary to identify what measures can be used at each to ensure that quality meets expectations. As service is often a difficult concept to define, and therefore measure, surrogate measures or indicators of performance may have to be used.

Targets

For every measure or indicator that is used, targets for performance have to be set. The targets need to be researched to ensure that they are within minimum and maximum levels of satisfaction for the market segment that is being serviced. One of the targets used by British Rail is the punctuality of trains. This they have found to be four times more important in the provision of customer satisfaction than any other measure. Following a study by Cranfield Institute of Technology of acceptable levels of service,

BR set itself the target of 90 per cent of all trains to arrive within 10 minutes of arrival time at destination. This it measures closely and follows up all instances of delays of greater than 10 minutes and attempts to deal with the causes.

In a competitive environment the targets that are set, and achieved, can then be measured against competitors and used as bench marks to indicate competitive advantages.

How and by whom

The task of measurement is traditionally left to operations managers to implement internal systems to control service performance. Some organisations have removed the role to some extent from the operation and use either senior managers or customers to provide systematic monitoring of the operation. For example some organisations use senior managers as 'mystery shoppers' who act as customers and appraise the goods and services using prepared forms. Other organisations convene 'focus groups', groups of senior managers and customers, to periodically review and discuss the operations performance. A third option used by many service operations is the use of periodic customer surveys to monitor certain service levels over a period of time. Such surveys not only provide valuable reflections on the performance of the operation but also provide valuable insights into customer expectations.

Staff development

The role of the contact staff is critical in the provision of customer service. Therefore, there is a need to communicate the needs for customer service and service standards to the operational staff and to develop procedures to deal with events where targets are not achieved or problems arise with customers. Training is also important, not only in terms of providing product and system knowledge but also in dealing with customers.

At all the points of impact and during the delivery system itself it is important for staff to understand the potential function of their activities, not only to provide service and to treat the customer as a guest and not an intruder, but also that each point of contact is an opportunity to sell. For example, one large multi-site, high-contact service operation when asked how many salespeople it employed replied 'four', ignoring the fact that it employed nearly 2000 contact staff who provided the goods and services to its customers.

Human resource management in service firms is critical to their success, as customer relations tend to mirror employee relations. Willard Marriott has been attributed with saying 'you can't make happy guests with unhappy staff'. The careful selection, training and motivation of staff, particularly contact staff, is an essential part not only of providing customer satisfaction but also achieving good resource utilisation. The next chapter deals in more detail with the human resource management issues.

Managing resources

The resources that the operations manager is responsible for managing include the facilities (the plant, equipment and machinery), the materials (input materials, supporting and facilitating goods) and the people (the staff and the customers). This section begins by considering the management task of co-ordinating the use of all of those resources to satisfy demand, capacity planning, then considers the management of one of the operational resources that is usually given little attention, the customer.

Capacity planning

'The objective of capacity planning is to match the level of operations with the level of demand so as to find the best balance between cost and service levels' (Voss, 1985). This involves the operations manager in acquiring, disposing of, and/or making the best use of resources to accommodate actual and forecasted changes in demand. This is a major issue in service operations as the service may be difficult to store (Sasser, 1982). Once an aeroplane takes off, for example, an unused seat cannot be stored for use later but is capacity that has been lost. A further issue is that many services require the participation of the customer. This creates some uncertainty about the arrival of customers and the processing time that may be required. There is, however, the opportunity to use the customer as a resource to increase the capacity of the operation. This issue is dealt with in more detail later.

Strategies for managing capacity

Capacity planning is usually considered in three time horizons, long, medium and short term, and the actual lengths of these horizons will vary from industry to industry. Long-term capacity planning is concerned primarily with investment decisions based on corporate objectives and corporate strategy and the nature of the service package. In the medium and short term, capacity planning is constrained by the long-term decisions and is concerned with meeting the demands of customers and potential (forecasted) demand by the allocation and control of resources to try and maximise productivity whilst providing good customer service.

In the long term, investment decisions need to be taken to ensure that investments in new locations, technologies or new businesses are consistent with or appropriate to the capabilities of the operation. Also that any change in the service package is appropriate for an identified market segment.

There are two basic strategies that may be employed, independently or in combination, in the medium and short term to manage capacity. One strategy is to vary capacity to follow changes in demand, sometimes referred to as a chase demand strategy. This may be achieved by changing the numbers of people employed or their hours of work, improving manpower efficiency, the improved use of the customer, a change in the layout of the operation to increase productivity or by transferring resources from one part of the organisation to another.

A second strategy is to influence the demand for the service whilst limiting changes to the operation's capacity. This may be achieved by the use of price or promotion mechanisms to stimulate or reduce overall demand, or demand for the service at certain times of day. Supporting or complementary services may be provided either to take pressure off the core service or to attract more customers to it. The use of reservation/ appointment systems or queues may allow a more even use of capacity over a period of time.

Each strategy has different costs and service level trade-offs that need to be understood and assessed before implementation. For example, the use of changing hours of work creates a considerable scheduling problem for operations managers though providing increased flexibility in manning. The use of appointment systems may effectively control demand to fit with capacity and indeed move demand from periods of high demand to low demand, but may create utilisation problems if customers do not keep their appointments.

Managing the customer

In a service operation the customer is not another 'resource' like a material resource that has to be processed through the operation, though this is frequently a feeling of customers in some service organisations. The customer is the individual who is participating in the service, and possibly paying for it and benefiting from it. The consumer is the customer for whom the organisation exists. In some operations the customer undertakes a passive role whose well defined needs and expectations have to be met by the system. In these cases, the main task is the correct provision of the service package. More often, the customer takes a more active role in the service operation, either participating in its provision, for example, self-service, or assisting in the process of diagnosing needs, for example in consulting or health services activities, or in providing information about the service, for example, calling the telephone fault reporting service. To ensure that the customer adequately fulfils his/her role in the operation, consideration has to be given to the management of the customer. In order to understand the issues involved in the selection, motivation and control of the customer, it is necessary to identify the roles that a customer may take in a service operation. This section will examine three roles of the customer; the provision of services, the creation of atmosphere and the provision of information.

Provision of services

It has long been recognised that the customer, as a part of the internal labour force, provides some of the services for him/herself. Lovelock and Young (1979) state that the customer is a source of capacity to the operation at the point it is required, at the time it is required. By involving the customer actively in the production of the service the organisation can effectively remove some of the labour tasks from the service operation staff. There are many examples of customer provision of service (self-service) including direct dialling on the telephone, self-service supermarkets, making your own tea in a hotel, and self-service in a restaurant.

The customer may also provide some services to the organisation's other customers. In an MBA class, for example, student interaction during the class and participation in group work are an important part of the learning process of every student. In a golf club, the customers may provide services to other members often in a rota, like bar services, or provide a pool of available partners for a game.

Customers may also undertake activities that are of no direct benefit to themselves or to other customers but are seen to be tasks undertaken for the general good of the organisation, for example returning supermarket trollies to the compound or returning reference books to the correct place on library shelves.

Creation of environment

The customers may also be involved indirectly in the provision of service through the creation of the atmosphere in the service system. Part of the 'service' provided by a restaurant, for example, is the gentle buzz of conversation and the existence of other, seated and contented guests. Their activities contribute to the restaurant's ambience. If the customers were acting in a rowdy fashion, it would alter the service package. As such, the customer not only provides the environment, the 'climate for emotional involvement' (Normann, 1984), but also demonstrates the rules and codes of behaviour for the other entrants to the system. The implicit customer role becomes that of being a trainer for the other customers.

Provision of information

As a source of internal labour, the customer may also be directly involved in the organisation's quality control systems. Not just by providing positive or negative feedback as one might expect of a customer, but by being directly involved in the improvement of the service delivery by active and positive participation. Some organisations involve the customer not only in an assessment of how good or bad the service was but in the identification of the criteria for assessment. Other organisations use 'focus' groups and invite customers, together with employees and managers, to discuss the quality aspects of the service and how it could be improved.

The criteria discussed above may also include other performance evaluations, like speed of delivery. The customer may also be involved in the original specification of performance criteria. This might be the case in a piece of consultancy or the development of in-company training courses.

Having identified the roles and duties that are required of the customer, the operations tasks become those of selecting, training and motivating their customers to undertake them.

Quality versus resource utilisation

Traditionally the effective and productive use of resources and the provision of customer service have been seen as a management trade-off. If you improve one you may well compromise the other. This trade-off is now no longer acceptable as productivity and quality are both seen to be necessary in the new competitive service environment. Customers now require both productive and efficient operations, *and* good customer service. The need to provide value for money is evident. This is particularly visible in the public sector where the divisions between payer, beneficiary and participant are being broken down by the creation of internal markets. In local government, health and, more recently, in education, funding is being allocated on the basis of the provision of good customer service and the efficient use of resources. The same issues are being recognised by the 'soon-to-be privatised' public utilities, who are recognising the need to become efficient to attract funds and the need to provide customer service to maintain customers. The major challenge for many service industries is to improve productivity *and* improve customer service. The main route to success in this area is for service firms to adopt a customer perspective not only to understand how the requirements of the customer can be met to provide good customer service but also to make the best use of the customer in the service operation. This perspective is important because the customer process is the part of the operation that is potentially the least efficient (Chase, 1978) and the part that directly provides customer service. By understanding the management issues in this area, from a customer perspective, the issues of quality and productivity can be tackled. This is a view being taken by many successful service companies, for example American Express claims that 'the most successful service businesses are customer driven' (Simonds, 1985).

Summary

This chapter has taken a predominantly customer perspective of the management of service operations. This is because service industries are primarily involved in dealing directly with, and in bringing about change in, the customer. Many of the management issues in service operations stem from the inherent uncertainty and variation of the needs and expectations of the customers, and the need, very often, to provide an immediate response to them. This is compounded by the difficulties of knowing who the customer is and the existence of conflicts between the different types of customers. The two main tasks of the operations manager, the provision of customer service and the efficient management of resources are particularly difficult because of the close involvement of the customer in the operation. Customer service because of the difficulty in specifying and measuring service quality, and resource management because of the need to provide a response to the customer inside the operation, and the need to select, train and motivate the customer to fulfil his/her role in the operation.

References

Chase, R. B. (1978) 'Where does the customer fit in a service operation?', *Harvard Business Review*, Vol. 56, No. 4, November–December, pp. 137–142.

Gronroos, C. (1984) 'A service quality model and its marketing implications', *European Journal of Marketing*, Vol. 18, No. 4, pp. 36–44.

Gronroos, C. (1987) 'Service management: the service package as a source of competitive advantage', Presented at the EIASM workshop on Strategies in Service Industries, Brussels.

Johnston, R. (1987) 'A framework for developing a quality strategy in a customer processing operation', *The International Journal of Quality and Reliability Management*, Vol. 4, No. 4, pp. 37–46.

Johnston, R. (1988) 'Service operations: Designing the operation for strategic advantage', in: Wild, R. (ed) *The International Handbook of Production and Operations Management*, Cassell, London.

Johnston, R. and Morris, B. (1985) 'Monitoring and control in service operations', *International Journal of Operations and Production Management*, Vol. 5, No. 1, pp. 32–38.

Lovelock, C. H. and Young, R. F. (1979) 'Look to customers to increase productivity', *Harvard Business Review*, Vol 57, No. 3, May–June, pp. 168–178.

Normann, R. (1984) *Service Management*, Wiley, Chichester.

Riddle, D. I. (1986) *Service-led Growth*, Praeger, New York.

Sasser, W. E., Olsen, R. P. and Wyckoff, D. D. (1982) *Management of Service Operations*, Allyn and Bacon, Boston, MA.

Simonds, J. (1985) 'Quality at American Express', *Proceedings of the 4th Annual Operations Management Association Meeting*.

Voss, C. A., Armistead, C. G., Johnston, R. and Morris, B. (1985) *Operations Management in Service Industries and the Public Sector*, Wiley, Chichester.

Wild, R. (1977) *Concepts for Operations Management*, Wiley, Chichester.

14 Human resource management in the service sector

DR PAUL WILLMAN

Introduction

Over two-thirds of the UK workforce are employed in the service sector and, if the current trends towards the expansion of the service economy and the contraction of primary and manufacturing employment continue, we may expect this proportion to expand in the long term. If this occurs, then the expansion of the service sector will alter employment patterns for the economy as a whole. We know that the nature of service sector employment is distinctive; while the sector employs two-thirds of the workforce as a whole, it accounts for over 80 per cent of female employment and for almost 90 per cent of part-time employment. It has lower levels of trade union organisation than the economy as a whole (Bain and Price, 1983) and higher levels of labour turnover than either manufacturing or the public sector.

The management of such a workforce thus poses distinctive problems. The sector contains a wide variety of organisations; large financial and retail institutions, small retail and leisure firms, and a burgeoning number of professional service firms which employ predominantly highly qualified, highly paid, highly mobile staff. Service workers include hairdressers, counter clerks, and drivers as well as social workers, lawyers and doctors. Nevertheless, the sector does possess distinctive workforce features despite this variance; service firms all tend to be labour intensive, this labour experiences direct and frequent contact with the customer and, in many cases, the behaviour of employees is itself part of the provided service. For example, the skill of the doctor or hairdresser, and the behaviour of the waitress or barman affect customer satisfaction with the service organisation (Mills and Margulies, 1980).

At the core, therefore, of any human resource management strategy within service businesses there lies the need to attract, retain and control the activities of a diverse workforce which both constitutes a major cost for the business and which may also be its major asset (Kravis et al, 1983; Sasser et al, 1978).

In this chapter, we shall look at the strategies which have emerged for managing this human resource in different types of service business. Section 1 outlines the main areas with which human resource management is concerned. Section 2 looks at the differing structures of organisations in the sector, and their influence on human resource management policies and practice. Section 3 looks more closely at human resource practices in large consumer service firms. Section 4 looks at the peculiar problems involved in managing staff who have considerable customer contact. Section 5 offers some general conclusions.

Human resource management

Human resource management is concerned with the set of decisions and policies through which organisations attract, recruit, motivate, reward and develop their employees. In addition, it is concerned with the ways in which the employment relationship is terminated, whether through retirement, dismissal or voluntary termination (Beer et al, 1984). It is thus concerned with the mechanisms through which the organisation attracts candidates for employment, selects them, introduces them to the organisation's structure and culture, motivates them to perform a given set of tasks, pays them for this and seeks to identify their potential for future development. It is then concerned with systems for promotion, manpower planning, succession planning, and coping with labour turnover of one form or another.

All organisations, of necessity, perform these activities at some point during their lifespan. However, there may be substantial differences between organisations in the degree to which such activities are:

(a) *integrated*, for example in the match between recruitment activity and manpower planning;
(b) *formalised*, in the sense that they are matched to some standard across the organisation;
(c) *strategic*, in that they are matched to the organisation's overall market objectives.

There may also be substantial differences between organisations in terms of the responsibility for such activities. In some firms, these activities are defined as the responsibility of the personnel department, and are separated out from line management activity; in others, responsibility for the management of people is explicitly a core line management function, for which managers at all levels have some responsibility.

As well as considering the *nature* of human resource policies in an organisation, we must also consider their *scope*. While it is fashionable to talk about a single standard of human resource management embracing all employees, and to point to 'excellent' companies as practical examples of its worth, in many firms one needs to distinguish the relatively sophisticated and expensive techniques used in the recruitment, reward and development of managers from the rough-and-ready, uneven standards applied to lower-grade, high-turnover categories of employee. This is particularly important in service businesses, where lower grades of employee often constitute the customer contact. Some firms, such as Marks & Spencer and the John Lewis Partnership, seek to embrace such employees within a single standard of management; the majority, however, restrict their human resource policies to managerial grades. This difference will be discussed in more detail below.

The human resource practices prevailing in an organisation at any given time will be influenced by its size, ownership, structure, and the market in which it operates. It is difficult to generalise; organisations in similar markets often have different human resource policies. Nevertheless, we can understand the major differences in such policies across the service sector by beginning with an analysis of organisational structure.

The structure of service businesses

Most of the service sector consists of small firms, often run by the founder, professional bureaucracies, in which the activities of highly qualified professional staff are co-ordinated by a smaller administrative cadre, and large bureaucratic retailing organisations, in which large numbers of white-collar employees, both in outlets and in head office, are managed in a formal manner according to centrally-defined objectives. In Mintzberg's (1983) terms, we have simple structures, professional bureaucracies and machine bureaucracies. These three types of structure define the parameters of workable human resource strategies. We shall look at each in turn.

Many restaurants, hotels, shops, transport firms and leisure businesses are *simple structures*. They are run by owner proprietors or are family concerns. Typically, such organisations strongly reflect in their objectives, activities and culture the preferences of the owner(s). As Scase and Goffee (1980) have pointed out, they tend to be run on an informal basis, with recruitment, rewards and labour turnover prompted by owner preferences. One of the central tensions in such organisations is that between the owners' preference for retaining control and the career aspirations of those brought in to manage; the former resist growth while the latter see in it a chance for career mobility. Such organisations tend to grow, and thus change in form, die or fragment; in the latter case, sous-chefs, assistant hotel managers, or foremen leave to set up their own businesses, often in direct competition. Human resource policies do not exist, although human resource practices do.

In *professional bureaucracies*, the central strategic problem for the organisation is the attraction, retention and control of highly qualified professional staff. There is little in the way of career structure or career development; typically there is only one major career jump, that to partner, and the organisations' training and development needs are deemed to be catered for by the acquisition of a professional qualification, often prior to joining.

Many of the human resource options are thus dictated externally. In the average general practice, the relative qualifications, status and often pay of doctors, nurses and receptionists are set by the various professions. In the legal profession, earnings may vary according to specialisation and skill, but the organisation is often not in a position freely to appraise, direct the development of, or dismiss individual professionals. On the one hand, the professional ethos often stresses the individual's choice about which areas of expertise to develop; on the other, disciplinary activity is often the preserve of the professional association, rather than of the firm itself.

In such circumstances, there may be no clear business strategy; organisational objectives are simply the sum of individual professional strategies. Where firms seek to pursue a defined strategic direction, they must move away from the pure model of a professional bureaucracy. This involves two major changes; first, the re-evaluation of managerial work, second, the development of a specialist personnel or human resource function.

In professional bureaucracies, managerial work is often defined purely as administration, and as of lower status than professional work. The office manager is typically not professionally qualified or at least not eminent, and exerts control over unqualified staff whose function is to support and co-ordinate, rather than control, professional activity. However, where the organisation seeks to expand or diversify, activities such as the recruitment and retention of good staff attain a high priority and place high demands on professional time. There arises a need for a specialised personnel function.

A good example of this may be found in the management consultancy business. Consultancy firms are typically partnerships, but several have become very large, and embrace a variety of skills, some supported by professional qualifications and some not. The major audit firms, which have diversified into management consultancy now, typically, have personnel departments whose activities embrace the high volume of annual recruitment activity in the graduate market, appraisal of those aspiring to partnership, and the development of competitive remuneration packages in order to retain and motivate the best staff. Since such organisations often limit the available number of partnerships, there also arises the problem of managing outflow of employees, many of whom go to competitors.

The final organisational form to consider is that of the large consumer service organisation, whether in retailing, financial services or the hotel and restaurant business. Such organisations are distinctive forms of *machine-bureaucracy* – distinctive in that they employ large numbers of staff, but often in relatively small establishments. Hence, while the average bank clerk or supermarket check-out operator works under systems of bureaucratic rules, he or she, typically, works in an establishment of less than 200 people.

Such organisations have distinctive forms of human resource issue. Typically also, they have developed distinctive human resource policies. Since such organisations employ the majority of people who work in private services, we shall look separately, and in more detail, at them.

Human resources in large-scale consumer service organisations

In the last decade, large-scale consumer service organisations have seen the introduction of professionalised personnel departments and sophisticated personnel systems. The use of psychometric tests for recruitment and assessment centres for appraisal and career planning, of formal graduate entry and fast-track programmes and of more sophisticated remuneration systems often linking pay to performance, have revolutionised what were once paternalistic or service-based approaches to human resources. In addition, the demand for professional management, and the difficulties of securing sufficient supply, have led to the growth of management development activities seeking to manage the internal managerial labour market in order to secure a reliable flow of talent. These changes are in response to growth, and have highlighted several serious human resource difficulties faced by large retailing organisations.

Once more the starting point for considering these problems is the organisational structure. A typical retailing operation's structure is outlined in Figure 14.1. It indicates the growth of large head office functions, the number of outlet managers required and the prevalence of customer contact. The human resource issues emerge from this; they concern the relationship between head office and outlet staff, the role of line manage-

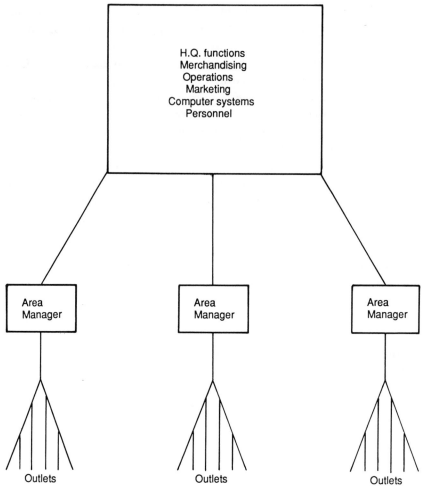

Figure 14.1   A typical large scale consumer service organisation

ment in outlets and the problems of managing staff with customer contact.

As this type of organisation has grown, it has tended to accumulate staff in head office functions such as purchasing, computer operations, business development, strategic planning, forecasting and financial management. Such staff are frequently graduates, often recruited directly from university via formal graduate entry programmes which offer access to fast-track career development. Retailers such as Marks & Spencer and John Lewis and most of the major UK banks have recently invested heavily in recruitment and assessment technology directed primarily at graduate entry, and have developed discrete career paths, often involving a concentration on head office work, for such employees.

The introduction of such staff poses problems. The first is that they pose a threat to older, perhaps non-graduate staff who have traditionally formed the backbone of management in such organisations. In UK banks, such head office staff seldom go to work in the branch outlets; the graduate/non-graduate divide thus complicates the natural tension between back office and staff in the retail outlets themselves. In UK retailers, more movement between stores and head office is encouraged. The second problem is that such staff develop high expectations at recruitment which may, if frustrated, lead to high turnover later on. The third is that a large graduate entry programme creates a career block for those who enter retailing organisations as school-leavers on a permanent basis.

Some of the problems here can be illustrated by examining Figure 14.2, which depicts the career planning system recently installed in a major UK

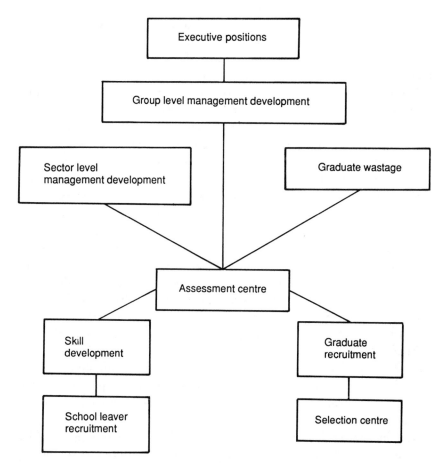

Figure 14.2   Career planning system: major UK bank

retail bank. In the past, such banks operated with a single-port-of-entry, internal labour market, in which slow, steady progression and high levels of job security were taken for granted, at least by male staff (Lockwood, 1958; Egan, 1982; Morris, 1986). Over time, this single labour market became fragmented through the importation of graduate entrants, initially on an unplanned basis, and subsequently through formal entry schemes. The Bank currently has to wrestle with the disintegration of the old career structure while implementing a new *streamed* career structure based on formal assessment through career potential centres.

The first major problem is to establish a reliable career potential database on which to base retention, discharge and promotion decisions. The second is to encourage employees to accept that these data are a fair reflection of their abilities and potential, and to plan their careers on the basis of them. The third is to encourage line managers to base promotion decisions on such data.

These problems are typical of many large-scale consumer service operations, where rapid growth has preceded the arrival of personnel systems to plan careers. They are complicated by the difficulty of developing and retaining sufficient line managers in outlets.

Large companies such as Marks & Spencer, Sainsbury and Trusthouse Forte require literally hundreds of line managers with responsibility for stock and financial control, customer relations, selling, and, importantly, the whole range of human resource functions. For many service staff, the first line manager *is* the organisation. This human resource aspect is vital, since many operations experience very high levels of labour turnover among lower grades. Unit or branch managers will tend to recruit, train and develop staff on a regular basis and, indeed, performance on human resource activity will generally form part of their appraisal.

However, the difficulty for many organisations lies in the development of career opportunities beyond unit management. Organisational structures tend to narrow markedly above this point; moreover many opportunities for promotion involve moves to head offices where jobs are very different and separate career structures prevail. Some organisations, such as Marks & Spencer, have in the past sought to integrate store careers with those at Head Office through formal systems of rotation. Others, such as hotel companies and banks, have motivated through regular promotion to jobs of increasing responsibility; a typical career might involve promotion from manager of a small operation to a large operation and subsequently to area or district manager.

The line management issue is a particular problem, because this level has responsibility for supervising staff with customer contact. Supervision and motivation of this level of staff is in some ways the key to successful human resource management in services, and it is worth discussing at some length.

The sector employs large numbers of staff engaged on various forms of selling activity, and personal service activity, in direct contact with customers. Many of these staff are, as we have seen, part-time. They may only work evenings and weekends; some, in banks in particular, work as part of a 'pool' of staff across several locations. Turnover among these grades is high, frequently over 100 per cent per year. Many are female, but of differing ages and status; some are school-leavers unable to find a permanent job, others students, others women with children seeking flexible working hours.

In effect, a dual labour market exists across the sector (Morris, 1986; Willman, 1986; Metcalf, 1988). On the one hand, there are career staff, often graduate and often male, who may move between organisations, but will in the first instance expect development opportunities and promotion through the managerial hierarchy. On the other hand, there are non-career staff, often female, part-time non-graduates, who work in important customer-contact roles, but who infrequently move up into managerial ranks.

These kinds of non-career employee have always been regarded as difficult to motivate. Their attachment to the organisation is fleeting, their pay often low, their job content often routine. However, the problem for service businesses is that, frequently, they are all that the customer sees. They define the quality of service the organisation can offer. This matters more in businesses where the service itself is the product, than in pure retailing, where poor service may be offset by good products. However, even in retailing, organisations such as the John Lewis Partnership and Marks & Spencer have spent considerable amounts incorporating such staff into expensive systems of welfare provision in order to sustain quality of service, while in highly competitive industries such as financial services and air travel, Trustee Savings Bank and British Airways have embarked on thorough and expensive customer care programmes with the same intent.

The motivation, skills and knowledge of these staff is a key issue for the quality of service offered by an organisation, and it is worth looking in more detail at the management problems involved.

Managing the point of sale

Essentially, there are five possible ways of controlling the behaviour of employees at work, whether in services or elsewhere (Ouchi and Maguire,

1975; Ouchi, 1977; Mills and Margulies, 1980; Trevino, 1986). These are as follows:

1 *Direct supervision*: This form of control, using close personal supervision, is externally applied, and can be used where the task is simple and easily observed, and where concentration of staff enables economies of scale in supervisory provision.

2 *Bureaucratic control*: Control through rules and procedures is appropriate where tasks are predictable and fully understood, and where the environment is relatively predictable.

3 *Machine pacing*: Employee activities may be paced by machines where the task is simple enough to permit automation; in many cases, rules and procedures previously learned by staff are simply programmed into the machine.

4 *Output control*: This is appropriate where the task is unclear or remote and unobservable, but the output, for example, sales volume, can be measured and related to a standard.

5 *Control through socialisation*: Through socialisation, members internalise the objectives of the organisation. The firm may either hire people who through previous training accept the necessary standards and objectives, or instil them through post-entry training.

These are pure types, and most organisations operate with a mix of controls. In manufacturing organisations, the primary determinant of the form of control is the task to be performed (Ouchi and Maguire, 1975); however, in services, choice of control mechanism is complicated by the nature of the customer interaction. Hence, it may make sense to employ socialisation control, even where tasks are simple and highly predictable, if staff/customer interactions are complex or difficult. Such controls involve considerable screening activity at the recruitment stage, and subsequent training which goes beyond mere technical training to an acquaintance with and acceptance of the values and culture of the organisation. They also require consistent line management role models for staff to emulate.

Many organisations in the service sector employ socialisation control. In fast-food operations like Macdonald's, and 'concept' restaurants like TGI Friday's, control through rules and by output is mixed with socialisation control. In airline bookings, technological control and socialisation control are also mixed.

Trevino (1986), has combined consideration of task complexity and customer uncertainty in ways which have considerable implications for human resource management. She classifies client contact roles in terms of these two dimensions of complexity, and in terms of the most suitable

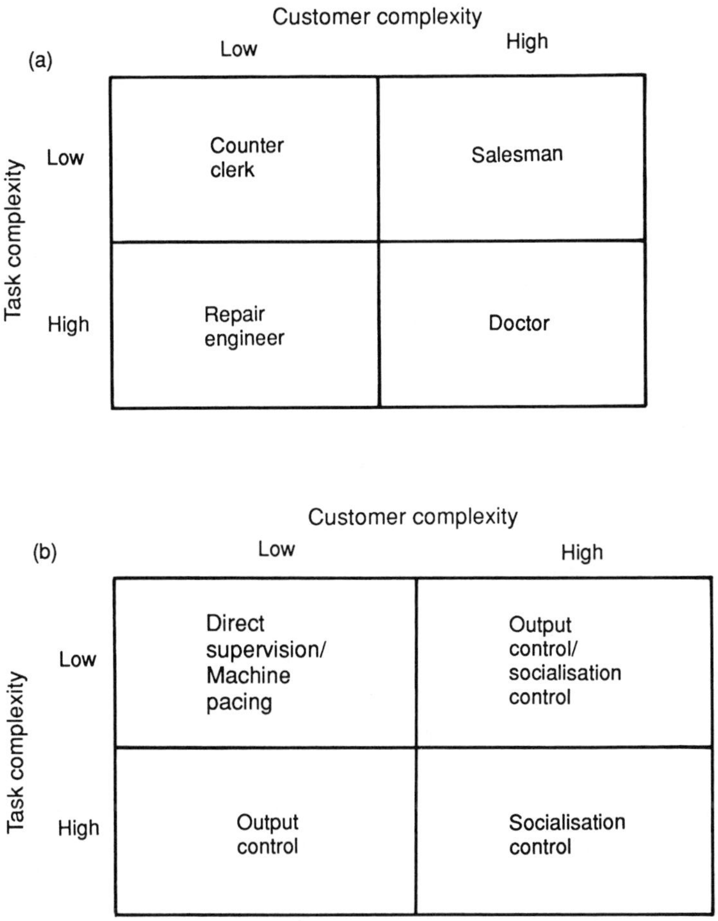

(a)

Customer complexity

	Low	High
Low	Counter clerk	Salesman
High	Repair engineer	Doctor

(b)

Customer complexity

	Low	High
Low	Direct supervision/ Machine pacing	Output control/ socialisation control
High	Output control	Socialisation control

Figure 14.3   (a) Task and consumer complexity; (b) Human resource implications
(Adapted from Trevino, 1986)

form of control; an adapted version of her approach is shown in Figure 14.3(a). From this, certain human resource practices follow, as in Figure 14.3(b). For example, where tasks are routine and customer contact short and predictable (cell A) control through technology and rules is appropriate. Where both task and customer contact are difficult (cell D), investment in lengthy socialisation and training is necessary. As an example, consider the difference in the financial services sector between the cashier operating a terminal to deal with a cheque transaction and the 'personal banker' negotiating a personal loan with a client (Willman, 1986). Such staff are recruited, trained, and paid in very different ways.

In professional service firms, most customer–staff interaction is in cell D, and the human resource policies of the organisation or the profession must deliver these kinds of staff. Such policies are likely to devote considerable emphasis to screening, training and development, to generate high staff commitment, and control through direct supervision or technology is unlikely.

In retailing, most customer–staff transactions are in cells A and B. Those in cell A are, where economies of scale and technology permit, often automated; for example, autoteller machines in banks. Those in cell B (simple task but high contact) may be assisted by technology, but, since the client's needs are uncertain, are unlikely to be paced by it. In fact, one of the key problems for retailing operations is to read the level of customer requirements and, then, to install human resource policies delivering staff to satisfy them. While many retailing firms are converging in their patterns of management development, one of the differentiating features is the scope of their human resource policies.

On the one hand, we may identify policies such as those of Marks & Spencer and some of the financial institutions, in which both career and non-career staff are embraced by the same human resource system and supporting culture, the object of which is to reduce labour turnover and to enhance quality of service. These policies are active and costly in relation to the overall pay of the staff involved. On the other hand, there is a low-cost set of policies followed in the UK by many employers in hotel and catering businesses, and by many large retailers, in which the presence of relatively low-paid, poorly committed high turnover staff is accepted, since it is not seen to affect quality of service. Commitment of lower level staff in such organisations is seen to be too costly or impossible to secure.

The former set of human resource policies, termed 'high contact' are depicted on the left of Figure 14.4; the latter, termed here 'low contact' are depicted on the right of the figure. The key distinguishing feature of these typified strategies is the extent to which staff behaviour is seen to be a key part of the service provided. Clearly, the problems of human resource management will differ between organisations which pursue these different strategies.

Conclusions

Service businesses, varied though they are, have distinctive sets of human resource problems. Some of these simply stem from growth, and might be experienced by any rapidly growing organisation in any sector. Others stem from increased competition, such as those in the retail financial

HIGH CONTACT	LOW CONTACT
Screening to ensure low turnover	Acceptance of high turnover
Socialisation	Limited technical training
Limited autonomy	Close direct supervision
Generous benefit system	
Performance- related pay	Payment of minimum wages
High staff commitment low turnover low absence low shrinkage	Low commitment high turnover high absence high shrinkage
Staff behaviour central to service	Staff behaviour marginal to service

Figure 14.4   High and low contact HR policies

services, and, again, have parallels outside the services. The truly distinctive feature of the service sector as far as human resource management is concerned is the management of staff with customer contact. Both professional service and consumer service firms are seeking to serve customer needs more fully in an increasingly competitive environment, but they differ in their definition of the problem. For professional service firms, the issue is to replace a knowledge or skill-based approach with a client-based one, which might require teams of professionals from different disciplines or even the breakdown of such disciplinary barriers. For consumer service firms, the issue is to improve the commitment, and thus the quality of service provided, by non-career staff in jobs which, while at the base of the organisation, are in direct contact with the market.

References

Bain, G. and Price, R. (1983) 'Union growth; dimensions, determinants, destiny', in: Bain, G. (ed) *Industrial Relations in Britain*, Blackwell, Oxford.

Beer, M., Spector, B., Lawrence, P. R., Mills, D. Q. and Walton, R. E. (1984) *Managing Human Assets*, The Free Press, New York.

Egan, A. (1982) 'Women in banking; a study in inequality', *Industrial Relations Journal*, Vol. 13, No. 3.

Kravis, I. B., Heston, A. and Summers, R. (1983) 'The share of services in economic growth', in: Adams, F. and Hickman, B. (eds) *Global Econometrics*, MIT Press, Cambridge.

Lockwood, D. (1958) *The Black Coated Worker*, Allen & Unwin, London.

Metcalf, H. (1988) 'Careers and training in tourism and leisure', *Department of Employment Gazette*, February.

Mills, P. K. and Margulies, N. (1980) 'Towards a core typology of service organisations', *Academy of Management Review*, Vol. 5, No. 2, pp. 255–65.

Mintzberg, H. (1983) *Structure in Fives: Designing Effective Organisations*, Prentice-Hall, Englewood Cliffs, NJ.

Morris, T. (1986) *Innovations in Banking: Business Strategies and Employee Relations*, Croom Helm, London.

Ouchi, W. (1977) 'The relationship between organisational structure and organisational control', *Administrative Science Quarterly*, 22, pp. 95–113.

Ouchi, W. and Maguire, M. A. (1975) 'Organisational control: two functions', *Administrative Science Quarterly*, 20, pp. 559–69.

Sasser, W. E., Olsen, R. P. and Wyckoff, D. D. (1978) *Management of Service Operations: Text, Cases and Readings*, Allyn & Bacon, Inc., Boston MA.

Scase, R. and Goffee, R. (1980) *The Real World of the Small Business Owner*, Croom Helm, London.

Trevino, L. K. (1986) 'The technology control relationship in service organisation', Paper to Academy Management Conference, Chicago.

Willman, P. (1986) *Technological Change, Collective Bargaining and Industrial Efficiency*, Oxford University Press.

15 The role of financial management in service organisations

BRIAN ADAMS AND PAUL COLEBOURNE

Introduction

Financial management is sometimes considered as a backroom clerical activity staffed by grey, pedantic individuals whose main purpose is making life difficult for the real workers in the organisation. Unfortunately this stereotype is often found, to some degree, in many organisations. However, we believe financial management has a more participative and positive role to play, especially in service organisations.

The purpose of this chapter is to explain the role of enlightened financial management. We have deliberately avoided detailed accounting techniques as these are covered in accounting textbooks.

The total service culture

First, we need to establish the key differences between service and other organisations. Conceptually the biggest difference is that service organisations satisfy a customer's needs without any tangible product, as such, changing hands. Service organisations are people-orientated, but this is not to say that they are not also capital-intensive. Consider, for example, the tangible assets required to operate a transport service or a computer bureau.

In a traditional manufacturing organisation the customer is mainly satisfied, or otherwise, by the product itself and arguably the service element is less significant. Increasingly, however, service is becoming an important element. For example, a manufacturer of electronic instrumentation may not have a technically unique product, but may be highly successful in providing a responsive design, advisory and installation service. In an increasingly competitive world economy, UK manufacturing industry has to become more service orientated and the distinction between service and manufacturing is therefore becoming less clear.

Most organisations can be broken down into departments on a functional basis. For example, between the frontline departments more closely connected with the customer, such as sales or operations, and other departments, such as personnel or accounting, which are often referred to as 'overheads'. This latter description rather misses the point, since it ignores the need for them to provide a valuable internal service to the frontline departments.

Consequently, there is often a tendency to curb the amount or quality of resources of the overhead departments to a bare minimum, often resulting in extremely poor value for money and inefficient services being provided to the frontline departments. Examples of this are where an under-resourced accounts department sends customers incorrect invoices and creates problems for the sales department, or provides misleading information on the performance of the organisation, or excessively accurate information that is too late to act upon.

There is a further important characteristic which profoundly influences the financial management of a service organisation and that is the degree of closeness to the customer. In a well run manufacturing organisation optimum levels of physical stocks of products and components are held which smooth out the fluctuations between demand and supply and allow customer orders to be satisfied within an acceptable timescale. In a service organisation it is not possible to hold a buffer stock of 'services' and the correct balance between providing a responsive customer service and having idle resources is more difficult to achieve. Idle resources cost money. Unsatisfied demand costs money. Delaying the satisfaction of the demand until resources are available eventually loses customers and also costs money in the long run.

This means that the need to forecast, plan ahead, manage customer expectations, acquire and retain staff resources, be flexible and responsive requires almost superhuman management ability. Because of this, everybody in the service organisation has to be committed to, and involved in, the delivery of the service. Autocratic and rigid hierarchical management structures are no longer appropriate – leadership and total commitment are paramount.

The financial manager, therefore, has to 'think service' – everything the finance department does has to be aimed at supporting the customer service team. Because everybody is much closer to customers rather than being insulated behind a warehouse of finished products, it is necessary for financial management to participate within a *total service culture* if it is to play a useful role.

Motivation and budgetary control

The key to success then, in a service organisation, is building a highly motivated team which identifies closely with the needs of its customers.

One of the key ingredients in any motivational programme is information and, in particular, information about how the individual employee is performing and how that performance is reflected in the performance of the team and of the organisation as a whole. Knowledge of this information will engender in the individual a sense of belonging, of being someone in the organisation who matters, which will lead to greater commitment and thus in time will encourage better teamwork. The customer will benefit directly from better teamwork and, therefore, so will the organisation. The ability to measure the performance of the business, and the individual's performance within the business, by applying financial techniques is where financial management can assist in employee motivation.

One method of applying this principle, which is becoming popular, is to inform staff of the annual or quarterly results in the form of an 'employee report'. This creates a sense of trust and involvement for the employees. These reports usually abbreviate the information contained in the statutory annual report and accounts and provide management with the opportunity to concentrate the employees' attention on key indicators of performance. The emphasis placed on different indicators of performance will vary between organisations, as will their relevance to the motivation of the individual employee.

Employee reports are essentially fairly general in nature and explain the overall performance of the organisation. It can be extremely useful to carry the process a stage further and have more regular and detailed feedback of performance. The ability to analyse and sub-classify the financial results of the business into meaningful figures for groups of individuals will enable them to identify with the organisation and see the relevance of their contribution. In the most successful organisations this process has been developed into budgetary control systems which have the following principal advantages:

1   involvement of management, supervisors and other key staff in agreeing realistic performance targets which they can directly control and to which they are thus committed;

2   allowing the planned activities of each department to be co-ordinated and appropriate funding to be obtained;

3   providing feedback on actual performance. The process of explaining

differences between actual and budgeted results encourages a constructive analysis of scope for improved performance;

4 providing a basis for rewarding people according to results achieved.

In preparing a budget a common failing is simply to 'add 10 per cent to last year'. This is the lazy way out and avoids the sort of penetrating analysis really necessary to arrive at a well thought out budget. A technique which we use is to start with a 'clean sheet of paper' and encourage management to prepare a 'zero-based' budget. In this way challenging questions have to be answered about the way service operations are carried out and often ideas about innovative, new and better ways to do things emerge.

In 'conventional accounting wisdom' it is normal to classify departments according to whether they earn a profit (profit centres) or are simply an overhead (cost centres). We believe that this approach should be changed to recognise that each department provides a service – the only difference is whether it is an external (direct customer) service or an internal (indirect customer) service. We have therefore coined the phrase 'service activity centres' for all departments.

We believe an organisation should set up service activity centres for individual departments, producing monthly financial and other relevant activity-based information by department, comparing actual with budget and with the same period of the previous year. The manager responsible for each service activity centre should explain any variances from the expected performance to their peers, and in turn should make a similar explanation to the staff in the department. Regular departmental meetings to discuss performance can identify areas for improvement and build on the team spirit.

Accountants need to be trained in communications skills, including the presentation of information graphically, in order that they can more effectively provide information to the managers of service activity centres.

The wider use of computers in recent years, especially in the smaller service organisations that had not been able to justify the expense in the past, has brought with it the greater accessibility of financial information. Compared with manually based systems, the use of computerised accounting and information systems means that information is available sooner, at more regular intervals, and that it can be sub-analysed into information relevant to specific individuals within the organisation.

Clearly, the greater capacity of modern computers could mean that individuals are swamped with information, much of which is meaningless to them. Great care and skill must be used to identify how much and how little information should be provided and to ensure that it is relevant to the role the person plays in the organisation.

Comparing actual results to budget can create an internal competitive spirit motivating individuals and teams to out-perform each other. However, this requires careful management because rivalry can be counter-productive and confusing for the customer, especially where shared resources or joint services are involved. The accounting information system, therefore, must be equitable. Unfortunately this often leads to complicated accounting arrangements which are error-prone and expensive to administer. If the accounting staff are not responsive to the needs of the 'accounted for' staff it can have an extremely demotivating effect. Helpfulness, imagination and a sense of perspective are vital characteristics of a good financial manager.

In summary, financial management has a key role to play in the motivation of staff. Careful selection of financial measures and the use of relevant information within a system of budgetary control designed for service activity centres, will improve the individual's commitment to the business. Improved commitment in a service organisation should mean greater commitment to the customer, which in time will ensure growth in the future.

Quality control

Unless the organisation is operating as a monopoly, poor quality of service will result in customer dissatisfaction and thereby low sales, high unit costs and low profitability. In an increasingly competitive environment 'high' quality is now a key factor in the survival of most organisations. There is, however, a danger that the pursuit of excellence may result in a 'bells and whistles' philosophy with technical excellence just for the sake of it. Quality therefore means the appropriateness and responsiveness of the service provided. Deciding the appropriateness of the service is part of the strategic and marketing planning of the organisation. Responsiveness is all about establishing service levels or measures of competitive performance and monitoring service activities to ensure that performance is consistently maintained.

For example, British Gas establishes and monitors target times for incoming telephone calls to be answered, visits to customers by fitters and replacement parts availability. Trends in measures of customer service such as these enable the finance manager to anticipate problems and highlight that action should be taken before financial performance is adversely affected.

In a service organisation all the staff who have contact with customers can be considered to be service providers and salesmen. A customer judges the quality of service provided by a service organisation as a function of the total contact with all employees, whether they be the telephonist, the accounts clerk or the service providers themselves. It is vital that each individual is aware of this fact and is trained to respond to comments made by customers at each point of contact. Even the credit control function can have a role in the quality monitoring procedures. By monitoring customer satisfaction levels, prompt communication to the service provider about quality problems that are causing non-payment, management can rectify any problems as they occur.

Thus, financial management has a role to play in quality control. Not only should the financial systems produce quality relevant data for the service providers, but also the operation of the financial systems themselves should be used to monitor quality. The staff operating the accounting systems that form the basis for financial management are a part of the total service culture.

Strategic planning

All businesses should plan ahead and service organisations are no exception. Being able to respond to market demand when it happens requires having planned in advance for that occurrence. It is the duty of management not just to manage the present situation, but also to manage the future and thereby give the organisation direction.

The requirement to plan should involve all the service activity centres within an organisation. Decisions may be required on future investment policy, on the likely costs of adopting a certain strategy or the financial implications of not adopting that strategy. The role of financial management in strategic planning is to provide the framework within which to reach these decisions, to provide the financial data for the different options under consideration and to present the anticipated outcomes in a readily comparable form.

For instance, if there are two similar market opportunities each with equal support within the organisation, but requiring investment in different technologies, the appropriate financial analysis can identify the preferred option. By establishing a required rate of return on investment, for example, by selecting the industry norm or one based on the organisation's own cost of capital, each different option can be analysed, evaluated and the outcomes compared.

When the Scandinavian airline SAS considered introducing the new generation of wide-bodied jets on its feeder routes to Europe, it rejected the proposal in favour of its existing narrow-bodied planes. Financial analysis showed that to maintain the necessary return on investment, the new planes would be required to make fewer flights each day. However, the reduction of flight availability would adversely effect the premium fare paying business passengers likely to interconnect with the international flights of the airline. It was concluded that the wide-bodied planes were more suited to the package holiday tourists who were not so sensitive to flight times or frequencies.

Sophisticated financial techniques also enable management to monitor the risk that is a function of all business activity. The successful understanding and management of inherent risk is a key feature of modern financial planning.

Preparing a strategic plan requires versatile financial systems that can quantify the financial impact of future decisions, enabling the management to take the appropriate action while they are still in control of the situation. Either a failure to plan for the future, or a failure to consider the necessary financial management requirements of the organisation in relation to those plans, may leave the business vulnerable to competitive situations to which it is unable to respond. Sound financial management is therefore a key constituent of strategic planning, and financial managers need to be trained so that they understand the commercial realities behind their numerical language.

Service activity costing

It is absolutely vital to know the cost of providing various services, because it is only when this information is known that decisions can be taken about the viability and methodology of providing a service within its market price.

Cost structures vary considerably among service organisations. For example, an airline will be completely different from a firm of architects or a hospital. Accordingly, the most appropriate type of service costing system will vary and examples of this are given below.

An airline is capital-intensive and, whilst control of its labour costs is very important, the costs of operating the aircraft are likely to be more significant. For instance, with the useful life of aircraft being directly affected by their use, profitability in airlines is highly dependent upon load factors. It costs much the same to transport 100 passengers on a Jumbo jet as 400 passengers, but the revenue effects are considerably different. By measuring, and controlling, costs per passenger mile, the airline will be able to identify poorly performing services. Low load factors and high passenger costs may be remedied by rescheduling flights or changing to smaller aircraft.

A professional practice, such as a firm of architects, is highly labour-intensive. Typically, in such organisations the financial controls should concentrate on the utilisation factors of staff and the efficiency with which staff are used to provide the services to clients. High utilisation factors generally mean that employees are being effectively used, and high efficiency factors generally mean that jobs are not overstaffed. The most appropriate financial systems will be those which include detailed estimates of task times, anticipated efficiencies and likely utilisation levels. From these it should be possible to determine the necessary staffing levels required, and thereby decide whether existing levels are adequate to exploit the market opportunity. A requirement for additional staff and/or lower utilisation or efficiency factors may be unacceptable.

For service organisations in the public sector, such as hospitals, there is no identifiable revenue and often no free market price against which to compare costs and assess financial viability or efficiency. A costing system based simply on the allocation of input costs is incomplete. In such organisations an analytical tool known as the 'value for money' (VFM) criteria has, therefore, been developed to deal with this problem.

VFM is based on the concept of evaluating three key aspects of the service provision. These are:

1 'economy' – are resources used which are acquired at least cost, commensurate with appropriate quality?

2 'efficiency' – are unit costs of providing specified service levels at a minimum?

3 'effectiveness' – are the specified service levels adequate for what is actually required or are they too high?

In practice economy and efficiency are relatively straightforward forms of cost analysis. Effectiveness, however, is more subjective and less easy to measure. It requires a much wider understanding of the context within which the organisation operates, its role, policy implications and consumer needs and expectations. The financial manager therefore needs to be well trained in order to understand market research findings and complex social policy implications.

The growth of VFM studies in the public sector has been in response to the requirement to provide a substitute for the lack of a competitive marketplace. Paradoxically, at a time when the public sector is being encouraged to learn from the private sector, the private sector could benefit from greater application of VFM techniques. Adopting the VFM approach could help any service organisation decide whether its cost structure could be improved and harmonised with the most effective form of service provision. This would be an exceptionally powerful technique for the financial manager if combined with zero-based budgeting described earlier.

To summarise, one of the key roles of financial management in service organisations is to develop flexible and relevant costing systems which enable short term and longer term decisions to be taken. These costing systems should reflect value for money principles.

Maintaining solvency and raising finance

Whilst most organisations would accept the need to keep some sort of financial record, there is generally a sense of confusion as to the purpose of accounting. Many see the accountant's role as just to 'keep the score'. Others view it as a legal requirement, indeed the Companies Act 1985 and the Insolvency Act 1986 lay down certain requirements for companies' accounting records. Financial management, as practised by the accountant, is an integral part of running any organisation. An organisation will not succeed without adequate controls over working capital, cash flow and longer-term financing.

Working capital is the funding required to finance 'current' or 'circulating' assets. In a service organisation this is mainly monies not yet received from customers for work done (debtors and work in progress) part of which, of course, is correspondingly financed by amounts due to suppliers and other short-term creditors.

Regular management accounts, in addition to reporting turnover, costs and profit, should always include movements in working capital and compare these with the budget. The management accounts should also contain working capital ratios such as debtor days (the number of days sales in debtors) or creditor days (the number of days purchases in creditors).

Working capital management is especially important in labour-intensive service organisations, because large amounts of salary costs have to be paid regularly and promptly. Those costs cannot be deferred and it is therefore very important to ensure that billing and cash collection procedures operate efficiently. Frequently, service organisations do not bill a customer for a service that is not complete at the end of a month. If a job is likely to take longer than, say, 6 weeks to complete, the payment terms should include a clause for part billings and the customer should be advised accordingly.

Underlying the control of working capital, and inextricably linked with it, is the need to prepare cash flow forecasts. These are not something just for larger organisations; all service organisations benefit from the information produced and the disciplines involved in preparing them.

Ideally, cash flow forecasts should be prepared as part of the budgetary process. The impact of the strategic decisions being contemplated may then be considered and the effects on the solvency of the organisation forecast. Each time management accounts are produced they should be accompanied by an updated and revised cash flow forecast. As noted elsewhere in this chapter, the timeliness of this information is crucial.

Regular cash flow reporting will highlight the effectiveness of the controls on working capital and will indicate when action is required. Together with the budget, cash flow reporting is one of the key areas which allow service management to look into the future. Unlike the budgetary process, which is usually once a year, cash flow forecasting is a monthly exercise and often needs to be carried out weekly or even daily.

A service organisation can generally raise additional finance in a number of different ways depending upon its legal constitution and past track record. Typically, a limited liability company may go to its bankers for short-term overdraft finance and medium-term loan capital and its share-holders for long-term equity finance (either by way of a capital injection or retained profits). The cost of raising additional finance, that is the rate of interest paid on borrowings or the number of shares that need to be issued, will depend entirely upon the confidence of the financial backers in the organisation, its management and its prospects – in other words confidence in the services it provides. Professional financial management has a leading role to play in managing the organisation's financial repu-tation and the ability to raise finance, when required, at an economical cost. Good financial managers 'sell' the strengths of the organisation to financial backers and 'deliver' reliable information about future financing requirements.

In summary, therefore, for a service organisation to be successful it must possess a sound strategy for continued solvency and the provision of longer-term finance. By managing the solvency of the organisation with budgetary control, working capital management and cash flow forecasting techniques, financial management has a leading role to play in its own right.

Conclusion

Financial management in service organisations is more than just producing accounts and saying 'no'. It embodies the whole system of accounting procedures, reporting and analysing not just past events, but also the future prospects. Its role spreads throughout the service organisation to cover motivation of staff, quality control, strategic planning, costing systems and continued solvency. In all these areas it provides invaluable knowledge both to those responsible for managing the organisation and to those who work in it. Its existence also gives outside backers confidence that the organisation is being effectively managed. Indeed, it is a valuable service in its own right and should be managed with that philosophy well to the fore.

16 Marketing services

FRANCIS BUTTLE

Introduction

Since the 1950s marketing has been acknowledged by major consumer goods manufacturers as an essential management function. Some have even embraced marketing as the core philosophy guiding their businesses. However, the service sector in general has been slower to come to terms with marketing, for a number of reasons. Many service organisations such as independent retailers and hair salons are small and have a well established and loyal customer base whose requirements they fully understand and meet. Some professional services operate codes of practice preventing the use of marketing techniques which might give one practitioner an edge over professional colleagues. Utilities such as electricity and gas have traditionally seen themselves as monopolists with no need for the competitive advantages which marketing can supply.

Hooley and Cowell's (1985) review of the status of marketing in the UK concluded that 'marketing in service companies lags some way behind that in product companies'. In particular they found that services made less use of marketing research and were more likely to base pricing decisions on cost, rather than demand, considerations. These conclusions were based on data supplied by 544 service organisations.

Some service organisations, however, are widely regarded as polished and successful marketers: Hertz, Trusthouse Forte, Burger King for example. Despite these illustrious examples, there is still considerable misunderstanding about the meaning and significance of marketing. Some equate marketing with selling or advertising; others think of it as market research. In truth it is all of these and much more.

The Institute of Marketing, an international professional body based in the UK, defines marketing as 'the management process responsible for identifying, anticipating and satisfying customer requirements profitably'. It is therefore the process which picks out target groups of customers, researches and forecasts their requirements, and then designs and delivers services to meet both the demands of these customers and the objectives of the service producer. Marketing ensures that the resources of the service producer are used to satisfy the expectations of the marketplace.

Marketing is not philanthropic; it is a means to an end. Customers are only provided with what they want because this improves the odds of long-term organisational survival in a competitive climate. Marketers believe that given freedom of choice a once-satisfied customer is more likely to become a repeat customer. They also believe in the power of word-of-mouth persuasion. A satisfied customer is likely to influence others to become customers. This is especially significant for services which, because of their intangibility, are often felt to be risky purchases. Consumers try to reduce perceived risk by seeking information from others who have had previous experience of the service.

From the inclusion of the word 'profitable' in the Institute of Marketing's definition, it might appear as if marketing has no role to play in non-profit service organisations. This is incorrect; profit is the usual objective of commercial service organisations, but marketing also has a role to play in the achievement of non-profit objectives. Universities and colleges are non-profit organisations which compete for the best of a limited supply of qualified school-leavers. By way of marketing they produce and distribute literature and audio-visual material; they advertise; they make presentations in schools; they modify course offerings to make them more attractive.

Is service marketing different?

There are several ways of looking at marketing. Marketing can be viewed as a philosophy; as a way of doing business. Companies run according to this philosophy are said to be marketing-orientated. A truly marketing-orientated business believes that its sole function is to create and retain customers. The whole business, its personnel and its technical systems, become geared to providing customer satisfaction and, in doing so, earning a profit. In this philosophical sense, the marketing of dry-cleaning services is no different from the marketing of detergents. Marketing can also be viewed as a management process. Typically, it involves these steps: investigating customer demand for a class of products; identifying a group of customers whose requirements could be better satisfied; developing a product to meet that demand; pricing the product at a level which the market will bear and which will return a profit; making the product available through channels accessible to the customer; promoting the product so that a desired unit or revenue volume of demand is achieved. Based upon careful analysis of alternative opportunities, and organisational strengths and weaknesses, marketing plans are compiled, implemented and controlled to achieve these marketing objectives. In this management process sense, the marketing of an employment agency service is no different from the marketing of computers.

Marketing can also be viewed as a set of tools used to manipulate demand. The term 'marketing mix', more popularly dubbed the 4Ps – product, price, promotion, place – is widely used to describe this toolkit. The marketer is seen as mixing these variables to achieve a targeted volume of demand. The marketing manager is a demand manager. The concept of the marketing mix was originally developed in the context of manufactured goods but has recently been extended into services. Whilst it is possible to argue that every marketing mix, whether for a tangible good or a service, is unique, some expert opinion argues that the distinctive characteristics of services – their intangibility, perishability and heterogeneity, and the inseparability of service production and consumption – exert a common influence on the types of marketing mixes that are appropriate to services (Berry, 1984). In this marketing mix sense there may be distinctive differences between the marketing of services and other products.

In at least one sense, therefore, service marketing may be different.

A services marketing mix

As noted earlier, the original 4Ps mix has come under the close scrutiny of service marketers. Many have found it wanting. Recommendations for change to the mix range from minor modification (Mindak and Fine, 1981) through major overhaul (Booms and Bitner, 1981) to dissolution (Lovelock, 1979).

Such recommendations are generally based upon the oft-quoted distinctive characteristics of services – intangibility, perishability, heterogeneity and inseparability. We now examine each of these in turn for its significance to marketing.

Intangibility

Services are intangibles. 'A good is an object, a device, a thing; a service is a deed, a performance, an effort.' (Berry, 1984).

It has been pointed out that there is a double intangibility to services. 'A service cannot be touched; it is also difficult to grasp mentally.' (Bateson et al, 1978). Services can not be experienced through any of the senses prior to purchase. Services can not be owned. 'No amount of money can buy physical ownership of such intangibles as experience (movies), time (consulting) or process (dry-cleaning).' (Shostack, 1977a). As Berry (1984) concludes, services are consumed but not possessed. This twin intangibility poses a number of problems for marketers. Services are difficult to demonstrate and describe; it is often hard for the marketer to set a price which demonstrates value for money; new service product ideas are not easy to test for consumer acceptance; neither can intangibles be protected by patent. The marketing difficulties are essentially those of communication and 'researchability'. A detailed examination of practice in ten service organisations concluded that 'intangibility does have a profound effect on the marketing of services' (Rushton and Carson, 1985).

Dual intangibility also has consequences for customers: as noted above they may perceive a high level of risk in service purchase which makes them prefer to seek product information from personal acquaintances rather than from marketer-dominated sources; and they may find services difficult to evaluate.

Perishability

Services are highly perishable. A dentist's chair, unfilled for 15 minutes is a revenue opportunity lost for ever. Time cannot be held over for future sale. Services cannot be inventoried. The critical marketing problem here is how to manage demand so that it is experienced at the times and in the quantities wanted. Over-demand may need to be diverted to less busy periods. New demand may need to be generated to fill seasonal or irregular over-capacity. Not only are service marketers managers of demand, they may also need to manage supply so that a profitable equilibrium is always obtained (Sasser, 1979).

Heterogeneity

Services are not homogeneous. A bank teller may provide courteous and efficient service on Monday but not on Tuesday. Two letters posted to a common address on the same day may arrive a week apart.

Because customers buying services meet face-to-face with service employees, and experience their behaviours and attitudes, service outputs cannot be standardised. Human performance cannot be fully controlled by management. If the service provider works to a variable standard, the service output will be of a variable standard. The marketing issue is one of quality assurance. In the absence of tangible attributes, it is hard to establish objective standards of service product quality; equally, quality is hard for consumers to assess prior to, or even after, purchase. Some marketing managements have responded by introducing systems and procedures to eliminate unacceptable variability of service outputs.

Inseparability

The consumption of services takes place at the same time as they are produced, often on the premises of the service organisation. This raises a number of problems which marketers of goods do not face: the participation of the consumer in the production process (e.g. when being fitted for contact lenses), or delivery process (e.g. when standing in line in a school cafeteria); the interaction between the service provider, the service environment and the consumer (e.g. when visiting the surgery of a medical practitioner); and the merging of operations, human resource and marketing responsibilities in one individual. A restaurant marketer, for example, must concern himself with menu planning, recruitment of customer contact staff and sales promotion.

Some service organisations such as retailers or passenger transport companies produce and deliver their service for many customers simultaneously. In these cases, customers interact not only with the service organisation but with each other. Other customers, therefore, are a part of the service consumption experience.

The marketing problems associated with these four characteristics are summarised in Table 16.1.

It should be noted, however, that there is some disagreement about whether services do possess these four common characteristics. Blois (1983) points out a problematic tautology: the claim that these four charac-

Table 16.1   Service characteristics and marketing problems

Service characteristic	Marketing problems
Intangibility	1 Services cannot be stored.
	2 Services cannot readily be displayed, demonstrated or communicated.
	3 Prices are difficult to set.
	4 No patent protection possible.
Perishability	1 Services cannot be inventoried.
Heterogeneity	1 Services cannot be standardised.
	2 Quality control is difficult.
Inseparability	1 Customer interacts with service production and delivery systems, and the service environment.
	2 Customer may be part of product, or of production and delivery systems.
	3 No clear distinction between marketing, human resource and operations management.

Source: after Zeithaml, Parasuraman and Berry, 1985

teristics are typical of services can only be regarded as valid if it is made on the basis of an analysis of a group of economic outputs which have already been classified as services. The problem is that classification is the intended *outcome* of such analysis. Others have claimed that 'there is really no such thing as a pure service or a pure physical good. Many physical goods have a facilitating service and most services use facilitating goods.' (Bateson et al, 1978). For example, purchase of a fork-lift truck comes complete with operator instruction, a service contract and delivery; and a restaurant's service would not be quite so enjoyable without eating and drinking the physical facilitating goods! Accordingly, Shostack proposed what she called a molecular model of market entities. Rejecting the dichotomy of goods and services, she explains that all 'market entities' contain both tangible and intangible components (Shostack, 1977a). Finally, it has been argued that heterogeneity, perishability and inseparability are also found in tangible goods and are 'not present in every service.' (Buttle, 1986a).

There have been remarkably few empirical studies of marketing problems in the service sector. One notable sample survey of 1000 American service organisations asked management to identify their major marketing problems (Zeithaml, Parasuraman and Berry, 1985). The 323 replies received rated eight problems mentioned in the services marketing literature on a scale of 1 (= no problem) to 5 (= major problem). The results, shown in Table 16.2 show that fluctuating demand, costing and quality control are perceived as the major problems, whilst transportation, storage and patent problems are deemed relatively insignificant.

Despite the arguments opposing there being anything special about services marketing, there is still a body of opinion lobbying for modification of the 4Ps. They argue that the original marketing mix was developed from observation of marketing practice in manufacturing companies; that there is patchy empirical evidence of marketing practi-

Table 16.2 Significance of service marketing problems

Marketing problem	Mean rating
1 Demand for services fluctuates	3.27
2 Costs of providing services are difficult to calculate	2.59
3 Quality of services is difficult to control	2.52
4 Customers themselves are involved during the production of services	2.13
5 Services cannot be mass produced	2.13
6 Services cannot be protected by patent	1.89
7 Services cannot be stored	1.87
8 Services cannot be transported	1.65

(n = 323; problems rated on 5-point scale; higher ratings indicate more significant problems)

tioners in the service sector facing problems not experienced by their colleagues in manufacturing; and that there is growing evidence that the four conventional elements of the marketing mix are insufficiently comprehensive for service marketing (Cowell, 1984).

Reformulations of the marketing mix have been industry-specific or general. Renaghan (1981), for example, proposes a three-element marketing mix for the hospitality industry: the product-service mix, the presentation mix and the communications mix.

The most influential general reformulation has been that proposed by Booms and Bitner (1981). Their new marketing mix for services comprises 7Ps. The old four of product, price, promotion and place plus three additions: participants, physical evidence and process.

Booms and Bitner define their additions thus:

Participants: all human actors who play a part in service delivery and thus influence the buyer's perceptions: namely the firm's personnel and other customers in the firm's service environment.

Physical evidence: the environment in which the service is assembled and where the firm and customer interact; and any tangible commodities which facilitate performance or consumption of the service.

Process: the actual procedures, mechanisms, and flow of activities by which the service is delivered.

Table 16.3 profiles the full revised marketing mix.

A banking example demonstrates the logic of modifying the marketing mix. How does a prospective customer select a bank with which to do business? Not only by its range of services (product), charges (price), location (place) and communications (promotion) but also by a number of other factors: the attitude and behaviour of its customer contact employees, the numbers and types of other customers, its appearance externally and internally, its systems for handling customer accounts, and its atmosphere. Since these additional influences on consumer choice behaviour can be managed, it makes sense to accommodate them in an extended marketing mix.

Participants

The conventional 4Ps does acknowledge the impact of personal influence on the buying behaviour of others, but only in the role of salesperson. In service marketing, however, customers are exposed to two groups of participants in the service production and consumption process – customer contact employees and other customers.

Table 16.3 Marketing mix for services

Product:	Quality	Brand name
	Range	Level
	Warranty	After-sales service
Price:	Level	Discounts
	Terms	Differentiation
Place:	Location	Channels
	Coverage	Accessibility
Promotion:	Advertising	Selling
	Sales promotion	Public relations
	Publicity	Merchandising
Participants:	Personnel	Attitudes
	training	Other customers
	commitment	
	appearance	
	incentives	
	social skills	
Physical evidence:	Environment	Facilitating goods
	colour	Tangible clues
	layout	
	furnishings	
Process:	Policies	Procedures
	Mechanisation	Employee discretion
	Customer involvement	Flow of activities
	Customer direction	

Customer contact employees

Customer contact employees have many identities: bank clerk, hairdresser, checkout operator, bus driver, hostess, receptionist, service engineer. They may have production (operational) or sales roles as in the examples of chiropodist and shop assistant respectively. Some service employees, such as waitperson, occupy joint roles of service producer and service salesperson.

Not all service organisations provide, or require, a high level of customer contact: television contractors and postal services are examples. However, some, such as private schools and nursing homes, do feature a very high level of customer contact. Indeed, very often, this is the key attribute on which the organisation competes for customers.

Customer contact employees are in a powerful position to influence buying decisions, particularly in services where there are few tangible facilitating goods which customers can use for evaluation of alternatives. Such employees become, in effect, the most tangible evidence of the quality of the service organisation and its products.

Lehtinen (1985) has identified three components of service quality:

1   Interactive quality. The quality of the interaction between the contact employee and the customer, inclusive of systems and persons.

2   Physical quality. The quality of tangible clues such as surroundings and facilitating goods.

3   Institutional quality. The profile or image of the service organisation, which is 'the only quality dimension that can be experienced by the customer before the service production process'.

Physical quality is easiest to define and maintain because objective standards can be established. Levitt (1976) has suggested that many services can be subjected to the same technologies as manufactured goods, thus effectively eliminating variations in physical quality. He dubs this the 'industrialisation of service'. Under this arrangement, a Big Mac in Los Angeles will be materially identical to a Big Mac in London. The quality of tangible clues, including facilitating goods, can be assured with some certainty. Indeed, it has been observed that McDonalds' success is due in some part to the company's adoption of industrial production processes which eliminate variation (Buttle, 1986b).

Institutional quality can be measured using conventional marketing research methods, and strategic or tactical remedies introduced if necessary.

However, in services where there are significant levels of customer participation in the production and consumption process, management can face major problems of assuring interactive quality. The source of the problem may not be the employee. The customer, through his interactions with contact employees, service production processes and other customers can also have a major impact on the quality of the service.

There are a number of ways in which marketers can affect interactive quality standards: by influencing human resource decisions, by minimising the number and significance of employee–customer interactions, and by customising the service.

Influence human resource decisions

So as to obtain some degree of control over interactive quality standards, marketers may become involved in the recruitment, training, motivation, appraisal and compensation of customer contact staff. Indeed, it has been suggested that 'the successful service company must first sell the job to employees before it can sell its services to customers.' (Sasser and Arbeit, 1976). This notion of marketing the organisation to employees has been termed 'internal marketing'. Gronroos (1983) suggests that service organisations adopt an internal marketing concept. This 'holds that an organization's internal market of employees can be influenced most effectively and hence motivated to customer-consciousness, market-orientation and sales-mindedness by a marketing-like approach and by using marketing-like activities internally.' The aim is to recruit, develop and retain employees who are committed to achieving the objectives of the organisation by providing an appropriate standard of customer service. As a consequence, service marketers find themselves involved in activities normally the domain of human resource management. Flipo (1986) has found that 'in big service companies, internal marketing may take up to 80% of the marketing manager's time'.

Manage employee–customer interactions

A second way of reducing the variability of interactive quality is to minimise the number and significance of employee–customer interactions. This is in part achieved by introducing technology to replace human endeavour in service *production* – computerised telephone directory enquiries and programmed learning materials stored on disk are examples. Service *sales and distribution* can also be mechanised, either wholly or in part. Vacations and hotel rooms are sold via computerised reservation systems; banks make their services available both through automatic teller machines and in customers' homes equipped with appropriate computer hardware and telephone connection.

Customise service

A third way to minimise unacceptable variation in interactive quality is to customise the service. Effectively, this turns weakness into strength. It is a suitable strategy for tailors, interior designers, consultants and architects. The strategy requires each customer to be treated as presenting unique problems which the service must meet with unique solutions.

Other customers

Contact staff are not the only interpersonal influences upon customers. They may also be influenced by other customers during production or consumption of the service. A diner in a self-service cafeteria produces part of the service himself: he selects and plates his own food, takes the meal to a table and maybe even returns his soiled dishes to the trolley. In the line, he will almost certainly come into contact with other diners; there may be conversation; he may share a table with others.

Cowell (1984, p. 220) points out the ambiguity of the service marketer's relationship with his customers. 'The customer is not just a buyer: he is a co-producer and a resource, without which the service could not function.' In the restaurant business, for example, the expression 'meal experience' has become common currency. It reminds restaurateurs that diners do not just buy food and drink; they experience a style and standard of personal service, convenience, reputation, dining environment *and* the presence and behaviour of other clientele. In some restaurants other diners are the major attraction: they can provide an establishment with a distinctive style. In these circumstances, food and drink may provide only secondary satisfactions to the diner.

Physical evidence

The second of Booms and Bitner's additions to the marketing mix is physical evidence. They claim that 'because customers must form their expectations about services through means other than actual physical contact with the product they are paying for, their perceptions are influenced by marketing messages (e.g. advertising, publicity, sales promotions) and by tangible clues (e.g. architecture, furnishings, layout and colour.) (Booms and Bitner, 1982). This is confirmed by Levitt (1981) who writes: 'Common sense tells us, and research confirms, that people use appearances to make judgements about realities.'

Advertising agency premises are brightly and contemporarily furnished; management consultants dress soberly and conservatively. Intangibility brings problems which service marketers have the opportunity to resolve, at least in part, by managing tangible clues. Customer perceptions of service products may be based upon impressions formed during exposure to physical evidence.

Shostack (1977b) notes that intangible-dominant products are presented in the marketplace in mirror-opposite contrast to tangible-dominant products. Physical objects are enhanced through abstract associations whereas 'a service itself cannot be tangible, so reliance must be placed on peripheral clues.' Thus, Coca-Cola is surrounded by visual, verbal and aural associations with authenticity and youth, whereas a banker's office is furnished in leather and mahogany in order to present an air of solid dependability.

Management of these peripherals not only helps customers to better understand the service they are buying, but may add value so that customer satisfaction is enhanced.

Since many services are produced and consumed on the premises of the service organisation, there have been recent attempts to understand how the service environment influences customer behaviour. Retailers have known for many years that self-service stores laid out in conventional grid pattern are the most productive floor-plans for merchandising packaged consumer goods. Stores are designed to expose shoppers to the maximum amount of merchandise. Those categories, brands and items providing the best profit opportunities have been put in the most visible and accessible parts of the store. Now retailers have begun to look more closely into shopper behaviour. Many components of the retail environment have been tested experimentally. There is evidence about the effects of colour, noise, temperature, air movement, lighting on shopper emotions and behaviour (Buttle, 1984). Much work still needs to be done before the effects of physical evidence, particularly environmental factors are fully understood.

Process

The third innovation in Booms and Bitner's marketing mix is process. In manufacturing industry, marketing has little interest in production other than researching what items, volumes and qualities are to be produced. The great majority of marketing resources are put into pricing, distributing and promoting the merchandise after manufacture. Services are different. Marketing is keenly concerned with how the service production and delivery processes function. If service consumption is inseparable from service production, then the customer inevitably must come face to face with the production system. Indeed, as we've already seen, the customer may actually be a part of the service production or delivery system.

Efficient, effective production and delivery systems provide competitive advantages to the marketer. For example, a food service chain advertises that if it cannot deliver the pizza of choice to a customer's table in five minutes, there will be a full refund; some hotels have introduced express checkin–checkout systems to court high-spend business clients. Marketers are therefore closely involved with issues which were once the domain of operations management. Marketing's ability to generate customer satisfaction is in part dependent upon the influence it has over operations decisions such as facilities location, inventories of facilitating goods, production processes, production scheduling, quality assurance systems and operations staff training (they too may come into contact with customers). Large multi-site service organisations, such as food service franchisors, drycleaners and copyshops often have operations manuals intended to eliminate inter-site variation in service production and delivery. Marketing normally has considerable influence on the contents.

In organisations with a great deal of customer involvement in service production and delivery, marketers are less able to ensure effective and efficient operations, for the simple reason that customer input to those systems can never be fully controlled. The long wait which many patients endure in doctors' waiting rooms is ample evidence.

A word of caution

The Booms and Bitner revision to the marketing mix has an attractive face validity but it can be criticised on two counts. First, there is no evidence to suggest that organisations who develop and implement marketing plans based on 7Ps are any more successful than those who work only with 4Ps; empirical data have yet to be collected. Second, and more fundamental, a case can be made that the original 4Ps subsumes the additions of Booms and Bitner. The argument is that the customer experiences a bundle of satisfactions and dissatisfactions which derive from *all* dimensions of the service whether tangible or intangible, animate or inanimate. From the consumer point of view that bundle of satisfactions and dissatisfactions *is* the product he buys; from the service producer's point of view the product is designed from tangible, intangible, animate and inanimate raw materials to deliver those satisfactions which the customer values.

The product and/or promotion elements of the traditional 4Ps may incorporate participants in service production/delivery/consumption. Equally, since customers also come into direct contact with the service organisation's physical evidence and processes, these may be thought of as being part of the product.

Services and the 4Ps

Although the case for an extended marketing mix may be suspect, examination of the way service organisations conduct their marketing highlights some interesting issues and commonalities. In the next few pages we look at each of the conventional 4Ps in turn.

Product

New services

New commercial services are developed for much the same reason as other products; the profit motive. This is reflected in a desire to improve market share or sales volume, or to avoid the profit erosion which progress through the product life cycle inevitably brings. There is some evidence suggesting that the conventional four-stage life cycle – introduction, growth, maturity, decline – applies also to service products (Laczniak, 1980; Wahab et al, 1976). Profits decline as competition hots up, markets become increasingly fragmented and prices keener.

In non-commercial and non-profit sectors, improved client service or changing user needs often motivate innovation.

Lovelock (1984) has identified 6 categories of service innovation: new categories of service designed to satisfy latent demand, start-up businesses, new products introduced to existing customers, product line extensions, product improvements and style changes.

New services such as these may originate from sudden, original insights or have their genesis in entrepreneurial flair. More often, they require 'continuous effort and appropriate organizational provisions.' (Johnson, Scheuing and Gaida, 1986, p. 163). As Rathmell (1974) comments, 'the conventional steps of exploration, screening, business analysis, development, testing and commercialisation apply to services as well as goods.'

There are, however, some special difficulties which service marketers face during innovation. Service *product design* involves careful consideration of several interrelated issues: tangible and intangible components; animate and inanimate components; participants, physical evidence and process; physical, interactive and organisational qualities. Service marketers typically are concerned with a broader range of considerations than goods marketers.

Since *services cannot be protected by patent*, there is considerable incentive to bring products quickly to the marketplace to prevent loss of competitive advantage. The temptation to inadequately pretest innovations for customer acceptance is strong. Services are relatively easy to copy, particularly those which need few facilitating goods. New insurance policies and new educational programmes are examples. Since service innovations often require very little venture capital, risks are taken in launching services which would not be tolerated in high-cost, tangible goods innovation.

Testing new service concepts for customer acceptance is no easy matter because of services' dual intangibility. The innovation may be difficult to grasp mentally. There is also the problem of presenting tangible evidence of the service to interviewees. In the absence of facilitating goods there may be nothing to see, taste or otherwise experience. Test marketing – launching the new service into a limited geographic market – is relatively straightforward only for multi-site operators. The success of the innovation can be judged by making inter-unit comparisons. Kentucky Fried Chicken recently introduced menu changes throughout the UK following tests in two geographic regions (Anon, 1983).

The generic term 'product' is increasingly used to encompass both goods and services. Given (1) that most items in the marketplace contain both tangible and intangible elements, and (2) that goods and services compete for the same disposable income (e.g. laundromats compete with appliance manufacturers to meet customer demand for clean clothing), the new terminology makes sense.

Price

Price is the second of the conventional 4Ps. Many service industries do not even use the term price: amongst the many substitutes are admission, commission, fare, fee, premium, rent, subscription and tuition.

Whether one is considering goods or services, pricing decisions are complex. However, there are several particular issues and problems facing service marketers: intangibility, perishability, heterogeneity, government regulation, self-regulation and an unusual cost/value/price relationship.

Intangibility means that customers cannot see what they are buying, and therefore cannot easily judge whether they are receiving value for money. Intangibility introduces more freedom into pricing decisions, but greater risk into buying decisions. The greater the proportion of tangibles incorporated into the service, the greater standardisation of price there must be; intangible-dominant services allow greater freedom because there are fewer objective criteria against which customers can compare prices.

Perishability imposes the need for flexibility of pricing decisions. Price discounts are commonplace in services. If rack rate for a hotel room is $50, and the direct costs (laundry, cleaning consumables, direct labour) of preparing that room for guest occupancy total $10, then any price between those two figures will contribute towards fixed costs and profit. Some buyers of services are becoming more sophisticated and delay purchase in the expectation of seeing prices fall, especially in markets where supply exceeds demand. Marketers respond by attempting to mobilise demand as early as possible. In order to stimulate early buying, travel agencies and tour operators have co-operated to offer for sale during the winter months a limited number of extraordinarily cheap summer inclusive tours.

Because services are *heterogeneous*, customers may expect prices to vary. For example, if a marketing research agency takes on an investigation and is unable to produce a satisfactory report, the client may wish to re-negotiate the fee.

In some service industries, there is national, regional or local *government regulation of prices*. This is true of air transport, education and health services, community services, postal and telecommunications services in many countries around the world. Intervention serves public policy purposes; pricing decisions are therefore subject to political and social, rather than strictly economic, influence. Deregulation, as introduced in 1979 in the American air transport industry has led to greater price competition, based in part upon improvements in productivity, and to no little consumer confusion.

Some services industries operate *self-regulation of prices*. Although practices vary from country to country, price regulation is common amongst road haulage companies, lawyers, real-estate agents, architects, doctors and dentists. Prices are maintained through professional codes of practice, cartels or conferences.

When the service is intangible-dominant as in consulting and education, or when the consumer is buying access to knowledge and skills, there is no simple relationship between the costs of producing and delivering the service and the price charged to the consumer. Many services of this kind are therefore not suited to cost-plus pricing methods, but instead are demand-oriented. Service marketers therefore need to understand the value that customers place on their product, and the price they are willing to pay. This makes for a complex *cost/value/price relationship*.

Promotion

Promotion is the third of the conventional 4Ps. The promotion mix includes advertising, selling, sales promotion, direct mail, sponsorship, merchandising and public relations. As in goods marketing, these techniques are used in communications intended to influence the buying process by achieving cognitive (learning), affective (feeling) or behavioural (doing) outcomes in target audiences. However, a number of distinctions can be drawn between the promotion of goods and services.

Promotional methods are not universal in services. Some professionals such as accountants and stockbrokers have traditionally prevented the use of advertising and sales promotion, regarding these techniques as unethical. Recently, there has been international relaxation of these prohibitions. Other service organisations are very small and may feel they have neither the need nor the resources for promotion.

In goods marketing it is assumed that the audience is the potential and actual consumer. Service marketers who have adopted the internal marketing concept also *target customer contact and operations employees*. The goal is generally to make them aware of their role in providing customer satisfaction and meeting corporate objectives, or to inculcate favourable attitudes or behaviour.

Rathmell (1974, p. 96) recognises the principal difficulty facing promoters of service consumption when he writes: 'it is difficult or meaningless to promote an intangible product as a tangible product. An intangible does not lend itself to visual presentation. In addition, either visualization of a service being performed or a word description, whether written or spoken, offers only limited opportunity to inform, persuade or remind the service customer or prospect. As a result, the intangibility of services leads to the adoption of what many believe to be a superior form of promotion.' Many organisations *promote the more controllable tangible components* of their service. Airlines promote their wider, more comfortable seats. Hotels focus on the in-room amenities package. Intangible-dominant services cannot focus on tangibles, and therefore have followed a promotional track which many marketing purists would applaud. This is the approach which Rathmell calls superior – an emphasis upon consumer benefits. Correspondence schools emphasise that education can enrich the successful student's lifestyle and present new opportunities for career advancement. A home delivery service for diapers emphasises convenience, hygiene and time-saving benefits. Both types of message are also present in goods promotion. The critical difference is that many services do not have the choice of promoting tangibles or consumer benefits.

As noted above the job of promotion is to influence the consumer's decision-making process. Although most research has focussed on consumer goods, Zeithaml's (1981) investigation of the processes used to evaluate services draws tentative conclusions which help guide promotion mix decisions. Because of intangibility and heterogeneity, service purchase is perceived as riskier than goods purchase. Accordingly, promotion could focus on assurances and guarantees of quality; on staff qualifications and training; on procedures designed to standardise the quality of the service. Consumers also prefer to seek information from *personal* sources prior to service purchase. Word of mouth influence has a significant role to play.

Selling plays an important role in service marketing. It has been observed that in services 'personal selling is the predominant component of this (promotion) mix.' (George, Kelly and Marshall 1983). This is primarily due to the nature of the service product. Consumption involves both direct consumer/service organisation interface and customer involvement in service production. This simultaneity not only permits but necessitates interactive marketing. A plastic surgeon who consults with a client to straighten her nose, is ideally placed to sell a face lift or breast implants. Dual intangibility can become a major barrier to purchase unless marketers take the time to explain the service's benefits. Advertising can rarely provide the amount of time required, nor the opportunity for interaction with the prospect.

Customer contact employees, if adequately trained in selling techniques can do much to stimulate demand and reduce the percentage of services perishing unsold. Despite these advantages of personal selling, a report in the American magazine *Sales and Sales Management* provides some evidence that service firms spend less on sales training and require a shorter period in training than manufacturers. Given the difficulty of selling intangibles the reverse situation might be expected.

Service expenditure on advertising is increasing. Banks, multiple retailers, hotels, restaurant chains, building societies, tour operators, travel agents are all spending more in media than ever before.

Place

Place is the last of the conventional 4Ps. In marketing manufactured goods, concepts of place are easy to understand. A consumer in Boston wants to buy a knife; the knife is manufactured in Birmingham. The item needs to be shipped cross-country, either direct, or into outlets patronised by the customer. Place decisions are therefore concerned with the physical movements of goods and the selection and management of intermediaries in a channel of distribution.

Place decisions provide time and place utilities to customers by making products available when and where wanted. These same utilities need to be offered to consumers of services and therefore in this conceptual sense there are no differences between goods and services place decisions. Confusions about the role of place in service marketing arise for two reasons: first, because inseparability of production and consumption implies that there can be no such thing as a channel of distribution for services; second, because intangibility implies that there are no physical flows through those channels. As we shall see both these assumptions are incorrect.

Service marketers are particularly concerned with two classes of place decisions: location and channel. Decisions of both types aim to make service products more convenient and available to their target markets.

Location

Location is described by Rathmell (1974, p. 104) as 'the distribution of people and facilities prepared to perform services.' The location of the service firm may or may not have a significant influence on marketing performance. Customers do not really care where their electricity, television programmes or telephone service comes from. However, either for reasons of customer demand or industry custom and practice, services may be geographically dispersed or concentrated. Pizza chains and secretarial agencies are dispersed where there is demand; private medical practitioners are concentrated in Harley Street, London. In the USA, advertising agencies concentrate in Madison Avenue, New York, together with complementary services such as printers, graphic design studios, film and video producers and independent copywriters. It is possible to distinguish between the location of a service organisation and its operations. With multi-site services such as copyshops and cinemas the organisation is often centralised whilst the operations are dispersed.

An inappropriate location decision can sound the death knell for services such as retail organisations. The founder of the Hilton hotel group is reputed to have said that there are three factors responsible for the success of a hotel: location, location, location! A number of hotel and restaurant chains have devised mathematical models to assist in decision-making, but these are very often no more than simple adaptations of more sophisticated retail models (Akehurst, 1981). Indeed, probably the most sophisticated in their location decision making are the multiple retailers who make two distinct, but interdependent location decisions: (1) the selection of a trading area and (2) the selection of a particular site within the trading area.

Simkin, Doyle and Saunders (1985) identified six different approaches to retail site selection in the literature. These ranged from 'look and judge' checklists through comparisons with analogous situations already encountered to complex mathematical modelling procedures. However, their survey of retailers concluded that 'techniques discussed in the literature are not regularly adopted by the retailer, excepting the intuitively assessed checklist and analogue comparison.'

Top quality sites are rapidly acquired when they become available. Location decisions are therefore often made under considerable time pressure.

Channels

The distribution channel comprises those organisations and individuals which make the service more convenient and accessible. At one end of the channel is the service producer; at the other the customer. Flowing through the channel are money, information and the tangible clues surrounding the service. Let us take the vacation product as an example. The vacation product is assembled by a tour operator who block-books hotel rooms, arranges meal plans, charters flights, organises airport–hotel–

airport transfers and access to tourist attractions. The product is sold by travel agents to individual or group vacationers. In this example, the distribution channel is three stages long (tour operator – travel agent – vacationer); information and tangible clues (brochures, video tapes) about the holiday flow through the channel from tour operator to vacationer; payment for the vacation flows from vacationer to the travel agent who retains a commission and passes the balance to the tour operator; feedback about the vacationer's satisfaction with the product flow back directly or through the travel agent to the tour operator.

Most writers generalise that because of the intangible and inseparable nature of services, direct sale is the only possible channel for most of them (Donnelly, 1976). Direct sale is certainly commonplace but by no means is it the only form of channel.

Direct channels are used to distribute the services of accountants, dentists, funeral directors and lawyers. The incentive to seek out indirect channels often comes from the organisation's desire to grow (e.g. American Express credit cards) or from the need to raise demand to match the service organisation's capacity (e.g. filling empty theatre seats). There are a wide variety of direct and indirect service channels, a sample of which appears in Table 16.4.

Table 16.4   Distribution channels

Hotel room		Guest
Hotel room ...... tour operator ...... travel agent		Guest
Credit card	retailer	Member
Insurance ...... master agent	local agent	Customer
Insurance	bank	Customer
Theatre seat	ticket agent	Spectator
Car rental	tourist information office	Driver
Rail transport	travel clubs	Tourist

There are a number of innovations in types and forms of service channels. Banks for example, once restricted to High Street locations, are distributing their services through full-service core branches, satellite service or 'thin' branches, remote self-service banking points, home banking and electronic funds transfer at the point-of-sale (EFTPoS) (Howcroft and Lavis, 1986). Accommodation is also being distributed electronically (hotel reservation systems). The Home Shopping Club, an American cable TV innovation, provides viewers with the opportunity to buy direct off screen by making a phone call and quoting a credit card number.

Some services have not recognised the additional business that could be generated through channel innovation. Restaurants, for example, conventionally sell direct to diners. Many of them barely break even on mid-week nights. There are no insurmountable difficulties in extending distribution to sell through travel agents, tour operators, tourist information offices, theatres, cinemas, motels, factories and offices.

Service provision, in fields like banking, retailing, industrial cleaning, and travel agencies, is becoming more concentrated. Independent service organisations are collaborating to fight the growing power of the chains by developing their own channels of distribution, e.g. the hotel consortium Best Western.

Franchising of services is growing extremely rapidly. There are franchises in fields as varied as accounting and tax services (H & R Block), drain cleaning (Dyno-rod), and slimming clubs (Weightwatchers). Franchising lends itself to any service that can be standardised – a major problem with heterogeneous services.

Management contracts are another innovation influencing the distribution of services. Under this arrangement, the service organisation, acting as agent, does not invest in the fixed assets necessary to produce and deliver the service. Capital is supplied by independent investors, whilst management and operations expertise is supplied by the service organisation. The agent normally retains a percentage of gross income and returns the balance to the property owner.

Table 16.5 provides a summary of marketing strategies that practitioners and academics have found suitable for service organisations, and the particular service characteristics which make them appropriate.

Marketing organisation in services

The aim of marketing organisation is to so define the authority and responsibilities of each employee that the firm will efficiently achieve its marketing objectives. The great difficulty in services is that decisions affecting marketing performance are made throughout the organisation. Inseparability of production and consumption means that there are interfaces between customers and the service production system. In manufacturing industry, marketers are not concerned with the interpersonal skills of production staff, nor are they much concerned with how the product is manufactured. In services these are major concerns because of the impact they can have on customer satisfaction. The marketing organisation should, therefore, explicitly acknowledge the requirement for marketers to have input into human resource and operations decisions.

Recommendations have been made for coping with these service-specific problems. Lovelock et al (1981) suggest that a matrix organisation could

Table 16.5 Marketing strategies for services
(*developed from an idea in Zeithaml, Parasuraman and Berry, 1985*)

Marketing strategies	Services features
Stress tangible clues	1
If no tangible clues, promote benefits	1
Create strong organisational image	1
If facilitating goods used, employ cost accounting to set price	1
Stimulate word-of-mouth	1
If intangible-dominant, use demand considerations to set price	1, 3
Use post-purchase communication	1, 3
Emphasise personal rather than non-personal communication	1, 4
Develop long-term customer relationships	1, 4
Develop empathic sales and operations staff	1, 4
Manage the service environment	1, 4
Use strategies to cope with fluctuating demand	2
Deflect over-demand	2
Make simultaneous adjustments to supply and demand	2
Industrialise the service	3
Maintain flexible pricing policy	3, 2
Develop and manage quality standards	3, 2, 1
Promote assurances of quality	3, 2, 1
Customise the service	3, 4
Invest in internal marketing	4
Plan production system to deliver customer satisfaction	4
Influence inventory, location, other operational decisions	4
Promote customer co-operation in the production process	4
Manage customers in service environment	4
Provide service from multi-site locations	4
Influence recruitment, training etc. of operations employees	4, 1
Influence recruitment, training etc. of other contact staff	4, 1
Co-ordinate promotional efforts of operations and sales staff	4, 2

Notes: 1 = intangibility; 2 = perishability; 3 = heterogeneity; 4 = inseparability. Several strategies are suitable for more than one reason. Most significant reason for strategy listed first.

ensure that there is multi-functional acceptance of responsibility for marketing performance. This, plus a healthy dose of internal marketing, adherence to quality control standards that reflect customer needs and the creation of inter-functional task forces to tackle marketing issues can do much to solve these organisational problems.

Notwithstanding this advice, the usual functional, geographic and customer organisation structures are found in service organisations.

Conclusion

Marketing, which is defined as the management process responsible for identifying, anticipating and satisfying customer requirements profitably, is applied in both commercial and non-commercial service organisations, yet marketing expertise is less pervasive in the service sector than in manufacturing.

There are several ways of looking at marketing: as a business philosophy, as a management process, and as a set of tools (called the marketing mix) used to manipulate demand. In this last way service marketing may be significantly different from goods marketing.

There is widespread agreement that services marketers face a number of special problems. Their products are intangible-dominant, making display, demonstration and communication difficult. Consumers find intangibles hard to understand and evaluate. Services are highly perishable. As services cannot be held in inventory, marketers need to be excellent managers of both demand and supply. Services are heterogeneous. Human job performances cannot be standardised. This makes quality control difficult to achieve. Production and consumption of the service take place simultaneously. This is known as inseparability. As a consequence, customers interact not only with sales staff, but also with production staff. Furthermore interaction often takes place on the service organisation's premises. Marketers of services are therefore concerned that operations and human resource decisions should be made with some sensitivity towards marketing needs. Not all students of marketing believe that these characteristics are unique to services.

There have been a number of attempts to reformulate the marketing mix to make it more applicable to service marketing. Such reformulations have been either industry-specific or generalised. The most influential suggests that service marketers can use seven controllable variables to manipulate demand – product, price, promotion, place (channel and location decisions), participants, physical evidence and process. Known collectively as the 7Ps, the last three are claimed to be variables used only by service marketers. Some observers claim that these three new additions are already subsumed in two of the other 4Ps, product and promotion.

New commercial services are developed for much the same reasons as other products, but there are some special managerial difficulties: service design involves consideration of intangible and human elements, unlike goods design; patent protection is impossible; services are relatively easy for competitors to copy; concept testing intangibles is a very difficult research task, and test marketing for single-site services may be out of the question.

Price decisions are complex for services. Intangibility means that cost inputs to price may be insignificant. Perishability imposes the need for flexible pricing. Because services are of inconsistent quality, consumers may expect prices to vary or to be negotiable. The prices of some services are regulated by government or trade organisations.

Marketing communication in the service sector is aimed not only at customers but at customer contact employees. This so-called 'internal marketing' aims to build behaviours and attitudes which promote the cause of customer satisfaction. Much customer-targeted promotion aims to tangibilise the service. Where this is impossible or difficult, copy strategy may emphasise consumer benefits. Personal influence is often more important than non-personal communication in building trial and repeat purchase.

Well conceived place decisions make services more convenient and accessible. The location of the service organisation is of critical importance to the success of some, but not all, services. Where location is important, services make two interrelated decisions: selection of a trading area, and selection of a particular site within the trading area. Many services are distributed through the simplest channel – direct from producer to consumer. However, there are many forms of indirect service channels, including some which are electronic. Service organisations are beginning to compete through channel innovation.

Inseparability presents special challenges when designing a marketing organisation structure. The interaction of customer with operations staff and the production system suggests that organisation structures should recognise the interdependence of marketing, operations and human resource functions.

In all, improving the quality of service marketing is an immensely challenging task which can only be successfully accomplished if there is a deeper understanding of the special problems facing this growing sector of industry.

References

Akehurst, G. P. (1981) 'Towards a theory of market potential with reference to hotel and restaurant firms', *Service Industries Review*, 1(1), February, pp. 18–30.

Anon. (1983) 'How KFC plan to fly back up the pecking order', *The Times*, 21 June.

Bateson, J. E. G., Eiglier, P., Langeard, E. and Lovelock, C. H. (1978) *Testing a Conceptual Framework for Consumer Service Marketing*, Marketing Science Institute, Cambridge, MA.

Berry, L. L. (1984) 'Services marketing is different', in: Lovelock, C. H. (ed) *Services Marketing*, Prentice-Hall, Inc., Englewood Cliffs, NJ, pp. 29–37.

Blois, K. (1983) 'Service marketing – assertion or asset', *Service Industries Journal*, 3(2), July, pp. 113–20.

Booms, B. H. and Bitner, M. J. (1981) 'Marketing strategies and organisation structures for service firms', in: Donnelly, J. H. and George, W. R. (eds) *Marketing of Services*, Proceedings Series, American Marketing Association, Chicago, IL, pp. 47–51.

Booms, B. H. and Bitner, M. J. (1982) 'Marketing services by managing the environment', *Cornell Hotel and Restaurant Administration Quarterly*, May, pp. 35–9.

Buttle, F. A. (1984) 'How merchandising works', *International Journal of Advertising*, No. 3, pp. 139–48.

Buttle, F. A. (1986a) 'Unserviceable concepts in service marketing', *Quarterly Review of Marketing*, 11(3), Spring, pp. 8–14.

Buttle, F. A. (1986b) *Hotel and Foodservice Marketing: A Managerial Approach*, Holt, Rinehart and Winston, Eastbourne.

Cowell, D. W. (1984) *The Marketing of Services*, Heinemann, London.

Donnelly, J. H. (1976) 'Marketing intermediaries in channels of distribution for services', *Journal of Marketing*, 40(1), January.

Flipo, J-P. (1986) 'Interdependence of internal and external marketing strategies', *European Journal of Marketing*, 20(8), pp. 5–14.

George, W. R., Kelly, J. P. and Marshall, C. E. (1983) 'Personal selling of services', in: Berry, L. L., Shostack, G. L. and Upah, G. D. (eds) *Emerging Perspectives in Services Marketing*, American Marketing Association, Chicago, IL, pp. 65–7.

Gronroos, C. (1983) *Strategic Management and Marketing in the Service Sector*, Marketing Science Institute, Cambridge, MA, Report No. 83–104, pp. 76–87.

Hooley, G. and Cowell, D. W. (1985) 'The status of marketing in UK service industries', *Service Industries Journal*, 5(3), November, pp. 261–72.

Howcroft, B. and Lavis, J. (1986) 'Delivery systems in UK retail banking', *Service Industries Journal*, 6(2), July, pp. 144–58.

Johnson, E. M., Scheuing, E. E. and Gaida, K. A. (1986) *Profitable Service Marketing*, Dow-Jones Irwin, Homewood, IL.

Laczniak, G. R. (1980) in: Mokwa, P., Dawson, W. M. and Prieve, E. A. (eds) *Marketing the Arts*, Praeger, New York.

Lehtinen, J. R. (1985) 'Improving service quality by analysing the service production process', in: Gronroos, C. and Gummesson, E. (eds) *Service Marketing – Nordic School Perspectives*, Department of Business Administration, University of Stockholm, pp. 110–19.

Levitt, T. (1976) 'The industrialisation of service', *Harvard Business Review*, Vol. 54, September–October, pp. 63–74.

Levitt, T. (1981) 'Marketing intangible products and product intangibles', *Harvard Business Review*, Vol. 59, May–June, pp. 94–102.

Lovelock, C. H. (1979) 'Theoretical contributions from services and non-business marketing', in: Ferrell, O. C., Brown, S. W. and Lamb, C. W. (eds) *Conceptual and Theoretical Developments in Marketing*, American Marketing Association, Chicago, IL, pp. 147–65.

Lovelock, C. H., Langeard, E., Bateson, J. E. G. and Eiglier, P. (1981) 'Some organizational problems facing marketing in the service sector', in: Donnelly, J. H. and George, W. R. (eds) *Marketing of Services*, Proceedings Series, American Marketing Association, Chicago, IL, pp. 168–71.

Lovelock, C. H. (1984) 'Developing and implementing new services', in: George, W. R. and Marshall, C. E. (eds) *Developing New Services*, American Marketing Association, Chicago, IL, pp. 44–64.

Mindak, W. A. and Fine, S. (1981) 'A fifth 'P': public relations', in: Donnelly, J. H. and George, W. R. (eds) *Marketing of Services*, Proceedings Series, American Marketing Association, Chicago, IL, pp. 71–3.

Rathmell, J. M. (1974) *Marketing in the Service Sector*, Winthrop Publishers Inc., Cambridge, MA.

Renaghan, L. P. (1981) 'A new marketing mix for the hospitality industry', *Cornell Hotel and Restaurant Administration Quarterly*, August, pp. 31–5.

Rushton, A. M. and Carson, D. J. (1985) 'The marketing of services: managing the intangibles', *European Journal of Marketing*, 19(3), pp. 19–40.

Sasser, W. E. (1979) 'Match supply and demand in service industries', *Harvard Business Review*, November–December, pp. 133–40.

Sasser, W. E. and Arbeit, S. P. (1976) 'Selling jobs in the service sector', *Business Horizons*, 19 June, pp. 61–5.

Shostack, G. L. (1977a) 'Breaking free from product marketing', in: Lovelock, C. H. (ed) *Services Marketing*, Prentice-Hall Inc., Englewood Cliffs, NJ, pp. 37–47.

Shostack, G. L. (1977b) 'Is service marketing the right way?' *Trusts and Estates*, November, p. 722.

Simkin, L. P., Doyle, P. and Saunders, J. (1985) 'UK retail store location assessment', *Journal of the Market Research Society*, 27(2), April, pp. 95–108.

Wahab, S., Crampon, L. J. and Rothfield, L. M. (1976) *Tourism Marketing*, Tourism International Press, London.

Zeithaml, V. A. (1981) 'How consumer evaluation processes differ between goods and services', in: Donnelly, J. H. and George, W. R. (eds) *Marketing of Services*, Proceedings Series, American Marketing Association, Chicago, IL, pp. 186–95.

Zeithaml, V. A., Parasuraman, A. and Berry, L. L. (1985) 'Problems and strategies in services marketing', *Journal of Marketing*, 49(2), Spring, pp. 33–46.

Part IV
Operational issues in service industries

The final part of this book focusses on key issues that managers in service organisations must consider. They pervade services at a strategic, operational and functional level and directly affect how and why the service manager makes decisions. Foremost of these issues is quality. In Chapter 17, Brian Moores explains why service quality is important and how service managers are attempting to achieve this elusive goal. But a review of other chapters of the book will reveal that many of the other contributors also recognise the importance and relevance of this issue and they discuss it in the specific context of their topic area.

Possibly of equal importance, but with a much lower profile, is the issue of productivity in service organisations. Robert Mill, in Chapter 18, explains why this should be a major concern and what service managers can do about it. To a certain extent it has always been believed that there is some sort of trade-off between quality and productivity, and in a simplistic way this is probably true. All things being equal, if a room maid is asked to clean 12 rooms instead of 10, or 3 instead of 4 tills in a bank are operating, then quality will suffer at the expense of productivity. But in most cases 'all things' do not remain equal, in which case both quality and productivity can be enhanced.

There are two main trends in services that enable this to happen. First, front-of-house activity is being decoupled from back-of-house, usually with the latter being automated in some way. Examples of this are central production kitchens supplying several outlets in the catering industry, and central data processing in banking. Productivity is enhanced by the economies of scale that can be achieved back-of-house that are not possible at the service contact point, and quality is enhanced by increased accuracy, speed or whatever that centralised, automated, back-of-house performance can provide. The second trend is increased customer participation in the service experience. In many service industries customers are doing very much more themselves as opposed to being served by a service employee. Clearly, this improves productivity as the customer is acting as an unpaid employee of the organisation. But quality is enhanced too, since customers seem to enjoy this participation, either because it speeds up the transaction, as with automatic cash dispensers, or introduces a high level of customisation, as with self-selection salad bars in restaurants.

Clearly, understanding, modifying and developing new service delivery systems requires effective decision making. In Chapter 19, David Targett looks at the way in which the management sciences can contribute to dealing with these complex decisions. Like many of the contributors, he identifies the facts that the focus of attention, and relevance of specific topics, are different when considering services in comparison wth manufacturing industry.

Finally, Paul Gamble, in Chapter 20, looks at the role and nature of management information systems in the context of service organisations. It is such systems that provide the service manager with the data he or she needs in order to determine whether or not they have been successful.

Such feedback is essential, for the issues, problems and challenges facing service management are exciting, demanding and dynamic. It is my hope that this book has demonstrated this and provided enlightenment with regard to how one may face the issues and meet the challenge.

17 Management of service quality

PROFESSOR BRIAN MOORES

Introduction

There are some cynics who incline to the view that the current obvious growing concern with total quality management is yet another in a long line of passing management fads.

Just as managers became obsessed with, say, job enrichment or critical path analysis in the 1960s so, runs the argument, the interest in quality-related issues will gradually dissolve to be replaced with whatever is next in vogue. Such cynics are probably wrong, for this newly emerged awareness is not focussed on a single management technique, but rather does it relate to a basic characteristic of the product on offer, which to a large extent can determine whether or not an organisation stays in business. Dissatisfied customers are likely to become ex-customers, and this is probably more so in service industries than elsewhere on account of the alternatives available. Certainly, this is much more the case in 1989 than it was even ten years ago when one had to be satisfied with what one got. It will doubtless come as a surprise to younger readers to discover that, if one holidayed at a Blackpool boarding house in the immediate post-war years, one had to be off the premises at 10.00 am and was not allowed back in until early evening. Imagine offering that level of service today! Again, it does not seem all that many years ago that one was left with the impression that a bank was actually doing the customer a favour in handling an account. What a difference to the present-day interest in putting-the-customer-first campaigns being mounted by many such financial institutions. Almost overnight they appear to have woken up to the fact that customers are now less likely, as a matter of routine, to stay with the same bank all their lives in spite of any difficulties they might have experienced.

However, let us not run away with the idea that all services have been turned on their heads. How many commuters board trains within 40–50 miles of London expecting that they will have to stand for the whole journey? Likewise, it is a fact of life that most individuals, if called for a hospital outpatient appointment, would schedule for a whole morning or afternoon away from the workplace. Before discussing why the picture on the service quality front is as varied as it is, let us first explore just what we mean by the term. That definitional exercise will be followed by a discussion of why the quality of service is so important, how it is offered or advertised, how it is monitored and how is it to be improved.

What is service quality?

It would be tempting to suggest that, while we might not be able to define exactly what is meant by the quality of service provided, it is easy enough to appreciate when it has been inadequate. However, the use of the term inadequate implies some element of comparison between the service experienced and that which had been expected.

Indeed, this idea of a user-defined level of service quality has led some writers to suggest that quality is the difference between expectation and reality. Personally, I would prefer to think of any such disparity as being a measure of customer satisfaction. It is difficult for me to come to terms with the fact that, if someone attends a hospital outpatient appointment expecting to wait needlessly for two or three hours along with other individuals who might well have been assigned an identical appointment time, then the quality is acceptable if indeed the duration is of two or three hours. In that particular context, it surely behoves the management of the unit to have aspirations of a higher standard of service.

Nightingale (1987) has captured the various issues in his use of the terms *Customer Quality Standards* (CQSs) and *Customer Service Standards* (CSSs). The former correspond to the perceptions that service providers have of what customers expect of every aspect of the service offered, while the latter term relates to the standards the service provider has in mind to provide. Observe, though, that both these measures pertain to *every* aspect of the service. In other words, the service experience cannot be neatly captured on a single dimension. Quite clearly, someone does not go to a pub merely to imbibe an alcoholic beverage. One could do that more cheaply and probably a good deal more comfortably in the privacy of one's own home. Likewise, when a couple set out for a meal at a restaurant recommended in one or other of the good food guides, they will naturally be anticipating that the food will be well cooked. However, they will also be setting out with some expectations about the wine, the ambience, the price and the friendliness of the staff. The same is just as true if that same couple decide instead to indulge in a 'Big Mac' from Macdonald's.

How would the perceptions of this couple change if they wanted to celebrate in real style at one of Britain's top dozen restaurants? It is difficult to imagine that the food would be all that much better cooked, but more than likely the choice of dishes would be different, although not necessarily any greater. The relationships with the staff would be very different in nature and certainly they would be anticipating paying considerably more for an experience that might well feature some musical entertainment.

In some instances, the Customer Service Standards are made explicit and might even feature in the advertising of the product. Thus, for example, one American supermarket chain announces that no more than three people will ever be waiting at a checkout. Likewise, a gasoline company, also in America, used to advertise that your windscreen would be cleaned within 20 seconds of arrival on the forecourt. In a similar vein, in their advertising of Business Class facilities, airlines increasingly incorporate very specific details of the legroom provided and the type of china off which one will eat.

When these standards are not made quite as explicit, how does the customer become conscious of them? Mechanisms, albeit subconscious, are clearly in place which provide appropriate clues and enable an impression to be formed in the customer's mind. Few people, for example, would arrive at a Macdonald's wearing evening dress, unless perhaps a previous engagement at a smart restaurant had turned out to be a complete disaster! Likewise, it would be a rare occurrence these days for a customer to blanch on seeing the extortionate prices charged for wine in a five-star restaurant. Travel companies have been quite successful in implanting in people's minds an image of the particular niche in which they are operating. A person taking a standard Intasun package, for example, has quite different expectations from someone going on holiday with Kuoni, and the difference will not only be financial in nature.

Of course, once an individual or group has been through a particular service experience, they will have a much more finely tuned set of expectations should they decide to participate again. Indeed, it is quite possible that a return visit will be associated with a welcome, which in turn adds to the experience and which becomes a major component of future experiences. From observation, it would appear that being recognised is an important component of service encounters as the 'cognoscenti' have always known.

What all this says in a nutshell is that while quality, like beauty, might well be in the eye of the beholder, the service provider is actually the person who ordains just what service standards are being offered. If the customer feels that the experience does not accord with his or her expectations, it might conceivably be because the provider has not maintained the standards, but it could be that the customer's anticipations were off target.

Why is service quality important?

In the manufacturing sector, companies have long recognised that quality, be it perceived or actual, impacts directly on sales. The impressive performance turnaround at Jaguar cars was in part explained by the massive increase in productivity following John Egan's appointment. This had a direct impact on costs, but what undoubtedly contributed more to sales was the emphasis placed on quality. This ensured that prospective customers, particularly those in North America, could be confident that their vehicles were more likely to be on the road than off. Increasingly, the quality of the finished product constitutes an important element in the marketing mix. One must give credit to the Japanese for having revolutionised our thinking on this front. From an immediate post-war image of producers of copies and garbage, they have moved to a position of standard-setters for a host of products, most notably in the electronics and automobile industries. The impact on Western producers has been nothing if not traumatic, but this increased quality of production has been paralleled by a growing public demand for higher quality products. This has undoubtedly been fuelled by the emergence of agencies which have set themselves up as evaluators of standards of quality and even safety. While Iaacoco might have poured scorn on Ralph Nader's well documented attack on the safety record of the Ford Pinto, the attendant publicity did not help sales of that particular model. When the Consumers' Association magazine *Which?* ranks toasters according to value-for-money, you can rest assured that that particular edition is read avidly, however dispiritedly, by all toaster manufacturers.

What the Japanese have done is to force manufacturers to recognise that the trade-off between quality and cost is, and was always, a myth. In terms of failing to meet specifications, a poor quality product represents an expensive unit of production, as the reported examples of *quality costing* exercises reveal. The cost of not getting something right first time as reflected in subsequent failures, be they identified internally or externally, can be and are absurdly high (Dale, 1986). As consumers, we should appreciate the fact that standards have improved and will continue to do so.

When we move across to the service sector, it could reasonably be argued that here quality is an even more important feature. At the simplest level, the choice of eating places is a whole order of magnitude greater than our choice of automobile manufacturers. It is also reasonable to postulate that in a service encounter the service is itself the product. If we accept that in hotels frequented by international businesspeople the traveller has a pretty sensible set of perceptions about what to expect, it is possible that price does not loom too large in his or her thinking. The traveller will have a set of minimum expectations which a Hilton, a Hyatt, an Inter-continental or a Sheraton can be expected to provide. The traveller can almost be guaranteed that there will be a bathroom en suite; the water will be hot; there will be a television and a drinks cabinet and, should a snack be required, some form of room service will be available. These all constitute explicit or implicit parts of the offer. However, all these chains have become aware that what could set them apart is the nature of the personal interaction on offer, hence the quite massive, and to some extent surprising, upsurge in training programmes aimed at alerting staff to the fact that the customer comes first. In the hospitality sector, one could perhaps steal an analogy from Herzberg. Such things as the television in the room, could be likened to 'hygiene' factors in that, although their pres-ence is unlikely to add to customer satisfaction, their absence or malfunctioning can occasion dissatisfaction. The personal interaction aspects of the service encounter would, using this analogy, be likened to the 'motivation' factors. That said, the advertisements run by the Hemsley Hotel chain in which Mrs Hemsley proclaims that one should be able to turn the television off from the bed or be able to wrap the bath towel completely around one, suggest that we have not yet reached saturation point on accoutrements.* Indeed, one customer on a residential manage-ment course run by the author recently registered her dissatisfaction over the fact that the en-suite bathroom in a university facility did not boast a bidet!

What service organisations now seem to appreciate is that, if there is a mismatch between what is offered and what is expected, then the customer is less likely to return. If this mismatch is attributable to the service not meeting the specified standard, then the organisation will have failed unless it is able to 'recover' constructively. Some failures do provide such recovery opportunities as when it culminates in a letter of complaint. Few complainants turn down the offer of a free meal, a free night's accom-modation or even a free flight to compensate for the bad experience. If, however, the mismatch stems from an irreconcilable difference due to the customer having a completely erroneous picture of what is on offer, then such compensatory devices would, of course, be a sheer waste of money.

Another reason why expectations and results should be brought into line is that there is now ample evidence that someone on the receiving end of what they consider to be a bad experience will broadcast this to a sig-nificantly larger number of people than if the experience had been positive. This 'broadcasting' ratio would appear to differ by product or service, but

* These adverts all feature a similar theme: 'I would expect . . . so why shouldn't my customers?'

it certainly appears to start at around four, i.e. we tell at least four times as many people about a sour experience than we do about one that has gone well.

How is the quality of service offered?

Reference has already been made to the founder's wife proclaiming the very specific qualities of Hemsley hotels from the pages of magazines and hoardings. The windscreen cleaning and the supermarket checkout guarantee examples were of a similar genre. Some organisations, most notably Federal Express, make great play of how short a time elapses before a telephone call is answered. Quite often this type of proclamation of standards is associated with speed of service, but it might also relate to consistency of product. In parts of the United States, for example, one can secure a particular hairstyle in any salon in one chain of hairdressers through the simple expedient of asking for say 'Freddy', which, in all the shops, is the identity assumed by the individual offering that particular style.

In other service sectors, the offer is less blatant. A travel company might suggest that your prospective companions might come from a certain section of society. A restaurant might imply that it is expensive and, to reinforce the notion, might even go so far as to provide menus bearing no prices for those diners who are being entertained to a meal by their hosts. The various shuttle-service operations both here in Britain and in the USA owe their success to the fact that prospective flyers know that they will not have to wait for too long for a flight. Pass a Rapide type coach on a motorway and one can read off the various features offered inside which certainly seem appealing towards the end of a six-hour motorway car journey. Federal Express is not unique in offering guaranteed overnight delivery. Carryfast and most other parcel delivery companies make such an offer but, as yet, none has had the courage to offer more than the cost of the transaction by way of compensation. In that business, the customer can go one stage further and pay a premium for guaranteed morning delivery or even delivery before 10.00 am. Here the customer is becoming involved in the specification or negotiation of the standard. The customer has a similar opportunity when negotiating service contracts, be it for domestic appliances or sizeable computer installations. This is an unresearched field, but it does seem to this observer that the growth of airline executive clubs or the various 'gold' credit cards points to the fact that people are increasingly prepared to pay a premium for what they consider to be a premium service. Certainly over four million people can't be subscribing to private health insurance schemes to secure a higher quality of surgery. The surgeons will be the same ones they would encounter were they to be operated on in an NHS facility. They, or more usually their employers, are clearly intent on introducing a greater degree of certainty into the date of the operation if not its being brought forward (Lee, 1986).

It is a virtual certainty that the standards being offered will increasingly feature in the marketing mix. The inclusion of performance characteristics in automobile advertisements is one example of this phenomenon which sometimes leans in the direction of 'copy-knocking'. Anyone who has suffered the 60- to 90-minute waits at Kennedy or Miami airports must have been very receptive to the recent advertisements placed by Piedmont Airlines, whose gateway airport Charlotte, North Carolina, is billed as having minimal queue lengths. As far as the customer is concerned, this expanding body of information enables him or her to make a better informed decision. Certainly it should reduce the likelihood of a gross mismatch between expectations and reality. The downside for the service provider is that having gone public, so to speak, with his standards, it inevitably begets mimickry. Worse, if the service provider fails to deliver on the standards, the customer's level of dissatisfaction can go off the scale. How many of us, for example, take the company's brochure with us on holiday to ensure that reference to a sea view did not merely suggest a glimpse between adjacent office blocks?

The mimickry issue is what companies have to live with. It is after all held to be the sincerest form of flattery. On the service quality front, there are, though, a couple of pertinent observations one might make. Companies can bring about a veritable revolution in an industry by introducing a radically improved quality related offer. Sainsburys set a new benchmark for supermarkets. Back in the early '60s Holiday Inns were trail-blazing in the motel field, which up to that point had a sleazy and unreliable image. Likewise, Macdonald's quickly established itself as the standard for hamburgers (Love 1987). While these initiatives have, in all three cases, resulted in the organisations capturing huge segments of the particular markets, competitors have inevitably been forced to rise to the challenge. Indeed, to remain ahead of the field, Holiday Inns have had to create a new tier of facility which is identified by the Crown Plaza title. It is also of more than passing interest to report that all three organisations engage in detailed performance monitoring of the units.

How is service quality monitored?

Given the earlier discussion relating to customer perceptions and operational standards, it will be obvious that there are two parallel approaches to this monitoring theme. The 27-page checklist approach adopted by Macdonald's is concentrated very much on the off-stage elements, i.e. these aspects which are invisible to the customer. Likewise, most of the data collected on the performance of clinicians is not placed in the public domain, although there is sufficient available in America for it to have generated the 'preferred providers' concept. Sainsbury's know centrally of stock-out occurrences in individual supermarkets through their sophisticated information technology which is what also enables companies such as American Express to monitor response times for personal transactions.

There is a sense in which these are 'hard' measures, somewhat analogous to figures which might be collected in a manufacturing environment. There has been a temptation in the service sector to assume that, because the actual service encounter is so rooted in a personal experience, any assessment of quality is necessarily going to be intangible in nature. This is a temptation which should be resisted. Every effort should be made to establish standards and performance measures of these harder issues. Not only is it important from the perspective of management control, but it is more than likely that if a service organisation gets these things right, then there is a distinct possibility that the actual service encounter will also proceed smoothly. A patient's confidence in the system isn't boosted if a hospital consultant has been issued with the wrong case notes.

When we move across to the softer end of things, we are in the domain of customer satisfaction, and here I would argue that the picture is, to say the least, improvable. Many agencies now solicit views and assessments from customers about the service they have received. Even university teachers are doing it and 'ere long they will actually be obliged to undergo such assessments routinely. Unfortunately, it is this writer's considered opinion that to date most of the questionnaires developed to assist in this endeavour have been far too nebulous in content. Next time you stay in any half decent hotel, examine the questionnaire left on the dressing table. It will typically feature a half dozen very general questions which do not really expose any deficiencies until these are judged so serious that the client is obliged to handwrite in a lengthy tirade. In general, if a customer resorts to that or actually goes so far as to produce a letter of complaint, one can assume that any monitoring system has not been functioning adequately. While complaints do provide valuable insights, systems should have been in place for ensuring that such complaints ought not to have occurred in the first place. I happen to believe that customer monitoring should be so designed that when the results are to hand, they point to where exactly the service is failing to achieve standards and/or match expectation.

Consider, for example, the following question taken from a 32-page questionnaire distributed to over 30,000 ex-hospital patients and completed by over 14,000 (Thompson, 1983).

Q   *If for any reason I had to return to hospital, given the choice I would*:

	Hospital C	Hospital F	Overall
Be very happy to return to the same one	75%	39%	61%
Not mind going back to the same one	23%	40%	32%
Prefer to go somewhere else	2%	21%	7%

While admitting that Hospital F is performing poorly on this 'holistic' measure, there is no indication as to what is going wrong. To find out we need to examine the response patterns to the other 240 questions. In contrast to this generalised approach consider the following two other very specific questions from the same document. One relates to toilets and the other to food, the latter question being but one of 22 on this culinary theme.

Presentation of food

	Hospital C	Hospital F	Overall
The meals were usually made to look tempting and appetising	37%	4%	17%
On the whole the meals were reasonably well presented	56%	47%	56%
From time to time the meals were not presented as well as they might have been	7%	49%	27%

The level of cleanliness in the bathroom and toilets was:

	Hospital C	Hospital F	Overall
Such that they were very pleasant to use	89%	34%	65%
Quite good, although not of a particularly high standard	11%	46%	29%
Barely adequate, leaving considerable room for improvement	0%	20%	6%

I would contend that the specificity of these questions directs management action to where it is needed. There isn't just one single question on food which solicits an overall evaluation on a scale from say 'poor' to 'excellent'. One wouldn't know what to make of the response if there were such a bland question.

Given the expectation/reality aspect, it would perhaps be desirable to solicit information on just what it is that people are anticipating, but there are obvious difficulties. In this same hospital work, we did actually ask some questions which sought the respondents' views about how the reality matched their expectations on such issues as food and medical treatment and the results were in line with what the more focussed questions would have led one to believe.

From my own experience, most service organisations, be they tour operators, banks or hotels, are still using what I would label as first generation, non-informative documents and I suspect that most customers realise this. Outside the NHS, one can report that the approach adopted by the British Airports Authority is of this more specific nature, as is the approach adopted by BMW to assess the perceived quality of the maintenance service their customers receive. These, though, are very much the exception. It is difficult for this writer to see how the material secured from many such surveys can provide management with useful insights. Only if they are in possession of such feedback can they progress to improving service quality.

How can service quality be improved?

It goes without saying that one needs to know where one is failing to deliver before one can set about instituting improvements to systems, procedures or facilities. How much money has been wasted improving the décor of restaurants to encourage customers to return, when a far greater priority was the fact that the staff needed social skills training? Information therefore lies at the cornerstone of service quality improvement. However, it lies alongside an equally important imperative namely the commitment of top management to excellence, which message was so capably preached by Peters and Waterman (1982). Marks & Spencer is synonymous with quality because everyone in that organisation knows that it is a top-level objective. The same is true of Sainsburys. Everyone within and without Jaguar cars knows of John Egan's obsession with quality, and Colin Marshall at British Airways feels so strongly about it that he addressed groups of staff located at diverse parts of the globe every other day on this theme for over a year.

However, this need for a hellfire and brimstone evident concern for quality at the topmost levels of the company does not mean that those lower down have no contribution to make. On the contrary, the evidence is that quality provides the ideal opportunity for inculcating genuine worker involvement, one vehicle for that being quality circles. These are essentially little more than groups of staff meeting in company time trying collectively to ascertain how problems which are adversely affecting the attainment of good quality or even zero defects can be reduced or eliminated. Several million Japanese workers are reported to be involved in such circle activities which are now beginning to feature in British manufacturing, having been pioneered here originally at Rolls-Royce. Over the past three to four years, a number of organisations in the service sector have experimented with this approach including banks, hospitals, American Express, British Airways, British Rail and Holiday Inns (Dale, 1986). They go under various guises, being labelled Service Chains at Holiday Inns for example and Customer Care Teams at British Airways. While the designations might differ, there is a uniformity of approach which is aimed at developing staff, while at the same time bringing about improvements in service quality. It is not difficult to comprehend why such initiatives are successful if one accepts that most rational individuals prefer to be associated with success rather than failure. Only a few people would surely derive more satisfaction from producing a poor product or delivering a poor quality service than a good one. Quality circles enable some of the barriers to good performance to be removed.

In many of these organisations, quality circle initiatives are run in parallel with more formalised putting-the-customer-first programmes which were pioneered originally by SAS. On reflection, it seems somewhat unusual that organisations whose very lifeblood is satisfied customers need to be educated to the notion that the Customer is King. However, the reality is that many people are making a nice living by putting across this message, and I for one would have to report that one does become conscious of the end results whether one is travelling by British Airways or British Rail.

In summary, the proper management of service quality calls for it to be specified and monitored and for the existence of appropriate mechanisms for effecting improvements based upon what this monitoring reveals.

References and notes

Dale, B. (1986) 'Experiences with quality circles and quality costs' in Moores, B. (ed) *Are They Being Served?*, Philip Allan, Oxford, Chapter 4. (There is now even a British Standard on Quality Costing, (BS 6143). Some experiences of using this approach are detailed in this reference.)

Lee, J. (1986) 'An empirical study of attitude formation towards private health insurance and private medicine', Unpublished doctoral dissertation, University of Manchester Institute of Science and Technology. (Some interesting insights were secured into why private health insurance is a growth industry.)

Love, J. F. (1987) *Behind the Arches*, Bantam Press, New York. (An interesting analysis of the Macdonald's phenomenon is to be found in this book. Not only does the author provide an insightful history of the company, but one section is given over to how standards are established, monitored and controlled.)

Nightingale, M. and Coss, J. (1987) *Managing Standards of Service*, Hotel and Catering Open Tech., P.O. Box 18, Wembley, Middlesex, HA9 7AP.

Peters, T. and Waterman, R. (1982) *In Search of Excellence*, Harper & Row, London.

Thompson, A. G. H. (1983) 'The measurement of patients' perceptions of the quality of hospital care', Unpublished doctoral dissertation, University of Manchester Institute of Science and Technology. (The questions and response patterns quoted in the text are taken from this dissertation. A succinct summary of the methodology is contained in 'What the patient thinks', Chapter 9 in Moores, B., *Are They Being Served?*, Philip Allan, Oxford.)

18 Productivity in service organisations

DR ROBERT CHRISTIE MILL

Introduction

According to the American Productivity Centre, productivity – how efficiently resources are used to create outputs – has increasingly declined since World War 2. The situation in service industries, some would argue, is far worse. The National Restaurant Association, for example, estimates that the restaurant industry in the United States is only half as productive as manufacturing industries. Government figures indicate that labour costs are outpacing sales in eating and drinking places. Between 1980 and 1985, sales increased an average of 2.7 per cent per annum after inflation. However, it took an average of 4 per cent more employee-hours per annum to produce that.

In the UK, manufacturing industry grew at a rate of 9 per cent between 1980 and 1986, whilst service industry output increased by 17 per cent. However, in the former industries, the number of people employed fell by over 20 per cent, whilst service increased their workforce by 13 per cent. The implication of this is that manufacturing for this period has been achieving productivity improvements ten times as great as those in services. It has been proposed that the service sector may well mirror what has happened in manufacturing if it fails to tackle this productivity issue, that is to say a significant decline, followed by major rationalisations to make a smaller, leaner and fitter sector (Quinn and Gagnon, 1986; Johnston, 1988).

The situation is particularly acute in service industries for several reasons. First, many of these industries are in the mature stage of the life cycle. In a typical life cycle, products, services and industries go through various stages. In the *introductory* stage an industry appeals to a rather small number of consumers. In the *growth* stage industry sales expand quite dramatically. In travel and tourism this began after World War 2 and is continuing today. Because of growing numbers of people (the baby boom) with greater discretionary income and higher educational levels, more people took holidays and ate out. The impact of this on consumer services was felt in the '70s in the United States and in the '80s in the UK. The growth stage is characterised by sales which increase at an *increasing* rate. Profits can be generated and efficiencies camouflaged in the growth stage simply by serving more customers.

There are signs, however, that many industries are moving towards the *maturity* stage of the life cycle. In the maturity stage sales are still increasing but at a decreasing rate. To a large extent this is what is happening in the United States, for instance the fast-food industry is already in the mature stage of the life cycle. At this point increased profits come from increased productivity – producing more from less – rather than from increased sales volume. Perhaps this is why we are seeing more innovation from this industry on the subject of increased productivity. If no action is taken, the industry will move into the *decline* stage of the life cycle. At this point a decline in sales is experienced unless the industry identifies a new market for the product – the movement of fast food into the breakfast business, for example.

Service industries cannot rely forever on market growth to fuel increased profits. In the future, industry profitability must come from increased productivity. A second challenge comes from the fact that the nature of the industry makes productivity difficult to measure, far less improve. The industry provides a combination of products and services – a hamburger and quick service; retail goods and a cheerful smile; an overdraft and a sympathetic ear. How do we quantify 'service'? In delivering a service there is only a limited amount of substitution of people for machines that can take place. This puts great pressure on management to increase the productive use of employees rather than rely totally on technological innovation to produce a more productive operation.

A third problem is that while, as stated above, employees are critical to increased productivity, service industries have traditionally placed little emphasis on employee development and training. Managers must come to see that ROI means Return On Individual as well as Return On Invest-ment (Mill, 1988).

What is productivity?

Productivity involves a relationship between the input of resources and output of goods and services. In the service industries management seeks to produce such things as healthy patients, well-groomed customers, well-fed diners. The resources at management's disposal are capital in the form of money, machinery, materials and tools, human resources and infor-mation resources. To an extent these inputs are substitutable. A highly paid chef may be substituted by a lesser paid cook, standardised recipes and commissary-produced convenience foods. The degree of substitutability is determined by the amount and dissemination of the information resources – the extent, for example, that management knows about new techniques or advances. The role of management is to develop and organise a system that increases the value of the output faster than the cost of the input.

Three trends can be identified. First, traditional measures of productivity have focussed on the effectiveness of the labour force. In primary and manufacturing industry, with outputs with standardised products that can be easily measured in terms of quantity, volume or weight, measurement is both relatively simple and meaningful. Where, as in any service industry, there is a great diversity of output, such physical measures cannot be used and money is used as the measure. Typically, the payroll ratio – payroll costs as a percentage of sales – was used. The fallacy here is that productivity can seemingly be increased simply by raising prices. The resulting payroll ratio is smaller and gives the impression that more sales are being produced at the same cost.

Better measures of productivity are inflation-proof and based on 'physical' characteristics. Examples are the number of customers served per employee-hour, number of sales per employee-hour or, as the Bureau of Labour Statistics defines it, sales receipts adjusted for inflation and indexed to a base year per employee-hour. But whilst these measures may be more effective, there are two problems. Management will also have to make customer satisfaction, service and quality part of the productivity equation. If more customers are processed, but in an impersonal, mechanical way, are we more or less productive? If more customers are served at a banquet by fewer waiters but service is slower and several guests have soup spilled on them, is the operation more or less productive? The key is to produce satisfied customers at a profit. J. C. Penney is credited with saying, 'If we satisfy our customers but fail to satisfy our business, we'll soon be out of business. If we get the profit but fail to satisfy our customers, we'll soon be out of customers.'

Second, such measures fail to recognise that two aspects of productivity are being measured. In manufacturing, the factory output is decoupled from actual sales since the products have the ability to be stored. This is not the case in services; usually production and consumption are simultaneous. Productivity measures in services therefore tend to measure both the ability of the operation to produce *and* sell the service.

Finally, we must take a holistic view of the workplace. The traditional view of increasing productivity in manufacturing has been to divide the job into specialised fragments and increase the efficiency of each of the

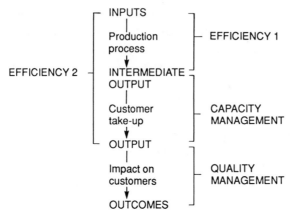

Figure 18.1 Model of service operations
Inputs: physical assets, such as plant and machinery, and labour which are combined in some way to create a series of intermediate outputs.
Intermediate output: the capacity to provide the service, which in the food service industry would be the output capacity of the kitchen and its staff and the seating capacity of the restaurant.
Outputs: the actual output achieved.
Outcomes: the impact which the service may have on the consumer.

parts. This rationale provided for the development of the assembly line. The modern view seeks to humanise the job – integrate worker and job to produce a satisfied employee who is performing productively.

Jones (1988) has proposed that one way to view the service operations is as a three-stage model as in Figure 18.1.

An example can illustrate how these factors relate to each other. An hotel's kitchen staff have available a range of commodities and foodstuffs, a level of expertise, and a range of equipment (inputs). Each day the head chef plans, prepares and serves a table d'hôte menu based on some assumptions about the level of demand (intermediate output). But not all of the dishes prepared are necessarily sold, only a proportion of them (actual output). The hotel's customers that have purchased the table d'hôte meal have a wide range of experiences, such as dissipation of hunger, comfort, social contact, security, and so on (outcomes).

In other cases, notably with service interactions such as with retail or public sector staff, inputs produce immediate output, bypassing the intermediate stage. These outputs tend to be less tangible and hence quickly transferred into outcomes by the consumer.

Thus, performance improvement is derived from managing inputs, or outputs, or both. This is the rationale behind the second stage 'intermediate output'. It enables the manager to differentiate between focussing on inputs and focussing on outputs. This leads to the idea of two types of efficiency:

'Efficiency 1' = the ratio of inputs to intermediate output, e.g. the unit cost of making a service available.

'Efficiency 2' = the ratio of inputs to output, e.g. the cost of providing the service in relation to actual sales generated.

This framework illustrates the reasons for the deficiencies of measures such as gross profit per cent and labour cost per cent typically used in some service industries. Both of these measure cost of inputs against cost of actual output. This encompasses both efficiency 1, i.e. how productive the inputs could be in producing an intermediate output, but also capacity management, how effective the unit has been in actually selling the intermediate output produced. This is not to say that from a business perspective both gross profit and labour cost are not useful measures. However, from an operations perspective it is clear that productivity and capacity are two different issues and should be measured as such.

Armistead et al (1988) identify that service managers can clearly control all three main influences on productivity – the input costs, the transformation of these resources into output (efficiency 1) and what they call utilisation of these transforming resources (or capacity management). They point out that managing capacity is not just the issue maximising the utilisation of the total operating system, but also the operating sub-systems. For instance, it is possible for a hotel to operate at 100 per cent but for parts of the operation to be underutilised.

The recognition of the importance of capacity as a strategy for managing productivity is significant. Managers are often under the mistaken impression that productivity gains can only be or are best achieved by cost cutting. In fact there are five potential ways of improving the efficiency of the relationship between inputs and outputs only three of which involve cutting costs (Figure 18.2).

Strategic determinants of productivity

It has been proposed that there are three significant strategic determinants of productivity in service industries (Armistead et al, 1988). These are the *volume* of demand, the *variety* of services offered, and the *variation* in the volume and demand over time. To these a fourth might be added, namely the *variability* of demand for the range of alternative services. Each of these impacts on the three major components of productivity mentioned above.

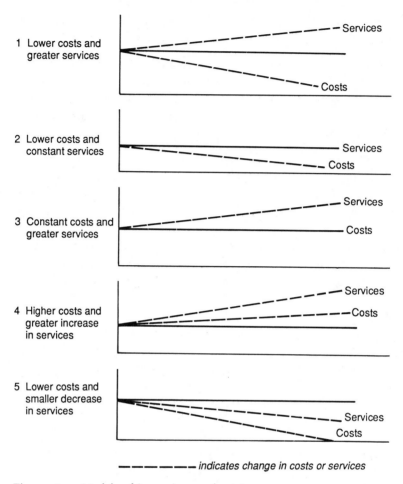

Figure 18.2   Models of increasing productivity
(*Source*: Merricks, P. and Jones, P. (1987) *The Management of Catering Operations*, Cassell)

The impact of *volume* on input costs are the traditional economies of scale. In services these relate in particular to increased purchasing power, spreading of central overheads, marketing economies and labour special-isations. There are similar influences on the efficient transformation of sources as well as 'Learning effects'. Furthermore high volumes also allow the delivery system to be balanced so that all subsystems are operating at optimum levels.

To some extent the potential productivity gains derived from high volume may be offset by the level of *variety* offered. As Armistead et al (1988) state: 'High variety reduces volume per service line and demands a wide range of skills, both of which increase input costs.' Variety may also require specialised plant, equipment and employees, which is likely to reduce the efficiency and make more difficult their full utilisation.

The impact of *variation* of demand requires that services adopt strategies and approaches that enable flexibility. Sasser et al (1978) propose two broad alternatives. The chase demand strategy is to design the service system so that resource provision is flexible enough to match fluctuations in demand. This strategy is considerably aided if accurate predictions of likely demand can be made. Thus in the fast food sector for instance, as many of the controllable variable cost elements as possible are managed in relation to demand. Staff are mainly part-time and multi-skilled; the shift patterns are varied and staff are hired to start on the hour, half-hour or even quarter-hour. The alternative broad strategy is the level capacity strategy. This is used where not all activity is dictated by the presence of the customer in the system. These tend to be services with relatively low content (Chase, 1981) or parts of service provision that have been decoupled from front-of-house. Thus, in banks the staff tended to be full-time and working to a normal nine-to-five routine. In periods of high demand, they undertake customer contact activities, but in quieter periods they switch to back-of-house tasks such as document handling and information processing.

Finally, the concept of *variability* suggests that not only will total demand vary, but also the demand for the range of services on offer will vary. Service managers are frequently faced with this fluctuation in sales mix. This has the impact in input costs of not only reducing potential economies of scale, but also making the implementation of strategies designed to cope with variety more difficult. With regards to efficiency, this provides additional pressure for accurate forecasting of potential demand on some 'last minute' flexibility over provision.

In summary, the management of service productivity will be significantly affected by the nature of volume, variety, variation and variability. We shall now go on to consider some specific examples of how service organisations manage and improve productivity.

Improving productivity

Employee productivity has been improved by focussing attention on three main areas – improved physical layout and task planning; tighter scheduling; and the motivation of employees.

Facility planning

Employee productivity is influenced by the interaction of the workers and the environment in which they work. The objective is to develop facilities that will enhance the productivity of the employees working there. This can be done through a process of facilities planning.

The goals of facilities planning are sevenfold. First, the planner seeks to ease the process of production. This means laying out space to ensure a smooth flow of people and things. A second goal relates to minimising the cost of and time required to handle materials. This can be accomplished by such things as moving items by mechanical means rather than by hand, routing things over straight-line paths while avoiding backtracking, carrying a minimum of inventory and ensuring that it is stored under the proper conditions. At the same time the planner seeks to minimise the investment in equipment. Cost-benefit analysis can be used to determine the extent to which machines should replace people. The planner must also work to make full use of both horizontal and vertical space. Space standards can be used to ensure that the work can be completed in a minimum of space without the feeling of being cramped. Equipment must also be maintained, so the wise planner will select surfaces that can be easily cleaned. Yet another goal of facilities planning is cost control. Portion control in restaurants, for example, can be made easier by the selection of serving utensils appropriate to the portions to be served. Lastly, facilities should be designed with flexibility in mind. The operation may need to expand, and considering this in the original development can save a great deal of time and money later on.

Once the facility has been planned and laid out in such a way that productivity is enhanced, attention can be paid to the way each employee performs his or her job. Task planning is the analysis of tasks involved in carrying out a job in order to establish a more productive procedure for completing that job.

The first step is to select the task to be analysed. It is logical to select tasks which are frustrating for employees or are causing bottlenecks in production.

A variety of factors affect each task to be analysed. Jobs are affected by the *accessibility* and *storage* of *the raw materials* used in performing the task. All materials should be easily accessible to the work area. In one hotel study it was found that 20 per cent of a room cleaner's time was spent in getting linen from the linen room. A shortage of linen made adequate stocking impossible. The answer was to establish a par system of stocking linen and other supplies for each floor closet. Making supplies more accessible, enabled cleaners to clean 16 rooms instead of 13. A key idea is that the handling of materials does not add to their value. Materials handling should, therefore, be kept to a minimum. The *steps used* in completing the task should be identified early on in the analysis. Identifying the steps involved in the process lets the analyst know where potential savings can come from. The *standard of desired performance* affects which tasks must be performed. A fine restaurant which emphasises its use of fresh ingredients will require different preparation methods for its menu items than a fast-food operation that relies heavily on convenience products. The process of performing a job is also affected by the *quantity to be produced*. For quantity jobs the capital investment for a piece of equipment may be less in the long run than the labour costs of several employees.

The cost of performing a task is affected by the *number and type of employees used*. Maximum efficiency results from having the least number of employees necessary. It may not, however, result in minimum cost. Keeping the staff at minimum levels may result in excessive overtime and reduced output due to tired employees. The skill level of the employee must also be considered. The key is to delegate tasks as far down the line as possible commensurate with the employee's ability to perform the delegated task.

Once the task has been selected, the answer to several questions will help determine the proper procedures to use in performing the task. If this task or step in the process is *eliminated*, will the end product or service suffer? Can it be *combined*? Are there *unnecessary delays*? Is there *misdirected* effort? Are *skills* used properly? Are employees doing too many *unrelated* tasks? Is the work *spread evenly*?

Holiday Inns found that wheeling a small cart into the guest room saved money when cleaning the room. The materials needed were easily accessible, limiting much walking. In addition, the room attendants felt more secure with the door closed. Energy costs were reduced since heat or air conditioning did not escape from the room as previously when carts were left outside the open door.

The work area can now be set up putting the above principles into practice. Ideally this will be done with the assistance of the person who does the job. Resistance to change is reduced by involving the employee in the process of change. It is also important because the work area for a small employee should be different from that for a tall employee. After a shakedown period the new procedure can be evaluated. The employee can be involved in determining whether any part of the process can be eliminated, combined or simplified. After the new procedure is agreed, new performance standards can be set and communicated to the employee. Employee performance may initially have to be supervised rather closely until the new procedure becomes a habit. At that point periodic coaching which stresses the positive as well as the negative can replace close supervision.

There is a danger involved in developing standardised procedures that employees must adhere to. For some employees standardised movements may lead to boredom with the job. The increase in productivity resulting from minimising unproductive movements may be offset by a loss in productivity resulting from employees who are less motivated because they are bored. The key is to ensure that there is an excellent match between the skills and abilities required for the task and those present in the employee.

Scheduling

As well as good layout and task planning, Industry Consultants have indicated that, in the restaurant industry alone, potential savings of 10 to 20 per cent of labour costs can be expected through better employee scheduling. This could represent savings of 3 to 6 per cent of sales.

The first step in establishing employee schedules is to determine a productivity standard against which to measure future performance. As we have discussed there are several ways to establish standards.

Time studies are useful for measuring repetitive activities involving the same product or service. This makes their use difficult in service industries where the work often consists of many different activities and the handling of many different customers. In work sampling, well-defined events are observed and recorded. An event might be a retail sale or the unloading of dishes from a dishwasher. As a result, data can be developed on times when service and quality were at a level which produced guest satisfaction with the fewest number of employees.

Forecasting is also a key to the successful control of labour costs. Employees are scheduled by applying the standard developed above to a forecast of customers, guests or covers. On the micro level a ten-day forecast starting on a Friday has advantages. It allows the forecaster to estimate customer counts for employee scheduling during a full pay period. It also allows a preliminary full weekend forecast. This is particularly important as so many service businesses have weekend business that is totally different from that experienced during the week.

Once a standard has been set using one of the methods outlined above we have a figure for determining how many staff hours are required for varying levels of forecasted business. A staffing guide shows how these hours should be scheduled to provide the required level of service with minimum unproductive labour. A staffing guide is usually prepared for the average level of business expected. Forecasted sales can be plotted for each half hour of operation and the appropriate number of staff hours per half hour can be scheduled.

Too often a system is set up without sufficient concern being given to maintaining it. Over a period of time small deviations from standard grow into major cost problems. The key in evaluating the system is to compare actual performance with the standard, to report any significant deviation in a timely manner and to take steps to correct any discrepancies.

Several approaches can be identified which, when put into practice, can produce more productive employee scheduling.

Schedule split shifts

A split shift refers to the concept of scheduling employees for two time periods during the day with time off in between. For example, employees may work lunch service, be off for a few hours, then return to provide service at dinner. This concept is feasible where employees live close to the operation. It does, however, make for a very long day for the employee. It would also encounter strong opposition if the employees were unionised.

Schedule irregularly

The idea of irregular scheduling is that an employee should be called in to work at the time business warrants rather than starting at the same time each day.

Part-time personnel

It is unproductive to staff for peak periods using full-time employees. Full-time personnel can provide a steady, well-trained core of employees to meet average business conditions, while part-timers can be used to supplement that core during peak periods.

Use staffing guide

As noted above, a staffing guide links forecasted business and productivity standards to determine the employees needed at each hour of the day. Its use is critical to establishing control of labour cost.

The flow of business in service industries is often erratic. At times during the day there are few customers; at other times there are lines of people waiting to be served. At times, then, employees have nothing productive to do yet they are paid for their time. The idea of storing employee labour is to utilise the employee's time when demand is low in ways that will contribute to the organisation when business is brisk. The first step in this process is to determine whose time is slack at what periods. Advance planning is then necessary to properly utilise the slack time which has been identified. Within the constraints of quality and safety, management can identify who has slack time and, utilising knowledge of short-term future events, can put that slack time to productive use. The products of the employees' efforts are then stored until the demand for them occurs. The employees' labour is, thus, effectively 'stored'.

Employee motivation

Finally, there is the management of the organisational climate or employee motivation as a means of improving productivity. Managers cannot directly motivate their employees, because motivation comes from within. Employees motivate themselves. Managers, however, can set a 'climate' within the company that will produce employees who are motivated or not.

What do we mean by the climate within an organisation? When employees say they never know what is going on, or they belong to a tightly knit group, or the only time they hear from the boss is when they have done something wrong, they are talking about the climate of the organisation. Climate can be defined as:

> 'A set of measurable properties of the work environment, based on the collective perceptions of the people who live and work in the environment and demonstrated to influence their motivation and behaviour.'

The above definition encompasses several things. First, climate is perceptual. It is the employees' perception of what exists rather than what actually does exist. These two may or may not be the same thing. Management may feel that high standards are set. The employee may feel differently. Whether or not high standards actually exist within the operation, it is the employee's perception that will influence employee action. If the perception is that high standards do not exist, the employee may decide: 'If management doesn't care about the standard of service given to the guest, why should I?' This perception of the standards set will colour the actions and motivation of the employee. Second, climate can be measured. A variety of dimensions have been suggested. Research has also shown that, while the climate within an organisation is stable over time, it can be changed by management action.

A model of how the climate within an organisation develops and influences job behaviour is suggested in Figure 18.3. The influences on climate – the external environment, differences in the style and behaviour of management – are moderated by the norms of the group of which the individual is a member, the task done by and the personality of the employee to produce, in effect, three types of climate. The individual has

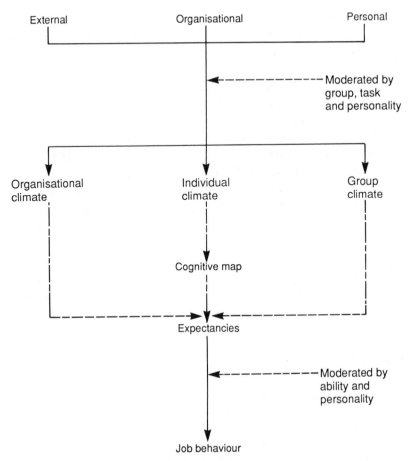

Figure 18.3   A model of organisational climate
(Adapted from: Field, R. H., George and Michael A. Abelson (1982) 'Climate: a reconceptualisation and proposed model', *Human Relations*, Vol. 35, No. 3, p. 195.)

a perception of the climate which exists within the company. To the extent that this is shared by the other employees in his or her department a group climate is formed. Where there exists a collective perception within the property an organisational climate can be described – one that is generally agreed upon to be a description of the operation as a whole.

The individual then develops a 'map' of the climate as perceived by him/her which acts as a screening device to reinforce the perception of the climate in his or her own eyes. Research has shown, for example, that the longer an individual has been working within a certain climate the more difficult it is to change that person's perception of the climate. On the basis of the individual, group and organisational climates, employees develop expectations which, moderated by the employees' ability and personality, affect motivation, satisfaction and job performance.

It has been shown, for example, that perceptions of climate vary among employees at different levels in the management hierarchy. Perceptions are also influenced by the type of job that employees perform and the type of person they are. One study found that when an experimental group was given more discretion to make decisions, they showed more responsibility and achievement motivations, felt a closer relationship to management and felt that rewards were more closely tied to performance than did a control group. They were also more successful in sales and profitability than was the control group. For employees who place great importance on the work situation certain climate dimensions are more important. Such employees prefer task-oriented management actions which seek to get the organisation moving. They also enjoy friendly social relationships while not wishing to be burdened with what they consider busy work. For those who see the work situation as being less important the emphasis sought is on main-taining pleasant relationships while reducing dissension and disruption.

References

Armistead, C., Johnston, R. and Slack, N. (1988) 'The strategic determinants of service productivity', in: Johnston, R. (ed) *The Management of Service Operations*, IFS Publications, Bedford.

Chase, R. B. (1981) 'The customer contact approach to services: theoretical bases and practical extensions', *Operations Research*, Vol. 29, No. 4.

Johnston, R. (1988) 'Service industries – improving competitive performance', *Service Industries Journal*, Vol. 4. No. 2.

Jones, P. (1988) 'Quality, capacity and productivity in service industries', in: Johnston, R. (ed) *The Management of Service Operations*, IFS Publications, Bedford.

Mill, R. C. (1988) *Managing for Productivity in the Hospitality Industry*, Van Nostrand Reinhold, Wokingham, Berks.

Quinn, J. B. and Gagnon, C. E. (1986) 'Will services follow manufacturing into decline', *Harvard Business Review*, Vol. 64, No. 6, November–December.

Sasser, W. Earl, Olsen, R. P. and Wyckoff, D. D. (1978) *Management of Service Operations – Text, Cases and Readings*, Allyn & Bacon Inc., Newton, MA.

19 Management science in service industries

DR DAVID TARGETT

Introduction

Just as it is difficult to make a clear distinction between manufacturing and service companies, so it is difficult to categorise the use of management science in the two sectors. Some approaches may be more likely to be effective in one sector than another, but no definite line can be drawn. The boundary is blurred, partly because the sectors themselves are blurred, but more importantly because the techniques deal with, in the main, decisions about the management of resources and these are not so very dissimilar once the contexts have been stripped away. The quantities and the types of resources may vary, for example, there is often more labour but less capital in the service sector, but as far as management science is concerned the principles are much the same.

What then can be said about management science in service industries? Perhaps three things. First, some techniques are more likely to be effective in service industries although they are not exclusively used there. This is because, by their nature, they are more able to deal with factors and issues that are of greater importance in the sector. In short, some methods can be applied more easily to the key tasks of service company management. Queuing techniques are an example, since they can deal with the major issue of setting and monitoring service levels.

Second, it may be more difficult to apply scientific methods to service industries because of greater uncertainties about problem structures and data. For example, people tend to be more unpredictable than machines and are therefore harder to encapsulate in a model. The decentralisation of many service companies is another source of difficulty. The converse of this is probably that the payoff from the application of management science is potentially great.

Third, these difficulties and the growth of the service sector have led to the development of techniques which are particularly relevant to the types of problem found in the sector. For instance, DEA (Data Envelopment Analysis) is a method for measuring the relative efficiency of operations at different locations. It takes into account all factors affecting performance, environmental ones as well as those under management control. It goes on to compare, for each location in turn, its inputs and outputs against those at other locations that DEA has defined as being 'similar', to determine relative efficiency. It is being applied, for example, to monitor staff levels at branches of a national bank.

This chapter will look at these three issues in turn, but as a background to these discussions, it is important first to review the distinctive characteristics of service industries and the implications they have for the application of management science.

The distinctive characteristics of service industries

The fundamental goals of management science are common to all sectors. Bleuel and Patton (1978) neatly summarise the commonalities as, first, the need for efficiency and economy and, second, the requirement to forecast demand and plan ahead. It is for this reason that management science techniques are applicable across all sectors. On the other hand there are distinctive characteristics of the service industry which makes management science different in the sector. The difference can be an important one, going beyond the realms of management science. Sasser (1976) warns: 'many writers assume that services are merely goods with a few odd characteristics . . . [but] the odd characteristics often make all the difference between prosperity and failure.'

These distinctive characteristics influence the application of management science and mean that the levels of usefulness and effectiveness of its techniques differ in the service sector as against other sectors. The following list of distinctive characteristics is taken from Fitzsimmons and Sullivan (1982) but it is in general agreement with other writers.

A *Measurement of output and performance is difficult.* Revenue and sales volume alone do not measure quality of service which is likely to have multiple attributes. In addition the attributes may not be easily quantifiable. For example, the performance of a health care organisation is a combination not only of financial results and patient throughput but also of the quality of care, the effectiveness of preventative measures and many other factors.

B *The 'product' is intangible.* Amongst the many effects of this are that quality control is not straightforward and that innovations are not patentable. For example, checking the quality of aircraft manufacture is probably a clearer task than checking the quality of a flight in an aircraft.

C *The consumer is part of the service process.* He or she may be an active participant, influencing what happens, and will care about the location and surroundings in which the service is given. Management education is a service industry in which the consumer plays a very active part.

D *Production and consumption are usually simultaneous.* A particular implication of this is that there can be no inventory of the service itself. For example, a shop assistant's advice to a customer cannot be stored. On the other hand the store can take steps to reduce the difficulty by, for instance, providing computerised information or a taped telephone message.

E *The 'product' is time perishable.* If a service is not used, it is likely to be wasted. For example, an empty berth on a cruise liner is potential revenue lost forever.

F *Site selection is governed by customers and demand.* Operations tend to be decentralised with limited opportunities for economies of scale. For example, fastfood restaurants are located where the customers are likely to be. On the other hand supermarkets do try to reduce the difficulty and achieve economies of scale by persuading customers to travel to them at their out-of-town locations, pointing out the advantages of doing so.

G *The industry is labour-intensive.* Labour is likely to be the most important resource and this importance is enlarged because of the consumer/employee contact in the delivery of the service. For example, banks, despite the introduction of automatic teller machines, are still heavily dependent on counter service.

These characteristics present the special challenges for service business management. Their importance gives impetus to a quest for management science methods for tackling them. As in all sectors an investment in management techniques is only worthwhile if the tasks they support are sufficiently important to provide a substantial payoff.

Management science tasks in the service sector

The characteristics described above suggest that there are a number of key tasks in the service sector to which management science can be effectively applied. Five key tasks are listed below but it is not meant to be an exhaustive list. Task 1, measuring performance, stems mainly from characteristic A above; task 2, quality control, from characteristic B; task 3, monitoring service levels, from C; task 4, planning, from D and E; task 5, ensuring operational efficiency, from F and G. Of course there is considerably more interaction between characteristics and tasks than this simple outline implies. For example, planning depends to some degree on most of the characteristics, not just D and E.

The five key tasks are outlined below. Two examples of techniques that can and have been applied are described for each of the tasks.

1 Measurement of output and performance

Typically, a service company has many dimensions along which it must measure output and performance. Some, such as costs and waiting time, may be straightforward to quantify; others, such as customer satisfaction present a much more difficult proposition, being difficult conceptually as well as expensive to measure accurately.

Cost-benefit analysis attempts to quantify intangible benefits. It is used mostly in the public service sector. For example, it has been used to balance the wide range of costs and benefits associated with an extension of the public transport subway system in London (Beesley, 1983). The benefits included the economic value of saved time and improved safety. Investments like this need cost-benefit analysis before they can be subject to standard capital expenditure evaluation procedures. Cost-benefit analysis can also be used in the private sector, for instance, to measure the value of a new training scheme for restaurant staff.

Work sampling measures how people use their time. It takes sample snapshots of what a person is doing at randomly selected instances during the day to build up a picture of how time is spent overall. Chase (1978) describes the use of activity sampling to determine how much time a sales manager is spending with customers as opposed to dealing with technical functions within the organisation.

2 Quality control

Whilst profits and other accounting data measure what is currently happening financially, the quality of the service is, for many organisations such as a public health service, a more important factor. For other companies the quality of the service will govern the return of customers and therefore future profits, costs and performance. Bleuel and Patton (1978) make the observation that quality control is much more of a management science issue in service industries in contrast to manufacturing where it is a specialist, i.e. engineering, matter.

Quality control charts are based on statistical methods and are a visual method of monitoring service levels. For example, Figure 19.1 is a quality

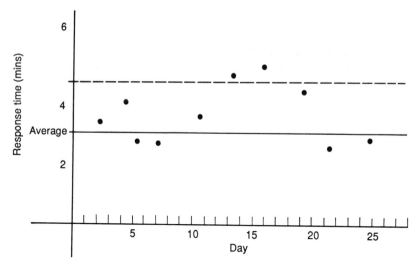

Figure 19.1   Quality control chart for fire service

control chart for the response time of a fire brigade. If there were a series of responses which were above the upper dotted line, then this would suggest some systematic (rather than random) reason for a worsening response and that corrective action was needed.

Statistical sampling methods are used in opinion polls of customer satisfaction. Sampling provides representative selections of customers to be questioned or given a questionnaire to find out information about the service. In this way systematic information is obtained as opposed to the biased information that would be obtained from complaining customers or customers who were personal friends of the owner of the company. In contrast, Targett (1985) describes the use of sampling in the banking sector to reduce corporate information available on mainframe computers to manageable levels.

3   Setting and monitoring service levels

It goes without saying that in a service organisation the customer's participation in the service process means that service levels need to be set carefully and then continually monitored and adjusted. This issue is exacerbated by the decentralisation of many service companies.

Queuing theory is a method of assessing waiting times, queue length, etc., in a service system. It is based upon knowledge of the pattern of demand for the service and the way in which the demand is met. For example, it has been used to estimate the numbers of till cashiers needed in a supermarket in order to ensure service levels meet certain minimum requirements.

The mathematics of queuing theory can be complex if reality is to be modelled in full. For instance, Serfozo (1985) describes the use of queuing theory in the routing of television transmissions where there is an 'over-flow station'. The complexity often means that it is preferable to use a less elegant but more comprehensible tool such as *simulation* as a substitute.

Inventory control can be used to keep stocks of supporting equipment to minimum levels subject to maintaining service levels (although the service itself cannot be stored). For example, a local education authority may use it to minimise the stocks of pencils, notebooks, visual aids etc. that it supplies to schools, subject to acceptable service levels which are likely to be expressed in the form: deliveries should be refused, because of a stock-out, at most 4 per cent of the time.

4 Planning

The uncertain nature of demand and the inability to hold stocks means that planning is of particular importance in service industries. The simultaneity of consumption and production means that the service operation cannot distance itself from the demand by holding inventories. Planning is the only way to be able to react to short-term changes.

Time series forecasting methods are useful in a situation where the 'product' is perishable and demand hard to predict. Time series methods can detect patterns and trends in demand from the past record of demand. They are used for short-term forecasting where the variable has a momentum of its own, i.e. before any management action has time to take effect. For example, changes in the macroeconomic environment or in a company's advertising policy will not have an immediate effect, and in the meantime forecasting may be best done by projecting the past record. Longer-term forecasting methods such as regression analysis would be needed in situations where management was intervening to influence demand or there were external changes affecting demand. For example, regression analysis would try to forecast the effect on demand of a new advertising policy.

CPM (Critical Path methods) and PERT (Programme Evaluation and Review Technique) are project management techniques for planning and monitoring progress on large-scale developments. They show the inter-relationships and timings of all activities involved in the project and thereby determine a critical path of activities, delays to which would delay the overall project. For example, CPM is used for management control purposes in the construction of new hospitals.

5 Increasing operational efficiency and productivity

The way a service is delivered can be viewed as a system which has to be operated to give a high quality service at lowest cost. Because service industries tend to be labour-intensive, the scope for improvement lies in the system rather than other factors such as economies of scale in purchasing.

Flowcharts can specify the process of the service operation in a lucid manner, making it easier for managers to understand what is going on and to search for inefficiencies. Sasser et al. (1978) describe the use of flowcharts in this context. Figure 19.2 is an example of a flowchart for a bank's branch operations and it was used in assessing manning levels.

Linear programming is a technique which optimises an objective subject to a series of constraints. It can be used, amongst other applications, for scheduling. For example, a road-based distribution company used it to plan optimal routings for their fleet of several hundred trucks. The objective which is minimised is the cost of operating the service; the constraints include the calls to be made, the number of trucks available and legal limitations on drivers' hours of working. Currin (1986) describes a route allocation problem when some routes are inadmissible.

Management science methods are of course also used outside this area of key tasks for more general purposes. For example, Lovelock and Young (1979) describe the use of operational research in designing the most efficient format for, as well as allocating, postal zip codes.

Difficulties in applying management science in the service sector

Arguably management science is easiest to apply and gives the most straightforward results when there is a clear and single objective (e.g. maximising profit), hard data (e.g. accounting information) and no more than limited and measurable uncertainties (e.g. normally distributed machine parts). Even then all may not be what it seems. For example, accounting data is sometimes far from accurate and this may cause an apparently optimal solution to be seriously suboptimal.

When the above three conditions are absent, management science is likely to be harder to apply. However, just because of the difficult conditions, management science may, if well applied, provide more valuable results than in a more straightforward situation. In general these three conditions do not hold in the service sector.

Service companies are likely to have *multiple objectives*, whether in the

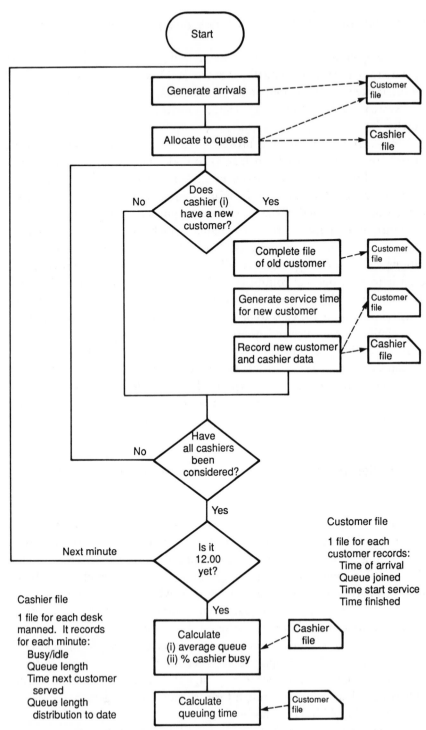

Figure 19.2   Bank simulation

form of the wide objectives of the health service or the many aspects of service quality in a fast-food restaurant. In both these cases the profitability measures used in other sectors are likely to be inadequate. Standard single objective techniques have therefore to be adapted or used to obtain only partial solutions to problems in full recognition of their limitations. However, the development of new multi-objective techniques is currently a growth area.

Data problems in the service sector are concerned with measurement and availability. The measurement problems occur because, for example, quality of service is harder to measure than sales revenue. The availability problem occurs because all companies have to collect accounting information, not least for legal reasons; softer types of data must be specially, and perhaps expensively, collected. Such data are unlikely to be available off the shelf. To obtain the data to support management science, money and effort have to be invested and there may be delays before work can start. There are also considerable problems in the allocation of costs to individual services. For example, how should a bank's extremely large data processing costs be allocated between different types of account and different financial products? Traditional accounting allocations may not be appropriate for the new circumstances of automated banking.

Uncertainty is a source of difficulty in all sectors. It is especially so in the service sector because of the closeness of the producer and consumer. It is difficult to put a buffer between them: the consumer is part of the production process and production and consumption occur simultaneously. One of the purposes of holding an inventory in manufacturing industry is to even up disparities between supply and demand. A manager in a service industry may be reliant upon the unannounced arrival of his customers and gets little warning of changes in demand. Statistical methods of handling uncertainty are therefore important. However, techniques such as queuing theory which specifically deal with decision-making under uncertainty tend to have a limited range of uses and even then are highly complex.

Some examples of newer techniques

The growth in the service sector and the above problems in applying standard management science methods in the area have encouraged the development of techniques which are able to handle these difficulties as well as other issues relating to the distinctive characteristics of service companies.

DEA (Data Envelopment Analysis)

DEA is a technique for measuring the relative efficiency of the different operating units of a service operation. As an example, it may be helpful to think in terms of the branches of a large bank. Each branch has several inputs which differ from branch to branch: manpower, property costs, promotional expenditure, etc. It also has several outputs: transactions processed, accounts handled, enquiries dealt with and so on. Assessing efficiency by the standard methods of measuring contribution and allocating costs is an almost impossible task. DEA takes a different approach and works as follows.

DEA gives weights to each of the inputs and each of the outputs and then for each branch considers the ratio:

$$\text{Efficiency} = \frac{\text{Total sum of weighted outputs}}{\text{Total sum of weighted inputs}}$$

It works one branch at a time and tries to see if there is a set of weights for which the efficiency ratio for that branch is not lower than that of any other branch. If so, the branch is said to be efficient relative to the other branches. If not, i.e. if whatever the weightings there are always other branches with a higher ratio, the branch is said to be inefficient. In this case DEA gives further information about the changes in input or output that are necessary if the branch is to become efficient.

DEA is based on fractional linear programming. It has been applied to branch banking, restaurant chains, hospitals and law courts. Sherman (1984) gives a good intuitive description of how DEA works; Sherman and Gold (1985) describe its application to branch banking.

Multicriteria methods

Standard optimisation techniques are designed to deal with the maximisation or minimisation of a single objective such as financial contribution or cost. A different approach is needed where there are multiple objectives. One way to tackle the problem is Goal Programming (GP), a technique for attempting to meet, or nearly meet, several objectives simultaneously. It has been available for many years, but the growth and problems in service organisations have led to a renewed interest, with further development and new applications.

It is useful to contrast GP with LP (Linear Programming). LP sets decision variables at levels which, subject to constraints, will make the objective function as large (or small) as possible. In GP each criterion, for example service level, customer satisfaction score, etc., is a constraint. Each constraint has a 'deviational variable' which measures the extent to which the criterion has not been met. If the criterion were met, the variable would have the value zero. All deviational variables are then included in the objective function, together with a weight reflecting the units of measurement and the importance of the criterion relative to others. The objective function then minimises the sum of the weighted deviational variables. In this way GP minimises deviations from goals taking into account the priorities between the goals.

Davis and McKeown (1984) give a clear description of GP with examples. However, basic GP is just the beginning of multicriteria methods and development is continuing all the time. In particular, the way in which priorities are handled within GP models has been the subject of much research. As an example of recent developments and for a review of the state of the art for multiobjective programming, see Hahn (1984). This article describes the use of multiobjective programming to an environmental problem with several goals.

Site selection

Site selection is particularly important to service organisations which typically operate at many decentralised locations, and management science techniques can help decide where a new site of operations might be placed. As with multicriteria methods, the fundamentals of site selection methods are not new but have been given added impetus by the growth of the service sector. Site selection techniques tend to be data-hungry, consequently a further impetus to progress has been the advances in computing power and reductions in costs which have overcome the expense and difficulties of using data-heavy methods.

Site selection might start with a gravity method. As its name implies, this determines the centre of gravity of some variable relevant to the location decision. For example, in the decision to locate a new fast-food restaurant, the centre of gravity of the population of the catchment area might be found. Alternatively, something other than population might be used, perhaps economic wealth or traffic flows. Having found alternative location sites, each would then be tested against other criteria, perhaps using multicriteria methods. For example, the restaurant sites would be investigated for traffic access, closeness to suppliers, amount of local competition, etc. Price and Turcotte (1986) describe the decision to locate a blood donor clinic using gravity site selection methods followed by multicriteria methods to make the final choice.

The blood donor clinic example dealt with the location of a single operating unit. On the other hand, there are methods for deciding the locations of a whole network simultaneously. This might be the case with a new service organisation setting up its operations from scratch but needing to open at several locations from the outset. For example, Ghosh and Craig (1986) describe the decision to open a network of service centres over a wide spread of geographical locations. The management science technique employed is network optimisation which is a form of mathematical programming.

Conclusions

The use of techniques such as DEA, multicriteria methods and site selection is increasing, as the service sector grows and recognition of the special problems that the sector faces also grows. Many of the techniques are highly complex and require specialists to run them. All this can disguise the fact that management science can be no more than part of the decision-making process. The technique does not take the decision, it merely does a first pass clearing and sorting of information and comes up with a provisional solution. This provides a properly informed base for discussions, judgement and fine tuning. It may be that management science will show the same pattern of development in the service sector that it has done in other sectors where the initial need for help has been followed by too high expectations, then disillusionment and finally by a new realism based on a mature view of its true role as an aid to the decision-making process.

References

Beesley, M. E. (1983) *Cost Benefit Analysis of London's Transport Policies*, Pergamon Press, Oxford.

Bleuel, W. H. and Patton, J. D. (1978) *Service Management*, Instrument Society of America, Research Triangle Park, NC.

Chase, R. B. (1978) 'Where does the customer fit in a service operation?' *Harvard Business Review*, November–December, p. 16.

Currin, D. C. (1986) 'Transportation problems with inadmissible routes', *Journal of the Operational Research Society*, Vol. 37, No. 4, April, pp. 387–96.

Davis, K. R. and McKeown, P. G. (1984) *Quantitative Models for Management*, Wadsworth Publishing Co., Belmont, CA.

Fitzsimmons, J. A. and Sullivan, R. S. (1982) *Service Operations Management*, McGraw-Hill, Maidenhead, Berks.

Ghosh, A. and Craig, C. S. (1986) 'An approach to determining the optimal location for new services', *Journal of Marketing Research*, Vol. 23, No. 4, November.

Hahn, R. W. (1984) 'On reconciling multiple goals: applications of multiobjective programming', *Operations Research*, Vol. 32, No. 1, January–February.

Lovelock, C. H. and Young, R. F. (1979) 'Look to customers to increase productivity', *Journal of the Operational Research Society*, Vol. 37, No. 4, April, pp. 387–96.

Price, W. L. and Turcotte, M. (1986) 'Locating a blood bank', *Interfaces*, Vol. 16, No. 5, September–October.

Sasser, W. Earl (1976) 'Match supply and demand in service industries', *Harvard Business Review*, November–December, pp. 45–6.

Sasser, W. Earl et al. (1978) *Management of Service Operations*, Allyn & Bacon, Inc., Newton, MA.

Serfozo, R. (1985) 'Allocation for servers for stochastic service stations with one overflow', *Management Science*, Vol. 31, No. 8, August, pp. 1011–18.

Sherman, H. D. (1984) 'Improving the productivity of service businesses', *Sloan Management Review*, Spring.

Sherman, H. D. and Gold, F. (1985) 'Bank branch operating efficiency', *Journal of Banking and Finance*, No. 9.

Targett, D. (1985) 'An experience in the design of a management information system for a bank', *Journal of the Operational Research Society*, Vol. 36, No. 11, November, pp. 999–1007.

20 Management information systems

PROFESSOR PAUL GAMBLE

Introduction

Information systems in service industries may be considered from three principal perspectives. The first of these is the size of the problem space. Services are often sensitive to a wide range of social and economic variables. This means that the factors which determine whether a service can or will be provided with commercial success are often hard to isolate. The second perspective concerns the judgements that managers may use in regulating the provision of services. Such judgements often incorporate a great deal of soft data, well understood in human terms but difficult to model objectively. Nevertheless, it might be argued that some manufactured goods share both these characteristics to some degree. However, the third perspective is the role of information in the service itself. In this respect information systems can play an important part in determining the structure of an industry and in transforming the very nature of the service. From this perspective, management information systems (MIS) in service industries both regulate and support the product itself.

Management information and management decisions

If a management information system is to support decision making, its design and function must take into account the way in which managers make decisions. The classic problem solving model is that proposed by Newell and Simon (1972). They argue that behavioural complexity in decision making is largely a function of the environment. Consequently, they propose a decision model which proceeds by a series of rational stages, a process which lends itself to machine-based procedures for problem solving. The first of these stages concerns intelligence to determine that a problem exists. The second stage is solution generation. The third is choice by which alternative solutions are evaluated and compared.

Much attention has been given to choice in the literature. The notion that managers control decisions through rational choosing is an attractive one. More careful consideration of the research tends to suggest that for managers, the choice stage may sometimes be relatively unimportant. Indeed, by manipulating the information system managers can influence whether a decision is made (Bachrach and Baratz, 1963), how a decision is made (Mechanic, 1962), and what kind of decision is made (Lee, 1985). In some situations the manager's decision simply confirms what is more or less already decided.

Newell and Simon's ideas have made a very important contribution to our understanding of human problem solving. In organisational terms, however, the picture of an orderly process moving through formal problem identification, a rational search for solutions and the exercise of choice, followed by precise implementation, is hard to support in practice. Researchers differ in their views about how decisions are made but are generally agreed that the process is confused and difficult to understand. In fact, in one study by Cohen and others (1972), organisations were described somewhat fancifully as 'garbage-cans for decision'. Envisaged in this way, organisations work by dropping something into the can where it is shovelled around until a decision emerges. Decisions thus produced are an outcome of four, relatively independent, streams of organisational activity.

The first stream involves identifying problems, equivalent to the intelligence phase. This is to do with recognising or defining problems. It would seem that a problem is anything which might warrant some attention. The way in which problems are recognised by managers is unclear. However, it is apparent that this can be a predominantly political process. Two managers might well interpret the same intelligence quite differently. Suppose it is discovered that a competing hotel is refurbishing its bedrooms. One manager might argue that no response is required, the competitor is moving out of our market. A second manager might think it important to match this investment so as to stay in touch.

For this reason, problem identification is often linked closely to the second stream which involves solutions. In many cases solutions are available before matching problems can be found. For example, a hotel might review its security systems after a manager has been attracted by a new electronic locking system. As Mintzberg (1976) puts it,

'An interesting phenomenon in recognition is that of matching. A decision maker may be reluctant to act on a problem for which he sees no apparent solution; similarly he may hesitate to use a new idea that does not deal with a difficulty. But when an opportunity is matched with a problem, a manager is more likely to initiate action.'

The third stream concerns who takes part in the decision. This is central to the operation of an MIS. Like any product, if it is to be successful, it must be tailored to the needs of its users. Unfortunately, it would appear that a participant can be anybody who comes and goes within the overall process. Participation in a decision is seen to be function of time, attention and availability rather than how much a person might know about the problem being solved. In other words, sometimes the person assigned to deal with a decision depends on who is around.

Finally, there are choice opportunities, which are the occasions when organisations are expected to produce what is called a decision. Very often, these choice opportunities are actually forced on the attention of a decision maker by a crisis situation. Even so, opportunities are often sublimated by managers into more routine situations and dealt with accordingly.

This somewhat confused picture is made more perplexing when the true behaviour of managers is taken into account. Many studies of managerial work, stretching over a considerable period of time, present a picture of management behaviour as reactive, tactical and frenetic. Thus Carlson (1951), Horne and Lupton (1965), Mintzberg (1973) and Stewart (1983) all indicate in studies of time-budgeting that even senior managers spend little apparent effort on planning and abstract formulation. They tend to hold many short face-to-face meetings which flit from topic to topic, are subject to constant interruptions and tend to respond rapidly to the initiatives of others. Indeed, they seem to become so accustomed to this pattern of work that where interference is not generated from outside, managers may create their own interruptions by switching tasks or making telephone calls.

Judging the effectiveness of this behaviour is more difficult. Brewer and Tomlinson (1964) have suggested that a work pattern of this sort allows managers to deal with complexity by rapid accumulation and synthesis of data. Kotter (1982) developed the idea by arguing that the absence of planning is more apparent than real and that such apparently opportunistic behaviour is a way of achieving a great deal in a short time.

Whatever the merits or demerits, it is evident that this kind of behaviour provides little observable opportunity to solve problems by means of thinking about a theoretical framework. Nor does it seem to provide for formal interaction with a passive and highly structured MIS. Butler and his colleagues (1980) summarised the position in these words.

'In short, decision making is an activity which muddles through incrementally within bounded rationalities to merely satisficing and transient ends in a manner that need not be all that consistent or logical.'

How do managers use information to make decisions?

If managers did not use information for making decisions then there would be little purpose in building management information systems. The question that arises is, what kind of information do managers want and how do they use it? Davis and Olson (1985) defined information along the following lines.

'Information is data that has [sic] been processed into a form that is meaningful to the recipient, and is of real perceived value in current or prospective decisions.'

Thus data are transformed into information as they acquire structure or meaning. A table of numbers may be described as data. A graph of that table showing trends and patterns becomes information. If the manager has to restructure items which are presented in order to understand and use them, perhaps by calculating some percentages or by making comparisons with other data, then he or she has not been given information. Most of the work to do with collecting and analysing data is purely mechanical. Within organisations, these activities carry low status whether or not they are carried out by a machine.

Primarily, therefore, it would seem that an MIS must offer structure. Structure is not the only attribute of information, however. The structure or meaning of the information must be recognisable, that is to say it must be perceived by the recipient. The act of perception has two elements in this context. First, the information must be accepted as relevant to the current problem by the recipient. The information must be wanted by the recipient, though what a manager thinks is wanted may not always be the same as what is actually needed (Aguilar, 1967). Second, the information must be understood by the recipient. To provide someone with information that they can neither understand nor use, is not going to help them make a decision. The other two important attributes are that the information must be received and that it must be received in time to affect the outcome of the decision to be made.

The process of interpreting the information in the form of a decision is regarded as more of a social process requiring the application of judgement. Some problems do not lend themselves to an objective answer and yet someone must choose. The manager makes the decision by applying a value judgement. To this extent a person is clearly central to a management decision and must therefore be regarded as part of the information system. The application of values carries much more status in the organisation, whether it be done by a man or by a machine. Perhaps, because of the higher status associated with value judgements, some people may feel threatened and uncomfortable if such judgements are the result of a machine-based process.

Elements of a management information system

A management information system can be conceived as three major elements. One element is a mechanical process that collects and transforms data. Nowadays, this mechanical element will very probably comprise one or more computer systems.

Another element is the characteristics of the information itself. Information characteristics have been categorised by Lucas (1986) in a number of ways; source, time frame, scope, frequency, organisation and accuracy. Thus, a projection from the boss using both internal and external data, produced once each year in a structured but perhaps relatively imprecise form, would get different treatment from the daily rooms report produced by the hotel front office. Situational factors will also affect how the information is used. If the consequences of using the information are thought to carry important implications either for the decision maker or for the organisation, then this might result in extra care or attention being given to the information.

Finally, there is an individual element which relates to the characteristics of the decision maker. Mason and Mitroff (1973) defined the contextual nature of management information systems quite well.

> 'An information system that serves an individual with a certain cognitive style faced with a particular decision problem in some organisational setting.'

While this definition refers to serving the decision maker, it must be emphasised that the decision maker is actually an influential part of the information system itself. Developing an effective MIS means that the organisation must develop the managers for whom it is intended. Meadow (1970) noted that users typically have only partial knowledge of the information that they want for a particular problem. They are often unaware of how the information might be structured or even what information systems might be available within the organisation. Where computer based systems are concerned, extra difficulties are encountered. Managers often have difficulty in formulating their problems in computer terms and may very well be ignorant of the penalties attached to particular search strategies.

The point can be illustrated in the context of travel agencies. The travel trade in the UK is often considered a leader in the use of information systems because of the speed with which it switched from using telephones to the use of on-line videotex systems. However, insufficient and inadequate training has resulted in many agents making partial, inefficient and over-expensive use of their computerised databases (Istel, 1987).

The cognitive affective approach to problem solving

From what has been discussed so far it should be apparent that, however much managers might seek to design management information systems which give black and white answers to black and white problems, this would be very hard to achieve. Organising a collection of 'facts' on a computer might be relatively straightforward. Difficulties arise in terms of attaching those facts to situations which might be described as problems.

In general, managers (and other people) respond to situations on the basis of knowledge and attitudes. 'Knowledge' refers to facts or cognitions that they have and the way in which those facts are organised. 'Attitudes' refers to the values which they attach to those facts. These affective elements denote preferences or liking for particular courses of action. The influence of value systems on decision making is beyond the scope of the present discussion.

Not all decision makers are equally inclined to use the same sort of information in solving problems. Psychologists term the difference between ways of thinking about problems as cognitive style. Broadly, cognitive styles can be categorised as analytical or heuristic. Analytical problem solvers favour a quantitative approach. Heuristic problem solvers are more inclined to look at broader issues and to solve problems intuitively. This is not to say that any individual will always use the same method for every type of problem.

Many real world situations, especially those in service industries, encompass a very large problem space. It is neither convenient nor possible to consider all the elements of a problem exhaustively, even if the decision maker were inclined to do so. Instead, decision makers tend to regulate the amount of cognitive effort they are prepared to make. Simon (1982) referred to this as satisficing, a term which connotes satisfy and suffice. He recognised that the range of rational choices that a manager might consider would be bounded by practicality. Thus, a (limited) search for an adequate or acceptable solution, rather than an exhaustive search for the one best solution, would meet most needs. Based on a proposal by Keen (1980) it is possible to identify six categories of cognitive effort. Each of these might be associated with a particular kind of information system support.

Computation

Problems involving computation are easily supported by computers or calculators. Mental calculations of this sort are in any case constrained by speed and intelligence, so that most managers can improve their response to this type of decision by using a machine.

Specification

Specification problems are those involving probabilities, priorities or conscious articulation of weights. Examples might include producing critical path networks to regulate the opening of a new supermarket, drawing up a set of schedules for dealing with different jobs or selecting a travel itinerary between several cities. Analytical decision makers rely on these techniques, but individuals often find it difficult to be consistent between problems, especially where subjective probabilities or weightings are involved.

Search

Search type of problems, or those which consist of creating alternatives, ideally require comprehensive examination. Most people are equally poor at dealing with this type of problem and tend to avoid rigorous analysis by using heuristics. A manager searching for a new Property Management System out of the 200 or so on the market in 1988 could narrow the search by drawing on advice or experience or by disregarding some possible options.

Assimilation

A manager's ability to make sense of data presented in numerical, verbal or graphical form is very dependent on cognitive style. Many managers do not enjoy reading long reports. The information system can help by providing the data in a variety of ways so that it can rapidly be absorbed in the most acceptable form. An example might be a graph supported by a table.

Explanation

Being able to justify or explain conclusions and methodology is often central to credibility. It can greatly affect the acceptability of an information system. When explaining their conclusions to other people, managers may use intuitive methods based on feedback and interpersonal skills. 'Sensing' approaches of this kind are beyond the scope of machine-based systems but more advanced information systems do seek to incorporate explanations of their own behaviour.

Inference

Inferencing refers to deriving conclusions from data using a process of statistical reasoning or by generalising from specific cases. The capabilities of the manager in this respect depend very much on education and training. Most people are not natural statisticians and tend to make over-simple, inaccurate deductions. However, trained personnel are often quickly able to classify and resolve some types of problem using heuristics. Such behaviour is typically characteristic of experts. Inferencing mechanisms are crucial to the operation of 'intelligent' information systems.

Judgement and management decisions

Simon (1960) originally distinguished two types of decisions labelled programmed and non-programmed. Keen and Scott Morton (1978) developed this further by introducing two categories of programmed decisions which they called structured and unstructured. A structured decision is one so well understood that it can be delegated to a low level in the organisation where it can be dealt with by means of a set of rules. Alternatively, the decision can be completely automated. Many problems to which the techniques of management science or operations research apply would fall into these categories, such as inventory reports or discounted cash flows. It might be noted that structured decisions correspond broadly with the cognitive styles of computation, specification and search. Assimilation, explanation and inferencing are more pertinent to unstructured situations.

Following these ideas it is useful to explore their implications for the design of a management information system. So far it has been suggested that the decision-making process itself is largely unstructured. It has been argued that value judgements play an important role, both in identifying situations when decisions are needed and in choosing solutions. It would also appear that managers may respond differently to information due both to their preferred cognitive style and to factors pertinent to the situation itself. Thus, even when given 'facts', managers tend to use judgement to select a course of action.

The role of judgement affects the design of an information system in two dimensions. The first dimension concerns beliefs about the cause of a problem. Where the problem space is large, or where it is not well understood, the cause of a problem may be very unclear. For example, restaurant sales may be declining because the food is of lower quality, or because the segmentation mix in the hotel has changed or because of competition from the restaurant around the corner.

The second dimension concerns the extent to which managers share preferences about what they are trying to achieve. In the example given, the chef may want a bigger food budget, the food and beverage manager a new sales effort and the rooms division manager the closure of the restaurant and conversion of the space to bedrooms. Since solutions are very important to problem definition, such preferences will have a major effect on outcomes.

When preferences and causation are both certain, the role of the MIS is to support cognitive style by performing the necessary calculations. If there is some difference of opinion about preferred outcomes, the MIS must be designed to support the manager by providing ammunition for a chosen course of action (Swartout, 1981). If there is some uncertainty about the cause of a problem, then it is the role of the MIS to help the manager assimilate data or explain the situation. In this case the MIS must be designed to help the manager learn about the problem (Winston and Prendergast, 1984). Finally, in circumstances where neither cause nor outcome can be agreed, the information system must somehow move into the realms of inspiration to help the manager rationalise choice. This framework is illustrated in Figure 20.1 and it is interesting to examine the extent to which current information systems in service industries are able to assume these varied roles.

Extent to which beliefs in causation are shared	Extent to which preferences for outcomes are shared: Completely	Partially
Completely	**Computation** Control inventory Cost products Calculate prices	**Search/specify** Identify holiday Select media schedule Fix new prices
Partially	**Assimilate/explain** Accept reservation Bid for contract Speculate on currency	**Inference** Reposition in market Change product line Modify image

Figure 20.1 Implications for the role of management information systems (After De Alberdi and Harvey, 1985)

The current role of information systems

It is evident that the computational power available from modern business computers can only affect directly one possible role for a corporate MIS. Without a corresponding development of people and systems, major advances in the operation of information systems are unlikely. Consequently, it is unsurprising that a study conducted in the mid 1980s (PA Management Consultants, 1985) revealed what was described as a 'disturbing mismatch' between the expectations of top managers and their companies' information technology (IT) strategies.

The survey was based on 156 returns from the chief executives of *The Times* top 1,000 companies. It found that while 61 per cent of chief executives expected to obtain improved information and communications, only 31 per cent explicitly targeted this kind of improvement in their corporate strategy. Fifty-two per cent expected more support for management from IT, and 32 per cent expected more support for sales strategy. However, only 22 per cent and 13 per cent respectively have addressed these issues when applying IT to their corporate needs.

The survey concluded that the orientation of most corporate IT strategies was a strong bias towards data processing. It found that,

> 'most of the companies have a technical rather than a business-orientated approach to the realisation of IT projects.'

In practice it appears that chief executives have minimal involvement with the framing of corporate information technology strategy, as a rule being brought in only at the final stage when financial approval is sought. The reasons put forward to explain this are based partly on caution, a reluctance to innovate with computers, and partly on ignorance. Most chief executives are ignorant of what IT has to offer, PA observing diplomatically, 'the general impression which was gained during the study was that they are not as well informed about IT as they might wish to be.' Such circumstances do not favour advances in the design and application of information systems.

MIS and competitive advantage in service industries

For service industries, the link between the systems that the organisation uses for day-to-day operations and the systems it uses for management decision making, can be very close. In an analysis of different organisations, Porter and Millar (1985) refer to the economic and technological

Information content of the product

	Low	High
Low Information intensity of the value chain	Local retailer	Insurance Betting shops Real estate sales Hotels
High	Multiple retailer Equipment hire Oil refining Automobile manufacture Retailing	Credit card company Tour operator Airlines Newspapers Banking

Figure 20.2   Information intensity matrix
(After Porter and Millar, 1985)

processes used as the value chain. Information may play a greater or lesser role in a value chain. However, information may not play a significant part of what the customer actually buys. This allows for the creation of what Porter and Millar call an information intensity matrix, such as that illustrated in Figure 20.2.

Service industries usually offer products with a high information content. This information content may be important both in creating the service and in making it available to the consumer. It is in these areas that information technology (IT) can be used to change the competitive position of service industries. Porter and Millar argue that information can be used to change the structure of industries, create competitive advantage and even create new products by changing information content.

In the PA survey, building societies came closest to integrating their information systems with sales operations. Elsewhere, Harvey (1985) has described how the tour operator Thomson Holidays has deployed an information system which both manages and sells its holiday packages more effectively than its competitors. Thomson has integrated management information and sales operations. In doing so it has specifically designed its TOPS reservation service to change the structure of the industry.

Perhaps the largest example of such integration would be airline reservation systems. Meiklejohn (1988) has described how Sabre, the American Airlines system, contains details of 674 airline schedules, 14,000 hotels, 30 car hire companies and almost 50 tour operators. The structural and competitive effects of airline information systems are so great that American Airlines took legal action against the British Airways Travicom system in 1988 due to alleged bias in the way that Travicom provides product information. The design and operation of Galileo and Amadeus, the new European airline reservation systems, are subject to close commercial scrutiny.

By contrast, the other major element of the tourist industry, the hotel and catering sector makes relatively little use of its information systems in either creating or marketing its products. A number of reasons might be proposed for this. Hospitality products are not differentiated by technological factors in a manner that affects the method of delivery, price or even the product. It may also be argued that units in one location are not affected adversely by the use of information technology in another location. Thus, hospitality organisations generally confine their applications of information technology to computational, clerical services. However, it seems likely that where these interact with airline reservation systems some changes are likely to take place. By 1988 yield management techniques incorporating artificial intelligence techniques were being tested by some hotel companies.

Summary

A management information system is intended to deliver relevant information to managers and to support decision making. However, managers may be disposed to use information in different ways according to personal and situational factors. This must be taken into account in the design. The importance of judgement and the complex nature of the problem environment in service industries mean that the manager's role in the information system must be considered integrally. Furthermore, it is evident that in service industries, information is important not only in operational procedures but in the creation of added value.

References

Aguilar, F. J. (1967) *Scanning the Business Environment*, Macmillan, New York.

Bachrach, P. and Baratz, M. (1963) 'Decision and nondecisions; an analytical framework', *American Political Science Review*, 57, pp. 632–642.

Brewer, E. and Tomlinson, J. W. C. (1964) 'The manager's working day', *Journal of Industrial Economics*, 12, pp. 191–7.

Butler, R. J. et al. (1980) 'Strategic decision-making: concepts of content and process', *International Studies of Management and Organization*, Vol. 9, No. 4, pp. 5–36.

Carlson, S. (1951) *Executive Behaviour*, Strombergs, Stockholm.

Cohen, M. D., March, J. G. and Olsen, J. P. (1972) A garbage-can model of organizational choice, *Administrative Science Quarterly*, 17, pp. 1–25.

Davis, G. B. and Olson, M. (1985) *Management Information Systems: Conceptual Foundations, Structure and Development*, 2nd edition, McGraw-Hill, New York.

De Alberdi, M. and Harvey, J. (1985) 'Decision systems', in: Christie, B. (ed) *Human Factors of Information Technology in the Office*, Wiley, Chichester, pp. 170–85.

Harvey, D. (1985) 'Why Britain's bosses are in the dark', *Business Computing and Communications*, November, pp. 26–8

Horne, J. H. and Lupton, T. (1965) 'The work activities of 'middle managers' – an exploratory study', *Journal of Management Studies*, Vol. 2, No. 1, pp. 14–33.

Istel Survey (1987) *Technology and the Travel Agent*, Travel Business Group, Istel Ltd., Redditch.

Keen, P. G. W. (1980) *Decision Support Systems and the Marginal Economics of Effort*, CISR WP 48, Centre for Information Systems Research, MIT Report, Cambridge, MA.

Keen, P. G. W. and Scott Morton, M. S. (1978) *Decision Support Systems: An Organizational Perspective*, Addison-Wesley, London.

Kotter, J. P. (1982) 'What effective general managers really do', *Harvard Business Review*, Vol. 60, No. 6, pp. 156–67

Lee, R. (1985) 'Internal politics' in: Elliott, K. and Lawrence, P. (eds) *Introducing Management*, Penguin, Harmondsworth, pp. 198–218.

Lucas, H. C. (1986) *Information Systems Concepts for Management*, 3rd edition, McGraw-Hill, New York.

Mason, R. and Mitroff, I. (1973) 'A program for research in management information systems', *Management Science*, Vol. 19, No. 5, pp. 457–87

Meadow, C. T. (1970) *Man-Machine Communication*, Wiley, Chichester.

Mechanic, D. (1962) 'Sources of power of lower participants in complex organizations', *Administrative Science Quarterly*, 7, pp. 349–64.

Meiklejohn, I. (1988) 'Airlines arm for on-screen war', *Business Computing and Communications*, February, pp. 36–40.

Mintzberg, H. (1973) *The Nature of Managerial Work*, Harper & Row, New York.

Mintzberg, H., Raisinghani, D. and Thêoret, A. (1976) 'The structure of "Unstructured" decision processes', *Administrative Science Quarterly*, 21, p. 253.

Newell, A. and Simon, H. A. (1972) *Human Problem Solving*, Prentice-Hall, Englewood Cliffs, New Jersey.

PA Management Consultants (1985) *Survey of Chief Executives and their Perception of Office Automation*, PA Management Consultants, Royston.

Porter, M. E. and Millar, V. E. (1985) 'How information gives you competitive advantage', *Harvard Business Review*, July–August, pp. 149–60.

Simon, H. A. (1960) *The New Science of Management Decision*, Harper & Row, New York.

Simon, H. A. (1982) *Models of Bounded Rationality: Behavioural Economics and Business Organization*, Vol. 2, MIT Press, Cambridge, MA.

Stewart, R. (1983) 'Managerial behaviour: how research has changed the traditional picture', in: Earl, M. J. (ed) *Perspectives on Management*, Oxford University Press, London, pp. 82–98.

Swartout, W. (1981) *Producing Explanations and Justifications of an Expert Consulting Program*, LCS, TR251, MIT, Cambridge, MA.

Winston, P. and Prendergast, K. (eds) (1984) *The AI Business: Commercial Uses of Artificial Intelligence*, MIT Press, Cambridge, MA.

Biographical notes on the contributors

Brian Adams, MBA, FCCA, MIMC, is a director of Grant Thornton Management Consultants Limited and has considerable financial management experience at director level in a variety of organisations. In addition to consultancy experience in many sectors, he has worked in management positions in the paint industry, process control, construction and a major enterprise board. His special field of interest is in structuring an organisation's finance function so that it performs a more valuable and creative role. His expertise extends beyond the finance function into service activities generally and, for example, he has carried out effectiveness improvement assignments in catering operations, environmental planning, the professions and a large State service organisation.

Professor Gary Akehurst is one of the Founding Editors of the *Service Industries Journal*, the only academic journal in the world devoted to service industries, published since 1981. He is also Head of the Department of Catering and Hotel Management at Dorset Institute, Poole in the United Kingdom. Previously, he was Associate Director of the Service Industries Management Research Unit, Cardiff Business School, University of Wales and Lecturer in Managerial Economics. He has also been a member of Faculty at the University of Surrey and Manchester Polytechnic. Current research interests centre on service management and corporate strategies in hospitality and retail industries.

Dr Jon Bareham is currently acting as Dean of Brighton Business School and permanent head of the Department of Service Sector Management at the Polytechnic. He is a member of the CNAA Committee for Consumer and Leisure Studies, Secretary of the International Association of Hotel Management Schools and external examiner at Oxford and Huddersfield Polytechnics and Surrey University. He has undertaken considerable consultancy work for organisations such as Marks & Spencer, United Biscuits and Ward Breweries.

Dr Michael Z. Brooke – an author, lecturer and consultant – is Managing Director of Brooke Associates (Manchester) Ltd, a contract writing company. He was formerly a Senior Lecturer in Management Sciences at the University of Manchester Institute of Science and Technology and Director of the International Business Unit. He has written 16 books including: *The Strategy of Multinational Enterprise* (with H. L. Remmers, 2nd edition, Pitman, 1978), *International Corporate Planning* (with M van Beusekom, Pitman, 1979), *Centralization and Autonomy* (Holt, Rinehart and Winston, 1984), *Selling Management Service Contracts in International Business* (Holt, Rinehart and Winston, 1985) and *International Management* (Hutchinson, 1987); he is also an editor of two handbooks for managers – *Handbook of International Trade* (Macmillan) and *International Financial Management Handbook* (Kluwer). Dr Brooke has carried out projects for numerous international companies and has spoken at courses and seminars in 15 countries.

Francis Buttle is Lecturer in Marketing in the Department of Hotel, Restaurant and Travel Administration, University of Massachusetts, Amherst, Massachusetts. He was previously attached to the University of Surrey, England. He has been involved in marketing research, management and education for over 15 years across three continents. He is author of the textbook *Hotel and Foodservice Marketing: A Managerial Approach*, and has written some 60 articles. He has a Bachelor's degree in Management Science, a Master's in Marketing and is completing a Doctorate in Communication.

Paul Colebourne, FCA, BSc, is an executive consultant with Grant Thornton Management Consultants Limited who specialises in helping organisations to improve the effectiveness of their financial departments, based on 15 years experience of financial management. He has an unusually broad perspective, having trained originally as a production engineer, then as a chartered accountant with Price Waterhouse, followed by financial management positions with the Guinness and Inchcape groups and Combined Technology Corporation. Latterly, he was the Finance Director of a Lloyd's insurance broking firm.

Dr Paul Fifield is Director of The Winchester Consulting Group where he specialises in the design and delivery of very senior management training programmes in strategy, marketing and international business. In recent years Paul Fifield has been extensively involved in consultancy and marketing management in the services sector, where much of WCG's work has been carried out for clients which include Mercantile Credit, Thomson

Holidays, Holiday Inns, Clerical Medical Investment Group, Tunis International Bank, Crusader Insurance plc, The Frizzell Group and Norwich Union Life Insurance Society. At the same time, Paul has maintained his interest in teaching, having lectured on strategy and international marketing at the Institute of Marketing, Brunel University, Henley Management College, Cranfield and IMCB, and in research into consumer behaviour and market segmentation; he is jointly responsible for developing context marketing at WCG. Previously Dr Fifield spent several years in marketing and sales both in the United Kingdom and Europe working in the DIY and leisure industries. Paul Fifield holds a BA degree in Business Studies and an MBA. He has recently completed his thesis on international market segmentation for his PhD from Cranfield Institute of Technology.

Norman Flynn is Lecturer in Public Sector Management and Chairman of the Public Sector Management area at the London Business School. He has degrees in economics from Sussex and Newcastle Universities and has worked in local government, Birmingham School of Planning and the Institute of Local Government Studies at the University of Birmingham. He is especially interested in strategic management performance measurement and managing under competitive tendering. He is Consultant to various public bodies and is a member of the Chartered Institute of Public Finance and Accountancy's Accounting Panel.

Professor Paul R. Gamble, BSc, MPhil, PhD, MHCIMA, is the Charles Forte Professor of Hotel Management in the Department of Management Studies for Tourism and Hotel Industries at the University of Surrey. Following a number of years management experience with international hotel companies, Professor Gamble developed his academic career with research into hospitality computer systems, a topic on which he has written widely. He has also developed several computer based systems which are used in Europe and the USA. As a consultant to companies, institutions and government bodies, both in the UK and overseas, he has been closely involved in the design and implementation of management information systems at many levels. His current research activity concerns the application of knowledge based systems to hotel operations.

Robert Johnston is a lecturer and researcher in service operations management at Warwick Business School in the UK. Mr Johnston has worked in industry, where he held several posts, more recently as an area operations manager in the tourism and leisure industry. He has worked in many parts of the service sector in both private and public organisations.

His current research interests include service strategy, performance measurement and service quality. He is Research Director of a project investigating control and performance measurement in a wide range of service industries, sponsored by the Chartered Institute of Management Accountants. He is also the adviser to a Home Office team investigating the standardisation of motorway incident procedures. Mr Johnston has published widely. He is author of two books, *The Management of Service Operations* and *Operations Management in Service Industries and the Public Sector* (with Voss, Armistead and Morris). He has organised several workshops and conferences of service operations and is Treasurer of the Operations Management Association, UK.

Peter Jones is a Principal Lecturer at Brighton Business School. He has degrees from the Open University and London Business School and worked originally in the hotel and catering industry both in the UK and Belgium. He is the author or co-author of four textbooks largely relating to operational management issues in the hospitality sector and is particularly interested in service delivery. He has been a consultant to a wide range of organisations, particularly in relation to developing strategic and operational responses to competitive tendering. He is a Fellow of the Hotel, Catering and Institutional Management Association.

Andrew Lockwood is a Lecturer in Hotel and Catering Management in the Department of Management Studies for Tourism and the Hotel Industries at the University of Surrey. He has experience of the hotel industry both as a manager with two major international companies and as an owner-operator. He has written two books with Peter Jones on management topics in the hotel and catering industry and has also published a number of articles in the field. His research interests centre around the effective use of manpower in hotels and the problems of achieving service quality.

Dr Robert Christie Mill, CHA is Professor of Hotel and Restaurant Management at the University of Denver. His teaching career began in 1972 at Niagara University. He consequently served on the faculties of Lansing Community College and Michigan State University. He holds a PhD and MBA from Michigan State University and a BA from The University of Strathclyde's Scottish Hotel School. Dr Mill earned the designation of Certified Hotel Administrator in 1985. His industry experience includes positions with Trust House Forte in Europe, on board ship as a cook with Canadian Pacific and as assistant to the Vice-President of Manpower Development with Inter-Continental Hotel Corporation in

New York City. Dr Mill has authored, or contributed chapters to, seven books including *The Tourism System, Tourism: Business and Pleasure* and *Managing Productivity in the Hospitality Industry*. He is currently conducting research in the area of selecting, training and motivating hospitable employees. He has conducted numerous workshops and seminars for both industry and trade associations ranging from Mr Steak, Dairy Queen and AIRCOA Companies to the American Hotel and Motel Association, the National Restaurant Association and the World Tourism Organization. He has spoken in Great Britain, Mexico and Canada in addition to his activities in the United States. His ability to translate academic principles into down-to-earth practical management guides in combination with his native Scottish wit have earned him enthusiastic praise from his audiences.

Professor Brian Moores originally trained as an aeronautical engineer with A V Roe. A research assistantship at UMIST was followed by two years' postgraduate work at Johns Hopkins University on a Harkness Fellowship. Upon returning to the UK in 1966 he was successively lecturer, senior lecturer and reader in the Department of Management Sciences at UMIST. In 1986 he moved to UWIST to a Chair in Management, and in 1988 went to Stirling to take up a Chair in Management Science. Much of his research has been focussed on the application of Operational Research concepts to management problems confronting the NHS. In addition to more traditional OR-type modelling, this has more recently involved the measurement of patient satisfaction with hospital care. This led to an interest in the wider issue of quality management in service industries which in turn has led to a wider interest in all matters germane to quality. He has published extensively on NHS matters and recently edited a collection of papers on the quality assurance theme (*Are They Being Served?*). Since arriving at Stirling, he has been putting together the Quality Management Centre, which body will provide an educational, research and consulting resource for Scottish industries and commerce.

David Rea was born in Kent in 1948. He studied at Brighton Polytechnic and qualified as a librarian in 1972. He then worked for two years each for a local authority, a manufacturing company and a voluntary organisation before returning to Brighton Polytechnic as a member of staff in the Department of Learning Resources. He registered as a part-time student with the Open University and studied social science courses. He graduated with first class honours in 1981, and had acquired an academic concern for health care and the role of professionals within the State. He became a Community Health Council member in Brighton and registered for a part-time PhD in Social Policy and Administration at the University of Kent. This developed into a study of power relationships within the NHS and was completed by early 1987. In the same year he transferred to Brighton Polytechnic's Department of Service Sector Management where he taught public administration. In December 1987, he took up a research post at UMIST to investigate implementation of the North West Region's 'Resource Management' initiative. He is also involved in research into information technology within health care organisation and management.

Sue Ricks moved to the Department of Service Sector Management, Brighton Polytechnic Business School from Ashridge Management College. She has worked as a teacher, civil servant and has had a variety of management and consultancy posts in the leisure industry. Along the way she has obtained an Open University degree, a Diploma in Management Studies and an MSc degree (Business Administration) from the University of Bath.

Susan Segal-Horn is Lecturer in Strategic Management at Cranfield School of Management where she runs the MBA course in International Business and teaches on executive programmes. Her research work focusses on strategy in the service industries and includes book and journal publications on trends in the retail sector, the management of professional service firms, strategies for coping with retailer buying power, and issues affecting globalisation and global service delivery. She was previously Principal Lecturer in Corporate Strategy at Brighton Business School.

Dr Leigh Sparks is a Lecturer at the Institute for Retail Studies, Department of Business and Management, University of Stirling. Dr Sparks has been researching retail topics for almost ten years and has published widely on many aspects of retailing and distribution. He obtained his PhD from the University of Wales for a study of employment in superstore retailing. Dr Sparks is the Deputy Editor of the *International Journal of Retailing*.

Professor John Stanworth has been the leading academic figure in franchising in the UK for more than a decade. He is Director of the newly formed Future of Work Research Group (incorporating the Small Business Unit) at the London Management Centre, Polytechnic of Central London. He has been active in the field of small business since the mid-1960s and for ten years ran the London Enterprise Programme for small business entrepreneurs in association with the GLC and the London Enterprise Agency. Professor Stanworth has, since 1975, pursued an interest in franchising which has involved, amongst other things, directing two major research programmes and pioneering Britain's first successful courses for prospective franchisees. Professor Stanworth enjoys an international reputation in this field.

Dr David Targett is a Senior Lecturer in Decision Sciences at the London Business School. Before joining the Business School he was a consultant in Operational Research with British Leyland. At LBS he lectures to students in both postgraduate and executive courses on the numerical techniques used in business. He is particularly concerned with ways in which the gap between users of statistics and producers of statistics that exists in many organisations can be minimised. He has regular consultancy contact with organisations in many sectors of business including the whisky industry, banking, central government and transportation. His research work has been concerned with problems of numerical control in nationalised industries and he has published papers on this and other topics in several journals. He is author of the books *Coping with Numbers*, *The Manager's Guide to Business Forecasting* and *The Economist Pocketbook of Business Numeracy*.

Dr Paul Willman is Senior Lecturer in Organisational Behaviour at the London Business School and incoming Director of the Sloan Fellowship Programme. Formerly at Cranfield School of Management and Imperial College London. Publications include *Fairness, Collective Bargaining and Income Policy; Innovation and Management Control; Technological Change and Collective Bargaining*. Research interests: technological change and personnel policy. Industrial relations in the financial sector.

Index